INCOME DISTRIBUTION AND ECONOMIC GROWTH OF JAPAN UNDER THE DEFLATIONARY ECONOMY

Theory and Evidence based on an Econometric Analysis

INCOME DISTRIBUTION AND ECONOMIC GROWTH OF JAPAN UNDER THE DEFLATIONARY ECONOMY

Theory and Evidence based on an Econometric Analysis

OSAMU NAKAMURA

The International University of Japan, Japan

NEW JERSEY • LONDON • SINGAPORE • BEIJING • SHANGHAI • HONG KONG • TAIPEI • CHENNAI

Published by

World Scientific Publishing Co. Pte. Ltd.

5 Toh Tuck Link, Singapore 596224

USA office: 27 Warren Street, Suite 401-402, Hackensack, NJ 07601

UK office: 57 Shelton Street, Covent Garden, London WC2H 9HE

British Library Cataloguing-in-Publication Data
A catalogue record for this book is available from the British Library.

INCOME DISTRIBUTION AND ECONOMIC GROWTH OF JAPAN UNDER THE DEFLATIONARY ECONOMY
Theory and Evidence on an Econometric Analysis

ISBN 978-981-4436-15-1

In-house Editors: Sandhya Venkatesh/Divya Srikanth

Typeset by Stallion Press
Email: enquiries@stallionpress.com

Printed in Singapore.

To
Dr. Daisaku Ikeda
Founder, Soka University

Preface

Recently, the term "Japanization" has found widespread usage throughout the world. Japanization implies the Japanese society is very mysterious in terms of its economic system, in which the supply-side is very strong with high technology, efficient capital and qualified labor. However, the demand-side of the economy is stagnant, therefore, the actual economic performance is weak and prices are declining, with a huge amount of deflationary gap, large current account surplus and fiscal deficits, which cannot be explained by economic theories. Indeed, the supply-side of the economy and factors of production, including capital, labor and technology, are viewed as sort of national assets and wealth of nations. Therefore, the Japanese people are automatically assumed to be rich; however, this is not the reality. It is said that, "Japan is rich, but the Japanese are not, economically."

The Japanese society has experienced this prolonged economic slump since the bursting of the bubble economy and the "Lost Two Decades". The Japanese people have experienced this prolonged stagnation for two decades, but can no more endure such a situation, fraught with uncertainty, in the future. However, most policy makers, business leaders, economists and politicians misunderstand the causes of the long-term stagnation and measures to improve this situation. It is noteworthy that we need to recognize the power of the domestic demand, which could revive the whole economy through improving distorted income distribution and reconsider a true great nation as an advanced one.

As Karl Marx believed, capitalism collapses through "inner contradictions", reducing corporate profit share for competition and substituting capital for labor, which result in decreasing effective demands. The prolonged stagnation of the Japanese seems to rely on inner contradictions, with lower wages and hence limited effective demands. It seems that the difference between the capitalism, as interpreted by Marx, and the current Japanese economy may be dependent on socio-economic environments in which *entrepreneurs* employ workers with lower wages and the workers continue to work with lower wages, as Keynes criticized in the second fundamental postulate of neo-classical employment theory. In other words, the current long-term economic deflation might be explained by the anticipation of Keynes rather than that of Marx.

This study, therefore, introduces the demand-side oriented growth model incorporated with the supply-side in order to analyze the current Japanese economy focusing on the prolonged stagnation and measures to improve its situation. So far, we might have been excessively dependent on the public policies and have ignored the importance of roles of the distribution of income, particularly between profits and wages. In other words, this study elucidates the structural impediments for growth of Japan and examines appropriate policies to solve these complicated problems with theories and empirical studies on an econometric analysis.

With respect to the results of scenario simulations and future forecasts in this volume, I utilized the econometric model of Japan which was revised in December 2010 (Dec. 2010 Version) based on the available data up to FY2009 and conducted the baseline projection and various scenario forecasts in January 2011. The actual Japanese economy and the world economy are changing day by day, and hence our research work continues unceasingly to cope with these changes.

Acknowledgments

I am indebted and grateful to many professors and colleagues, in particular, to Professor Shuntaro Shishido, who has supported my studies and provided many insightful comments on this project; Professor L. R. Klein, who gave us useful comments and instilled some directions in our research projects; Professor Takao Shimizu, who has supported my research works, including this project, since I was a graduate student; and to Mr. Tadashi Kido, Mr. Norifumi Shimizu, and Mr. Katsunori Nagao, who have conducted econometric modeling and forecasting works for the Japanese economy and regional economies of Japan within the HEPCO-IUJ Project along with me for over 15 years.

Contents

List of Figures and Tables

Figures

Tables

CHAPTER 1

Introduction

The Japanese economy has had a structural deflationary gap since the mid-1970s. Although the gap was decreasing in the bubble period, the deflationary economy has become more serious since the bursting of the bubble. The gap is estimated to exceed 95 trillion yen as of FY2009, according to the estimation of this study. With the strong supply side of the economy, nevertheless, the demand-side has been stagnant, which has resulted in the structural deflationary economy. As a result, the annual average growth rate of real GDP has remained stagnant at around 0.86 per cent during the past two decades, which is referred to as the "Lost Two Decades". Accordingly, the growth performance of Japan is extremely weak compared to that of the other developed countries, with large trade surplus even after the Plaza Agreement held in 1985 and large amounts of fiscal deficit.

In addition, with a huge amount of financial assets in the household sector, domestic demands, particularly household expenditures, have been dormant since the bursting of the bubble. Moreover, household disposable income has also remained stagnant as an aftereffect of the bursting of the bubble. At the same time, household financial liabilities have remained at a higher level and become a heavy burden for the household sector and its expenditures. A number of financial corporations suffering from financial insolvency overcame a bad loan problem with public funds by the end of the1990s, while a number of households have continued to face the financial difficulties associated with debt under the deflationary economy. The persistency of high financial insolvency is one of the leading causes of the stagnation of household expenditures in Japan.

1.1.   **Research Objectives**

Accordingly, this study attempts to examine the causes of the Japanese deflationary economy, characterized as a structural deflation, and discusses how to alleviate the prolonged slowdown in order to restore Japan to a trajectory of high economic growth, with a special focus on the function of income distribution. In addition, not only income distribution flows but also accumulation of assets and debts in the household sector are taken into account for improving the prolonged economic stagnation of Japan by employing an econometric analysis with modeling and forecasting techniques. Furthermore, this study makes a long-term forecast of the Japanese economy up to the FY2030 with policy scenario simulations in order to capture the long-term growth path of the Japanese economy and analyze the effects of alternative policies on the economy.

Concerning the extensive Japanese deflation, many studies have emphasized the importance of Keynesian demand stimulus. For example, Klein *et al.* (2007) and Shishido *et al.* (2010) have stressed the significance of combined conventional fiscal and financial policy to recover the Japanese growth performance. However, due to the large national fiscal deficit, the central government has had a pessimistic view of the conventional Keynes policy. Thus, the government investments have been declining since the mid-1990s under the domestic policy for a reform of public finance and administration.

On the other hand, some studies analyzed the causes of the deflationary economy of Japan from the viewpoints of income allocation and asset and debt accumulation in the household sector and found that distorted income allocation resulted in the stagnation of the demand-side economy in Japan. For example, Ando (2002) and Ando *et al.* (2003) examined the stock basis SNA (System of National Accounts) structure in the non-financial corporate sector and found that the corporate sector's policies to increase accumulated savings distorted the income allocation for the household sector based on Tobin's q and its flow-basis measure. Hayashi (2006) supported Ando's thesis as the "over investment hypothesis," and Saito (2008) discussed this conjecture with Tobin's q ratio employing the latest Japanese SNA and examined substitutability between consumption and investment from a supply-side viewpoint.

On the contrary, Horioka (2006) examined the causes of the prolonged stagnation of the Japanese economy, focusing on household consumption expenditure with a demand-side approach. He summarized that the stagnation of household disposable income, the declines in household wealth and future uncertainty are the major causes of the stagnation of household consumption. Hence he stressed the importance of the demand-side approach to analyze this issue. In addition, Nakamura (2008) examined the causes of the Japanese stagnation of the demand-side economy from the viewpoint of income distribution, including both income flows and asset and debt accumulation in the household sector, and analyzed the effects of these factors on the Japanese economy using an econometric analysis. In Nakamura (2008), the regression analysis of household expenditures on disposable income in addition with three stock variables, such as financial assets, non-financial assets and financial liabilities, revealed that debt effects were more than asset effects, on a static basis.

This book also analyzes the causes of the Japanese deflationary economy, focusing on the influences of not only income distribution flows but also asset and debt accumulation to the household expenditures from both the demand-side and the supply-side points of view because many studies underestimate the role of stock variables in the demand-side economy. This study also examines the role of the supply-side to stimulate the demand-side, considering the interactive relations between income, demand and supply and the national economic framework. Econometric analysis is conducted on all three aspects with a view toward understanding the deflationary economy within Japan.

Concerning econometric modeling and forecasting analysis on the Japanese economy with respect to the long-term economic stagnation, there exist many research projects in Japan. In particular, with regard to the econometric study on the deflationary economy of Japan by explicitly utilizing GDP capacity, some projects including Japan–US Global Modeling Center (Shishido and Adams, 1990; Shishido *et al.*, 2011), Cabinet Office of the Japanese government and the Hokkaido Electric Power Company (HEPCO) Research Institute — the International University of Japan (IUJ) Project (Kido, Shimizu, Nagao and Nakamura, 1997–2010) have continued their research activities on this issue and published economic forecasts periodically.

The Japanese macro-econometric model employed in the present study has been developed for various research projects on the Japanese economy. It has been utilized as the core model for the HEPCO-IUJ Project and for prefecture-based regional econometric modeling and forecasting projects (Nakamura, 1993, 2002, 2010), and its calendar year base model has been employed as a national framework in the IUJ Global Model (Nakamura, 2007, 2011), which is in turn used as a pilot model for the JETRO-WEIS Global Model Project (Nakamura *et al.*, 1996; WEIS, 2005).

1.2. Methodology

As discussed earlier, in the present study, we employ econometric modeling and forecasting techniques as a methodology for analyzing the growth performance of the Japanese economy. Particularly, in order to understand the nature of the structural deflationary economy of Japan, a multi-equation structural model system with a demand–supply integrated-type logic has been developed. Here, we explain the econometric modeling and forecasting techniques briefly.

As shown in Table 1.1, at the first stage in modeling and forecasting, we consider an intuitive model, which is a kind of conceptual scaffolding constructed on the above-mentioned research objectives with a direct injection of the knowledge and experiences in our actual economy. With this intuitive base model, we design a theoretical model based on economic theories in economics and data availability. Based on this, at the second stage, econometrics and available data along with a database are input into the equation. Thereafter, we conduct a regression analysis, based on the theoretical model framework, by examining fundamental statistics, determining whether or not there exist biased estimates and investigating unit root test results. In this process, if we obtain the expected regression results for all behavioral equations, we move to the next stage. However, if we do not get good results, we return to the theoretical model and improve it. Then, we continue to implement the regression analysis until we obtain the expected plausible results.

Thereafter, we perform some dynamic simulation tests to determine whether the model can explain the actual economy with some model

Table 1.1: Econometric modeling and forecasting.

I. First Stage: Modeling for Theoretical Model

Intuitive Model $\rightarrow$ Theoretical Model

- Research Objectives
- General Knowledge
- Experience, etc.

- Economic Theory
- Literature Review
- Data Availability
- Actual Economy

II. Second Stage: Modeling for Econometric Model and Regression Analysis
               "Yes", next stage.

Econometric Model $\rightarrow$

           If "No", return to the previous stage.

- Econometrics
- Data Base
- Unit Root Test
- Regression Analysis

III. Final Stage: Forecasting for Forecast and Simulation Analysis
            "Yes."   "Yes."

Dynamic Simulation Tests $\rightarrow$ Forecasts $\rightarrow$ Analysis

          If "No", return to the previous stage.

- Goldberger Tests
  (Partial, Total and Final)
- Keynes Multiplier Test
- Dynamic Simulation Tests, etc.

- Baseline Forecast
- Scenario Forecasts
- Alternative Policy Analysis, etc.

Source: Compiled by the author.

reliability tests based on the Goldberger Test, including Partial Test, Total Test and Final Test, and with various dynamic simulation tests, including a dynamic Keynes multiplier test and financial and monetary policy tests. In the final stage of the Goldberger Test, all endogenous variables are interpolated during the regression sample period as a Final Test and continued until we can obtain good results by comparing the record of the estimated values to the actual values in terms of per cent deviation. The final test procedure is important for improving the econometric model at this stage, in which we can improve biased estimates, as well as in the regression analysis stage. When we obtain good results in the final test and in some dynamic simulation tests, we can advance to the next stage.

At the final stage, we implement a baseline forecast, which is a most-likely scenario for the future forecast. It is important to make the baseline forecast since it is a foundation for various scenario simulations. However, the econometric model with well-performed regression results and dynamic simulation tests may not necessarily perform the plausible baseline forecast. If we cannot make the plausible baseline forecast, we return to the regression analysis and improve the model again. Then, we start scenario forecasts after satisfying the baseline. Thereafter, we make scenario simulation analyses based on the results of the baseline forecast and scenario simulations.

As we discussed, the econometric modeling and forecasting techniques, as a methodology, are heavily dependent on our econometric studies and experience. Therefore, we need not only sufficient data but also extensive experience in modeling and forecasting.

1.3. Structure of this Study

With respect to the structure of this study, following Introduction, Chapter 2 reviews the cotemporary Japanese economy after the high-growth era and Chapter 3 analyzes the structure of the Japanese deflationary phenomenon by estimating GDP capacity and the deflationary gap. Chapter 4 discusses the causes of the long-term deflationary economy, from viewpoints of income distribution and asset and debt accumulation with reference to the supply-side and the demand-side economy, and Chapter 5 explains the theoretical model framework for empirical analyses in the present study. Chapter 6 discusses the demand–supply integrated macro-econometric model of Japan and examines the causation of the deflationary economy, and Chapter 7 performs a regression analysis for major endogenous variables related to the demand-side, the supply-side, income distribution and prices. Chapter 8 makes dynamic simulation tests including a model reliability test with the Goldberger Final Test, Keynes dynamic multiplier test, monetary and financial policy test and yen appreciation scenario simulation test, to analyze the dynamic causation of the deflationary economy of Japan. Chapter 9 conducts long-term scenario forecasts with a baseline forecast and three alternative scenario forecasts examining the growth performance of Japan under the deflationary economy. Finally, Chapter 10 summarizes the results concluding this study and presenting policy implications and finally discusses further research and simulation studies in the future.

CHAPTER 2

The Japanese Economy After the End of High-Growth Era

From the ashes of war, the Japanese economy was reconstructed and achieved high growth rates in the 1950s and 1960s. However, the economic miracle was underwritten by favorable conditions stemming from households, private corporate sector and public spending, with extensive sacrifices made to overcome post-war difficulties. Even after the end of the high-growth era, the Japanese economy continued to experience similar difficulties in which macro-environment constraints slowed the economy to a crawl. This chapter reviews the Japanese economy, with special attention to the relations between economic expansion and income distribution in the decades after the Japanese high-growth era, which may be one of the key concerns in the present study.

2.1. Period of Oil Crises and Transition to the Floating-System

In the 1970s, the Japanese economy experienced a couple of great environmental changes in the world economy, including the collapse of the dollar-gold standard system, in which the IMF-GATT Regime was substantially eclipsed, and several oil crises. In order to analyze the current Japanese economy and its problems, it is indispensable to discuss the Japanese economy in the period of the 1970s.

By achieving a high economic growth at over 10 per cent per annum in a couple of decades in the 1950s and 1960s, the Japanese economy attracted world attention at that time. However, in the early 1970s, two large international economic changes damaged the Japanese economy. These were, as well known, the Nixon administration's decision to move away from the gold standard and the first oil crisis. After these developments, many countries adopted the floating system in 1973 by way of the Smithsonian Agreement, and the exchange rates of major currencies fluctuated. The Japanese yen rates also fluctuated drastically, and the yen rate against the US dollar, which was fixed at 360 yen in 1949, appreciated sharply.

On the other hand, one more obstacle for the Japanese economy was the first oil crisis, which took place in 1973. Oil prices were stable during the decades in the 1950s and the 1960s, even during the world economic expansion after the end of WWII. However, the crude oil prices started to rise by the triggering of the Fourth Middle East War in October 1973. Thereafter, oil price hikes substantially affected the world economy.[1]

Facing such a situation in the early 1970s, Japan responded to these environmental changes quickly. Table 2.1 demonstrates the performance of the Japanese economy with real GDP growth rates, inflation in terms of CPI and WPI and the yen rate to the US dollar (EXR(¥/$)) in comparison with the US during 1970–1985.

From Table 2.1, it can be seen that the Japanese economy coped with yen appreciation and oil price hikes and sustained fairly stable economic growth at around 3–5 per cent in this period, in spite of being heavily dependent on the imports of natural resources, including crude oil from the rest of the world. Indeed, even in the second oil crisis period from 1979 to 1981, the Japanese economy sustained a positive economic growth at 3–4 per cent per annum, while the US experienced negative economic growth in 1980 and 1981.

At that time, the Japanese economy overcame these exogenous shocks through economic policies and collaborative efforts between the private and public sectors. In fact, some national projects by the central government were suspended and major labor unions compromised to terminate conventional wage-determining systems in order to avoid hyperinflation and to secure long-term employability. On the other hand, the Japanese corporate sector continued its investment and R&D expenditure to cope with severe competitions in world markets, thereby strengthening the supply-side economy. As a result, the relative wage income was stagnant, but, on the contrary, the corporate income rose in the latter half of the 1970s, as shown in Table 2.2.

Table 2.1: Growth performance of Japan in comparison with the US during the period of oil crises, 1970–1985.

	Oil Price ($/b)	Japan				US			
		GDP (%)	WPI (%)	CPI (%)	EXR (¥/$)	GDP (%)	WPI (%)	CPI (%)	EXR ($/—)*
1970	2.18	9.4	3.6	7.7	360.0	0.1	3.6	5.9	149.8
1971	2.66	4.2	−0.7	6.4	350.7	3.3	3.3	4.3	14539
1972	2.89	8.4	0.8	4.9	303.2	5.5	4.4	3.3	134.9
1973	3.24	7.9	15.9	11.7	271.7	5.8	13.1	6.2	125.3
1974	11.60	−1.2	31.4	23.1	292.1	−0.6	18.8	11.0	128.5
1975	10.96	2.6	3.0	11.8	296.8	−0.4	9.2	9.1	128.5
1976	12.23	4.8	5.1	9.4	296.6	5.4	4.6	5.7	133.6
1977	13.28	5.3	1.9	8.2	268.5	4.7	6.1	6.5	131.7
1978	13.39	5.1	−2.5	4.1	210.4	5.4	7.8	7.6	119.0
1979	30.21	5.2	7.3	3.8	219.1	2.8	12.5	11.3	117.4
1980	36.68	3.6	17.8	7.8	226.7	−0.3	14.1	13.5	117.7
1981	35.27	3.6	1.4	4.9	220.5	2.3	9.1	10.3	128.9
1982	32.45	3.2	1.8	2.7	249.1	−2.1	2.0	6.2	142.7
1983	29.64	2.7	−2.2	1.9	237.5	4.0	1.3	3.2	147.9
1984	28.55	4.3	−0.3	2.2	237.4	7.0	2.4	4.3	158.1
1985	27.37	5.0	−1.1	2.0	238.5	3.6	−0.5	3.6	163.4

*Nominal effective exchange rate, IMF formula (index, 1995 = 100).
Source: International Financial Statistics (IFS), IMF.

Table 2.2: Nominal GDP, wage income and corporate income of Japan in the 1970s.

	FY1970–1980	FY1970–1975	FY1975–1980
Nominal GDP Growth (a)	12.55 (%)	15.14 (%)	10.00 (%)
Wage income rate of changes (b)	14.84 (%)	20.29 (%)	9.63 (%)
Ratio of (b) to (a)	1.18	1.34	0.96
Corporate income rate of changes (c)	6.94 (%)	−6.34 (%)	22.10 (%)
Ratio of (c) to (a)	0.55	—	2.21
Ratio of (b) to (c)	2.14	—	0.44

Source: Compiled by the author, based on SNA68, ARNA, ESRI, Cabinet Office.

According to Table 2.2, the rate of changes in wage income drastically declined from 20.29 per cent, on average, in the first half of the 1970s, to 9.63 per cent, on average, in the latter half of the 1970s, while the rate of changes in corporate income rose from −6.34 per cent, on average, to 22.10 per cent, on average, in the same periods. Considering the declines in the growth performance of the economy between the first half and the latter half of the 1970s, we can easily understand that the income distribution pattern between profits and wages shifted in this period. As a result, the ratio of rate of changes in wage income (b) to that of corporate income (c) declined to 0.44 in the latter half of the 1970s.

2.2.   Period of the Plaza Accord and Bubble Economy in the 1980s

The 1980s was the turning point when the Japanese economy became matured, but its prosperity was disturbed by the currency realignment led by the US government. In September 1985, at the Plaza Hotel, New York, a consensus was reached to depreciate the US dollar and reduce interest rates to restore the world economy and to improve trade imbalance of major countries with coordinated fiscal, monetary and financial policies among G5 countries, known as the Plaza Agreement. Indeed, the US economy was suffering from stagflation (stagnation plus inflation) and the twin deficits of trade deficit and fiscal deficit in the early 1980s, just after the second oil crisis.

At that time, Japan was requested to accept this agreement since the Japanese economy could recover its growth performance in the early 1980s with large trade surplus, particularly to the US. The currency realignment was originally planned to depreciate the US dollar against the Japanese yen and Deutsche mark by around 10–15 per cent, but world markets responded vigorously to this currency realignment, and the US dollar depreciated sharply beyond expectation. The Japanese yen appreciated sharply in reverse, from around 240 yen/$ to 120 yen/$ within a few years.

In the yen appreciation, the Japanese economy incurred severe losses, and the central government implemented a large-scale fiscal policy with a six-trillion-yen spending package to avoid yen appreciation recession in

FY1986–1987. However, owing to depreciation of the US dollar, declines in oil prices and lower rate of interest, the "three low phenomena," the Japanese economy ultimately benefited from the Plaza Accord, which offset declines in real exports and increases in real imports. On the demand-side, the Japanese government continued large-scale fiscal policies to alleviate the yen appreciation damages, which brought forth the bubble economy and asset price hikes in the latter half of the 1980s.

Even following the structural changes in the 1970s, the Japanese economy prospered well into the 1980s. Table 2.3 demonstrates such a situation. The annual average growth rate of real GDP was 4.67 per cent, and private consumption and investment also achieved a high growth at 4.05 per cent and 8.82 per cent per annum, on average, respectively, in the 1980s. Particularly during the bubble period in the latter half of the 1980s, the annual average growth rate of real GDP and its components were strong, except for real exports due to the yen appreciation. In addition, the household disposable income increased consistently in terms

Table 2.3: Growth rate of real GDP, its components, real household income and real corporate income in the FY1980s.

	(%)		
	FY1980–1990	FY1980–1985	FY1985–1990
GDP	4.67	4.32	5.02
Priv. Consumption	4.05	3.49	4.61
Disposable Income*	3.50	3.01	3.99
Business Investment	8.82	6.75	10.93
Corporate Income**	2.13	3.60	0.68
Housing Investment	3.46	−1.27	8.41
Gov. Consumption	3.80	3.99	3.61
Gov. Investment	0.98	−1.85	3.89
Exports	5.59	7.23	3.98
Imports	6.08	0.80	11.64

*Deflated by consumption deflator.
**Deflated by business investment deflator.
Source: Compiled by the author, based on SNA93, chain-linked, ARNA, ESRI.

of constant prices, and corporate income also continued its high ratio to national income although its annual real growth was limited to 0.68 per cent since the corporate sector employed a lot of workers in this period, which constrained rises in corporate income. Indeed, the monthly averaged effective rate of worker-wanted was increasing in the bubble period and it exceeded 1.4, on average, in the year 1990.

However, even at the peak of the bubble, the inflation rate in terms of general deflator (PGDP) was relatively mild at 2.6 per cent in FY1989. That is, with the strong supply-side measures, the macro demand–supply condition seemed not to be tightened during the peak of the bubble during 1988–1990. Nevertheless, the Bank of Japan raised the official discount rate to 3.25 per cent in May 1989 to alleviate the heated economy.

2.3.   The Lost Two Decades after the Bursting of the Bubble

Following the tight monetary policy of the Bank of Japan, the central government also introduced "real estate loan restrictions" in March 1990, in which the Ministry of Finance forced financial institutions to limit real estate loans. At the same time, the official discount rate was raised to 6 per cent in August 1990. With tight monetary policy in place, this kind of intervention by the government paved way to the collapse of the bubble in 1990, and the major indicators turned negative in the summer of 1991.

Since then, the Japanese economy has experienced prolonged economic slump. Meanwhile, the government implemented various policies, including fiscal, monetary and financial policies, all of which were not very efficient or effective. Particularly, the large-scale fiscal stimulus planned to be implemented from FY1989 with 430 trillion yen for nine years, which was decided as an outcome of the Structural Impediments Initiatives (SII) between Japan and the US,[2] was cut short, and government spending declined from the mid-1990s onward. In addition, since the early 2000s, the central government has drastically reduced government investment under the policy of a reform of public finance and administration. On the other hand, the Bank of Japan introduced zero per cent interest rates and quantitative easing policy, but they have failed to boost the domestic demand.

After the bursting of the bubble economy, the Japanese economy suffered from long-term recession. Even during the long global boom from 2002 to the year 2008, before the onset of world financial crisis, the Japanese economy could not stimulate domestic demand, while exports and investments recorded strong growth in the situation of the world economic expansion, in particular in Asia and the Pacific.

As a result, the annual average growth rate of real GDP was 0.79 per cent and of nominal GDP 0.25 per cent in FY1990–2009, which represents the "Lost Two Decades", as shown in Table 2.4. During these decades, most of the indicators were deteriorating in terms of growth by decade except for real exports and real corporate income, in which real private consumption expenditure as the largest share in GDP was stagnant, along with the declines of real household disposable income. On the other hand, real private business investment recorded negative growth

Table 2.4: Growth rates of real GDP, its components, real household income and real corporate income in FY1990–2009.

(%)			
	FY1990–2009	FY1990–2000	FY2000–2009
GDP	0.79	1.09	0.46
Priv. Consumption	1.04	1.29	0.77
Disposable Income*	0.65	0.86	0.41
Business Investment	−0.81	−0.36	−1.21
Corporate Income**	0.80	−1.64	3.06
Housing Investment	−3.74	−2.38	−5.23
Gov. Consumption	2.46	3.05	1.80
Gov. Investment	−1.56	1.97	−5.33
Exports	3.80	3.08	4.46
Imports	2.42	3.92	0.78

*Deflated by consumption deflator.
**Deflated by business investment deflator.
Source: Compiled by the author based on SNA93, chain-linked, ARNA, ESRI.

in spite of positive increases in real corporate income in the 2000s. As discussed earlier, the corporate sector had increased accumulated savings, which distorted income distribution between profits and wages and resulted in Japan's deflationary economic predicament. Moreover, government investment, which would usually be employed for stimulating the demand-side, declined sharply in the 2000s. In addition, it seems that revision of dispatch labor law to extend the type of job might accelerate the distorted income distribution since 1999, which enabled the corporate sector to increase its savings and investment in the longest boom period between 2002 and 2008.

In summary, the Japanese economy in the past decades has weakened decade by decade as a result of macro-economic environment changes, in particular, yen appreciation in the floating system. In the high-growth era, the Japanese economy allowed the improvement of price and non-price competitiveness and expanded exports to the rest of the world. However, the highly appreciated yen with respect to major currencies resulted in competitive disadvantage, and many private corporations shifted their production base to the other countries through foreign direct investment (FDI).

Nevertheless, the corporate sector has continued vital domestic investment R&D and expenditures and further improved non-price competitiveness within Japan. As a result, the growth of the Japanese economy was led by exports in spite of the yen's appreciation. On the contrary, domestic demand has been stagnant with lower wage income increases. Therefore, the prospect of having domestic-demand–led growth has not been actualized for Japan, despite it being a matured and advanced nation with a strong currency. Japan could realize its domestic-demand–led growth with disinflation only in the bubble period, but this has become impossible since the bursting of the asset-led bubble in the early 1990s.

The growth performance, as noted, has been weakened from around 10 per cent, on average, in the 1950s and 1960s, to 4–5 per cent in the 1970s and 1980s, and to less than one per cent in the 1990s and 2000s, as shown in Figure 2.1. Interestingly, the growth in the past decades was led by foreign demand increases and non-housing investment related to increases in exports. The domestic demand increases have been relying on the increases in exports, which has not been changed at all as compared to that of high-growth era.

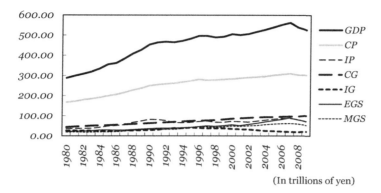

(In trillions of yen)

Figure 2.1: Real GDP and its major components, FY1980–2009.

Source: Developed by the author, based on SNA93, ESRI, Cabinet Office.

We will examine the Japanese economy and ways to improve this prolonged deflation in the following chapters.

End Notes

[1] Prices of the other primary commodities were also rising as well as oil prices, along with a trend of the natural resource nationalism in the 1970s.

[2] The Structural Impediments Initiatives was reconsidered by Japan and the US, and additional demand stimulus with 200 trillion yen was reinforced by Murayama Cabinet in 1994.

CHAPTER 3

The Deflationary Economy of Japan

3.1. Economic Structure with an Inflationary and Deflationary Gap in the Process of Economic Development

Through Rostow's (1960) view, we recognize that there exist various stages in the process of economic growth and development and, as Rostow defined, classify them into five stages, including the traditional society, the precondition for take-off, the take-off, the drive to maturity and the age of mass-consumption. In these stages, Rostow emphasized the importance of both the precondition for take-off and the take-off stages with an accumulation of capital and technology to achieve economic maturity for economic development. After the end of the take-off stage, however, most of the economies experienced lower economic growth rates.

In the case of Japan, its economy experienced the take-off stage in the fourth quarter of the 19th century and achieved the stage of the drive to mutuality in the prewar period according to Rostow. However, during the war period, around 80 per cent of the social assets, including capital assets and social infrastructure, were destroyed, therefore, the Japanese economy was forced to restart its economic development from ashes, but the accumulated technology which carried Japanese prosperity in the prewar period played a significant role in achieving economic development and entering the age of mass consumption and production within a couple of decades after WWII.

Here, we introduce a conceptual model for examining a macroeconomic growth performance of a country with respect to the macro demand-side and supply-side and major determinants of economic growth. In the process of economic development, we can observe an inflationary and deflationary gap in an economy. Figure 3.1 demonstrates the

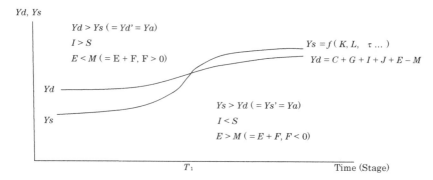

Figure 3.1: Demand-side economy (Yd) and supply-side economy (Ys) in the process of economic development.
Source: Developed by the author.

determinants of a demand-side and supply-side of a nation and the relationship between the demand-side and supply-side GDP during the process of economic development. In Figure 3.1, the vertical axis represents an aggregate demand and aggregate supply, and the horizontal axis represents time.

Generally, in the initial stage of economic development before T_1, the level of the supply-side GDP (Ys), which is a function of capital stock (K), labor (L) and technology (τ), is lower than that of the demand-side GDP (Yd), which depends on consumption (C), government expenditure (G), investment (I), inventory changes (J), exports (E) and imports (M) in an open economic system. The aggregate demand, however, cannot exceed the aggregate supply, so that the demand-side GDP is depressed to the level of the supply-side GDP, as Yd', and the actual macro GDP (Ya) relies on the supply-side GDP (Ya = Ys = Yd'). Therefore, Yd is a potential demand-side GDP, which cannot be realized in the actual economy. (Please see left-hand-side in Figure 3.1.)

On the other hand, when the economy is advancing, the supply-side (Ys) is getting stronger with capital accumulation and technical progress, and exceeds the demand-side GDP (Yd) at time T_1, in the take-off stage. Since then, the actual GDP (Ya) depends on the level of the demand-side GDP (Yd) because the supply-side cannot exceed the demand-side, and the supply-side GDP is depressed to Ys' (Ya = Yd = Ys'). Therefore, Ys is a potential supply-side GDP after T_1 in the actual economy. (Please see right-hand-side in Figure 3.1).

In the stage before T_1, saving (S) is smaller than required investment (I) to meet the demand-side of the economy ($I > S$), so that the inflationary gap ($Yd > Ys$) results in a demand-pull inflation and trade deficit ($E < M$). In addition, net capital inflows are positive ($F > 0$) because of trade deficit ($E < M$) and of $I > S$. On the contrary, in the stage after T_1, there exist the deflationary gap ($Yd < Ys$) and trade surplus ($E > M$) because of $I < S$. In this stage, we may not observe a demand-pull inflation but a cost-push inflation with higher labor cost in line with the economic growth. Basically, the growth rates are expected to diminish after T_1, since the economic growth depends on the demand-side growth performance, as Japan, West Germany and the other countries experienced in the 1970s.

Generally speaking, the economic structure before T_1, in which the demand-side GDP is larger than the supply-side GDP, is a "developing-country–type economic structure," and after T_1, on the contrary, a "developed-country–type economic structure." In general, therefore, a demand-side–oriented type model is employed for a developed country and a supply-side–oriented type model is utilized for developing countries (Klein, 1978). Nevertheless, both the macro demand-side and supply-side economy are important concepts for determining the growth performance of an economy considering the IS balance, as explained in Figure 3.1. Accordingly, a demand–supply integrated-type growth model is essential and useful for both developed and developing economies.[1]

In the case of Japan, its economy achieved high growth in the 1950s and the 1960s, and Japan became one of the OECD member countries in April 1964. In that sense, it seems that Japan experienced T_1, in the mid-1960s and was able to host the Tokyo Olympic Games in 1964 and Osaka World Exposition in 1970. In general, before T_1, it may be difficult to have large world events such as Olympic Games within the inflationary gap economic structure.

However, after T_1, the deflationary gap decreases since the supply-side GDP tends to meet the demand-side GDP again. Thereafter, the macro demand-side curve and supply-side curve cross again and again with a business cycle, and the economy reaches the steady state. Therefore, generally, we may not observe the long-term deflationary gap as a result of the structural deflation. In the case of Japan, however, we have observed the long-term structural deflationary economy since the mid-1970s.

The structural deflationary economy itself is not necessarily a problematic issue since the supply-side is stronger than the demand-side, in which we do not observe the demand-pull inflation. The structural deflation, however, may result in excess labor and trade surpluses in the longer-term period and may lose its economic dynamics, with increases in net capital outflows to the rest of the world.

3.2.   Deflationary Gap in Japan

In the 1970s, the Japanese economy did strengthen its supply-side by improving technologies with induced technical progress to cope with hyperinflation and economic recessions during the period of oil crises. With a huge amount of investment and R&D expenditure in the private sector, the Japanese economy overcame the oil crises by reinforcing the supply-side of the economy. Since then, the gap between the demand-side and the supply-side increased. As a matter of fact, Japan was able to cease the imported cost-push inflation in the early 1980s earlier than the other developed countries, and general price level was very stable even during the bubble period. Indeed, since the bursting of the bubble, prices have been declining in terms of GDP deflator.

Figure 3.2 shows the actual real GDP (GDP), which may be the demand-side GDP and the GDP capacity (GDPC) estimated by

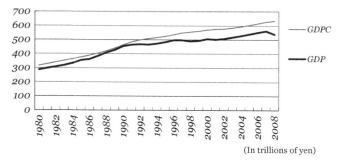

(In trillions of yen)

Figure 3.2:   Real GDP (GDP) and the estimated real GDP capacity (GDPC), in FY1980–2008.
Source: Estimated by the author, based on SNA93, chain-linked.

the Cobb–Douglas production function, adjusting the rate of capacity utilization of capital, unemployment rate and labor working hours to full capacities of each. (We will discuss how GDPC was estimated in Section 3.3.) Therefore, as shown in Figure 3.2, the deflationary gap is the gap between the actual real GDP and the estimate GDPC.

According to our estimation, the deflationary gap increased after the mid-1970s, and the gap itself was 28 trillion yen in FY1980 and 32 trillion yen in FY1985 in terms of 2000 year constant prices. In the bubble period from FY1987 to FY1990, however, the gap drastically declined to around 10 trillion yen at the peak of the bubble in FY1990, since the demand-side economy, in particular private consumption expenditure, was heated by asset price hikes. In this period, the GDP capacity growth rate also rose sharply in line with the high growth rate of real GDP through vital capital accumulation, in which we could see the economic dynamics of both the demand-side and supply-side, as shown in Figure 3.2.

After the bursting of the bubble, however, the gap widened again. Thereafter, in the longest boom period from FY2002, the gap slightly narrowed due to increases in exports and investment, but remained a large value at 60–70 trillion yen. In FY2008, the world financial crisis damaged the Japanese economy, particularly its demand-side, and, as a result, the deflationary gap started widening more and was estimated to exceed 95 trillion yen, as of FY2008, which was around 17 per cent of annual real GDP.

In general, the supply-side GDP, which is the GDPC in Figure 3.2, might be narrowing with a reduction of capital stock, as far as the demand-side is not boosted. However, in the case of Japan, many private corporations have continued their vital investment to improve the quality of their products in order to stimulate consumer demand. This might be inevitable in order to cope with severe competition in the world economy, as we experienced during the oil crises period in the 1970s. Therefore, the Japanese deflationary economy may be a result of a sort of structural deflation, and not simply a short-term deflation caused by the business cycle.

3.3. Estimation of GDP Capacity and Deflationary Gap

As discussed earlier, in the present study, we estimated the GDP capacity, because we explicitly utilized the estimated GDP capacity for our research.

Therefore, this section explains the procedures of estimating the GDP capacity and hence the deflationary gap and examines the reliability of the estimated GDP capacity time series with some measures.

In the first step, based on the Cobb–Douglass production function employing actual real GDP time series with a vintage model and time trend, real GDP is regressed on capital stock (KP) with capacity utilization rate of capital (CUR), which is the capacity utilization rate with the weighted average of the share of manufacturing and non-manufacturing sector, the number of employed $((1 - UR)*NL)$ adjusted by the ratio (LHRAT) of overall working hours (LHT) to legal working hours (LHL), the ratio of the recent three-year summation of real private non-housing investment to capital stock $((IP + IP(-1) + IP(-2))/KP)$ and time trend (TIME),[2] as follows:

ln (GDP)

$$= f((+) \ln (KP^*CUR/100), \quad (+) \ln (NL^*(1 - UR/100)^*LHRAT),$$
$$(+)(IP + IP(-1) + IP(-2))/KP, \quad (+)TIME)$$

According to the regression result from the labor productivity function, the coefficient of capital stock (capital share) is 0.30176 and hence the coefficient of labor (labor share) is $0.69824(= 1 - 0.30176)$. The fundamental statistics, including the t-value in parenthesis, adjusted R^2, standard error (SE) and Durbin–Watson ratio are significant and performed well with the Cochrane–Orcutt (C-O) procedure.

$$\ln (GDP/(1 - UR/100)^*NL^*LHRAT)) = 0.267797$$

$$(12.03)$$

$$+ 0.301759 \ln ((KP^*CUR/100)/(1 - UR/100)^*NL^*LHRAT))$$

$$(5.63))$$

$$+ 0.238326(IP + IP(-1) + IP(-2))/KP + 0.00412 \ TIME$$

$$(2.48) \qquad\qquad\qquad\qquad (3.06)$$

C-O(1981 − 2008)

$$\text{Adjusted } R^2 = 0.993 \quad SE = 0.00955 \quad DW = 1.708$$

In the second step, utilizing this regression result, time series of GDP capacity (GDPCHAT) is estimated from FY1981 to FY2008 by adjusting CUR, UR and LHRAT to employ the peak values in FY1990 at 100(%) for CUR, at 2.09(%) for UR and at 1.099 for LHRAT which are the values of the final fiscal year of the bubble period, as follows.

$$\ln (\text{GDPCHAT})$$
$$= 0.267797 + 0.301759 \ln (\text{KP}^*100/100)$$
$$\quad (12.08) \quad (5.63)$$
$$+ (1 - 0.301759) \ln ((1 - 2.09/100)^*\text{NL}^*1.099)$$
$$(^{***})$$
$$+ 0.238326(\text{IP} + \text{IP}(-1) + \text{IP}(-2))/\text{KP} + 0.00412 \text{ TIME}$$
$$\quad (2.48) \qquad\qquad\qquad\qquad (3.06)$$

In the final step, the estimated GDPCHAT was adjusted by the residuals between the actual real GDP time series and the estimated real GDP (GDPHAT) time series by the production function. Then, the GDPC and the deflationary gap (DGAP) time series were generated from FY1981 to FY2008, as follows.

$$\text{GDPC} = \text{GDPCHAT} + (\text{Actual Real GDP} - \text{GDPHAT})$$
$$\text{DGAP} = \text{GDPC} - \text{Actual Real GDP}$$

As discussed, Figure 3.2 shows the actual real GDP, the estimated GDP capacity (GDPC) and the deflationary gap (DGAP), and these time series are utilized to examine the Japanese macro-economic structure in this study. Concerning the assumption to estimate the GDP capacity including the peak value of capacity utilization rate of capital (CUR) at 100 (%), the rate of unemployment (UR) at 2.09 (%) and the ratio of total working hours to legal working hours (LHRAT) at 1.099(%), it seems these values may be reasonable. As a matter of fact, these values are the peak values of the bubble period and the highest value for each over the sample period from FY1980 to FY2009 in the present study.

For example, it seems that the value of rate of unemployment at 2.09 per cent may be the natural rate of unemployment of the contemporary

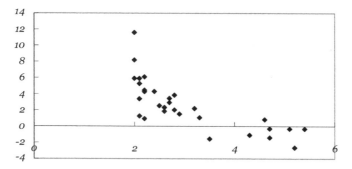

Figure 3.3: Phillips–Lipsey curve trade-off relation of Japan, FY1980–2009 (horizontal axis means rate of unemployment (%) and vertical axis changes in nominal wage rates (%)).
Source: Developed by the author.

Japanese economy after the end of the high-growth era of Japan, which could be observed within the Phillips–Lipsey curve (Phillips, 1958, Lipsey 1960) trade-off relation by employing data series from FY1980 to FY2009, as shown in Figure 3.3. In accordance with the Phillips–Lipsey curve trade-off relation of Japan, the curve may demonstrate to be vertical to the horizontal axis at around 2.0 per cent, which might be seen as if the natural rate of unemployment hypothesis (Freidman, 1968) were applicable to the Japanese economy. Certainly, in Figure 3.3, there are seven dot marks with less than 2.3 per cent rate of unemployment in horizontal axis, in spite of a wide range of nominal wage rate changes from 1.3 per cent to 12.5 per cent in vertical axis, which is in between around 2.1 to 2.3 per cent in horizontal axis.[3]

With respect to the reliability of the estimated GDP capacity, the time series of the estimated GDP capacity may be proven by the other measures. Here, we employ the concept of the natural rate of growth, which was introduced into economic theory by Harrod (1939) as the rate of growth of productive potential of an economy. According to his theory, it was defined as the growth composed of labor force growth and labor productivity (technology) growth. For the empirical analysis, therefore, we employ Okun's law (1962) to examine the natural rate of growth related to the relation between growth rate and changes in unemployment.

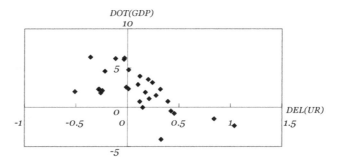

Figure 3.4: Correlation between growth rate of real GDP (DOT(GDP)) and changes in rate of unemployment (DEL(UR)) in FY1980–2009.
Source: Developed by the author.

Based on Okun's law, we define the natural rate of growth as the growth rate keeping the rate of unemployment constant, as demonstrated in Figure 3.4. The figure explains the correlation between growth rate of real GDP on the vertical axis and changes in rate of unemployment on the horizontal axis. According to the concept of Okun's law, the intercept of the correlated curve across the vertical axis represents the natural rate of growth. Employing this causation, we conducted regression analysis and estimated the natural rate of growth.

Based on the Okun's law, the natural rate of growth is estimated employing the following equation, in which, the constant coefficient (α_1) explains the natural rate of growth when the changes in rate of unemployment is zero (DEL(UR) = 0).

$$DOT(GDP) = \alpha_1 + \beta_1 DEL(UR) + u_1$$

where DOT(GDP) in the left-hand-side is real GDP growth rate, DEL(UR) means changes in rate of unemployment and u_1 refers to an error term.

Based on this model specification, we made a regression analysis by usually employing an instrumental variable (IV) method or two-stage least square (2SLS) since both real GDP growth and rate of unemployment are determined simultaneously in the actual economy. In regression, we employ the 2SLS and the DEL(UR) estimated by changes in labor productivity (DEL(GDP/L)) and previous year's DEL(UR) is utilized for this regression. In accordance with the regression result, the estimates are very significant in terms of t-value (value in parenthesis) of each coefficient. It is expected, by definition, that the natural rate of growth is 2.706 (α_1) per cent on average during over the period from FY1980 to FY2008, since we assume the growth rate is the natural rate of growth when the rate of unemployment change is zero (DEL(UR $=0$)).

$$DOT(GDP) = 2.706 - 7.395 \ DEL(UR)$$

$$(4.79) \qquad (-5.99)$$

2SLS (1980–2008) Adjusted R^2 = 0.705 SE = 1.412 DW = 2.020

Next, based on the same logic, we tested the natural rate of growth for two periods, such as the period from FY1980 to FY1990 and the period after the bursting of the bubble, utilizing a dummy variable (D_{9091}) of the lost two decades, as follows.

$$DOT(GDP) = \alpha_2 + \beta_2 \ DEL(UR) + \gamma_2 D_{9091} + u_2$$

where D_{9091} denotes the dummy variable with 1 before FY1990 and 0 after FY1991 and u_2 refers to an error term.

According to the regression analysis, it seems the result may be reliable and significant in each coefficient. Therefore, the average natural rate of growth is assumed at 1.912 (α_2) per cent during the period of the lost two decades from FY1991 to FY2008 and at 4.275 ($\alpha_2 + \gamma_2$) per cent during the period from FY1980 to FY1990.

$$DOT(GDP) = 1.912 - 5.596 \ DEL(UR) + 2.363 \ D_{9091}$$

$$(4.29) \quad (-4.69) \qquad\qquad (2.98)$$

2SLS (1980–2008) AdjustedR^2 = 0.739 SE = 1.321 DW = 1.919

Based on the estimated natural rate of growth of Japan, we can compare the estimated GDPC growth with the natural rate of growth and actual real GDP growth rate. Table 3.1 shows the annual average growth rate of actual real GDP, real GDP capacity (GDPC) and the annual average natural rate of growth by period. Indeed, the concept of the natural rate of growth may be a little bit different from the GDPC growth since the GDPC growth considers the growth with full-capacity utilization of capital, full employment and technical progress while the natural rate of growth takes

Table 3.1: Annual average growth rate of actual GDP, the estimated GDP capacity and the estimated natural rate of growth based on Okun's law.

Period(FY)	1980–2008	1980–1990	1990–2008	1990–2000	2000–2008
GDP growth	2.27(%)	4.67(%)	0.97(%)	1.09(%)	0.65(%)
GDPC growth	2.51(%)	3.80(%)	1.78(%)	2.13(%)	1.34(%)
Natural rate of growth	2.71(%)	4.28(%)	1.92(%)	—	—

Source: Estimated and compiled by the author, based on SNA93, chain linked.

account of the growth with full employment and technical progress, based on the actual real GDP realized in an economy. Nevertheless, we may be able to compare both the potential growth rates.

In accordance with the results shown in Table 3.1, the annual average growth rate of the estimated GDP capacity and the natural rate of growth are similar at 2.51 per cent and 2.71 per cent, respectively, during the period of FY1980–2008. As compared to the actual real GDP growth, both the GDPC growth and the natural rate of growth are higher than the actual real GDP growth by 0.24 per cent point and by 0.44 per cent point, respectively. On the other hand, during the period of the 1980s, the natural rate of growth is 4.28 per cent, which is lower than the actual real GDP growth at 4.67 per cent, and the estimated GDPC growth at 3.80 per cent is also lower than that of the actual real GDP. This may be because the actual real GDP growth was heated by expanded consumption with asset price hikes in the bubble period, which relied on demand-side expansion, not on the supply-side. This could be seen in the analysis of Thirlwall (2002) employing the same method to examine the natural rate of growth of 15 OECD member countries over the period 1961–1995, in which the average natural rate of growth of Japan in the boom periods was 8.7199 per cent, which was lower than the actual growth of Japan with over 10 per cent annual average growth rate in the 1960s.

On the contrary, the annual average growth rate of the estimated GDPC is 1.78 per cent during the period from FY1990 to FY2008, while the natural rate of growth is 1.92 per cent on average, both of which are higher than that of the actual real GDP growth in this period. The difference between the GDPC growth and the natural rate of growth may depend on different concepts of potential growth, irrespective of whether the full-capacity utilization of capital is taken into consideration. In this test, we employed the 2SLS to introduce the natural rate of growth utilizing Okun's Law and its plausible results.[4] It seems that the estimated GDP capacity may also be reliable, based on this comparative test.

Some research institutes also have estimated potential GDP and its growth. For example, the Bank of Japan (Ito *et al.*, 2006) estimated potential GDP utilizing the Cobb–Douglas production function, in which TFP (total factor productivity) was defined as the Solow residual. In addition, capacity utilization of capital and labor utilization rates were estimated based on the past averaged rates in calculating the potential GDP. Therefore, the rate of deflationary gap estimated was very low, at around 10 per cent of the actual GDP in FY2002, just before the longest boom. On the other hand, ESRI (Kitajima, 2011) also estimated potential GDP by utilizing a similar method employed in the BOJ, in which the gap was also less than 9.5 per cent of the actual real GDP in FY2009. These estimated values may be lower than our estimated deflationary gap in the present study since the estimated deflationary gap is 66.3 trillion yen (13.1 per cent in GDP) in FY2002 and 105.1 trillion yen (19.9 per cent in GDP) in FY2009.[5]

In summary, this chapter examined the deflationary economy of Japan through introducing the GDP capacity and hence the deflationary gap in the past three decades. According to our study on this issue, the large deflationary gap can be observed, and the growth performance has been declining in spite of the strong supply-side economy. However, this scenario means the growth potential is still strong as far as there is sufficient room to stimulate the demand-side economy, as we experienced in the 1980s, when the demand-side followed the supply-side and the supply-side ceiling (capacity) and its growth were sufficiently flexible to be boosted up in line with demand-side increases. In other words, we can realize a much higher growth since the supply capacity is not given but is endogenized.

End Notes

[1] Nakamura (2011) examined the aggregate demand–supply and economic growth performance of Vietnam utilizing a demand–supply

integrated-type model. In Vietnam, the aggregate demand is larger than the aggregate supply, $Yd > Ys$ ($= Yd' = Ya$). In other words, there is the structural inflationary gap in Vietnam which may be one of the major constraints on the long-term sustainable growth.

2 Nakamura (2008) examined the causes of macro-TFP being explained by the ratio of output price to input price (Px/Pz), ratio of labor cost to user cost of capital (Pw/Pk), ratio of intermediate input cost to user cost of capital, vintage of capital stock ($(IP+IP(-1)+IP(-2))/KP$) and time trend (TIME), based on Shishido and Nakamura (1992a), as follows.

$$\ln(\text{TFP}) = 2.465 + 0.0113 \ln (Px/Pz) + 0.068 \ln (Pw/Pk) - 0.0042 \ln (Pr/Pk)$$

$$(68.01) \quad (2.01) \qquad\qquad (7.03) \qquad\qquad\quad (1.78)$$

$$+ 0.029 \ln (IP + IP(-1) + IP(-2))/KP + 0.0059 \text{ TIME}$$

$$(6.74) \qquad\qquad\qquad\qquad\qquad (44.86)$$

C-O (1981 − 2007)   Adjusted $R^2 = 0.997$ SD $= 0.0010$ DW $= 1.414$

TFP: total factor productivity derived from the Cobb–Douglas production function as the Solow residual.

3 Interestingly, the Japanese rate of unemployment remained at around 2.0 per cent in the bubble period, which was fairly higher as compared to the lower rate of unemployment in the 1970s. As is well known, Friedman (1968) criticized the Keynesian fiscal policy employing the natural rate of unemployment hypothesis. In this hypothesis, the rate of unemployment (UR) relies on labor productivity (GDP/L) but not on the effective demand and hence the rate of changes in nominal wage rate. Friedman employed real wage rate (W/P) for this hypothesis in place of nominal wage rate changes, as follows.

$$\text{DOT}(W/P) = f(\text{UR}), \ (f' < 0) \quad \text{Therefore, DOT}(W) - \text{DOT}(P) = f(\text{UR})$$

Price (P) changes depend on expected nominal wage rate (W^*) changes and labor productivity (GDP/L) changes.

$$\text{DOT}(P) = \text{DOT}(W^*) - \text{DOT}(\text{GDP/L}).$$

Therefore, $\text{DOT}(W) - \text{DOT}(W^*) + \text{DOT}(\text{GDP/L}) = f(\text{UR})$.

In the long run, the expected nominal wage rate changes equal actual wage rate changes.

Therefore, $UR = g\,(DOT(GDP/L))$, $(g' > 0)$ and the Philips curve is vertical at the natural rate of unemploymentx (DOT means rate of changes). Indeed, we got this causation with employing GDP capacity (GDPC), instead of GDP, as follows.

$$UR = -19.33 + 0.5249 \ln (GDPC/NL)$$

$$(-4.99) \qquad (5.87)$$

$$OLS(1980 - 2008) \quad Adjusted - R^2 = 0.554 \; SE = 0.071 \; DW = 1.210$$

However, this issue of endogenizing the natural rate of unemployment is still under consideration in the present study, so we will discuss this issue in another opportunity.

[4] As noted, in the test we employed a 2SLS to improve bias because both the GDP growth rate and changes in rate of unemployment may be simultaneously determined in the economy and therefore an independent variable has a correlation with an error term. Both OLS and 2SLS estimates are listed below.

Estimates within OLS and 2SLS to introduce the natural rate of growth

	$DOT(GDP) = \alpha + \beta_1\,DEL(UR) + u_1$			
Method	OLS		2SLS	
α_1	2.402	(3.43)	2.706	(4.79)
β_1	−4.389	(−3.92)	−7.395	(−5.99)
Adjusted-R^2	0.713		0.705	
	Sample: FY1980–2008			

	$DOT(GDP) = \alpha_2 + \beta_2\,DEL(UR) + \gamma_2\,D9091 + u_2$			
Method	OLS		2SLS	
α_2	1.395	(4.09)	1.912	(4.29)
β_2	−3.620	(−4.58)	−5.596	(−4.69)
γ_2	3.404	(5.64)	2.363	(2.96)
Adjusted-R^2	0.746		0.739	
	Sample: FY1980–2008			

[5] Interestingly, these studies employ the method to estimate the inflationary gap in a business cycle, utilized by the US and European countries. Therefore, the indicator of the deflationary gap in terms of percentage

rate is defined, as follows.

$$\text{Gap}(\%) = [(\text{Actual GDP} - \text{Potential GDP})/\text{Potential GDP}]*100$$

As a result, the calculated deflationary gap is negative when the potential GDP is larger than the actual real GDP. In other words, this equation is an identity not to calculate the deflationary gap but to calculate the inflationary gap. Indeed, in the ESRI and BOJ research, the deflationary gap is assumed as negative values estimated when the capacity is larger than the actual GDP, based on the equation to calculate the gap, as mentioned earlier.

CHAPTER 4

Causes of The Deflationary Economy

As discussed earlier, the Japanese economy has been in structural deflation, which is different from a short-term deflationary situation that depends on a business cycle. In this chapter, therefore, we discuss the causes of the structural deflationary economy of Japan, with a special focus on the supply-side and demand-side economies incorporated with income distribution patterns. Distributed income flows between profits and wages have strong influences on the performance of both the supply-side and the demand-side economies associated with asset and debt accumulation in the private corporate sector and the household sector.

4.1. Income Distribution Patterns

In the 1970s, the supply-side of the economy was strengthened drastically to overcome hyperinflation and to cope with the severe competition in world markets. With a huge amount of investment and R&D expenditure even during the oil crises period, the Japanese economy overcame difficult situations. As a result of the complication of the inflationary spiral in the hyperinflation period, labor unions voluntarily compromised with their management to accept changes in the conventional wage system, which relied on the conventional management system of Japan, including lifetime employment and seniority wage system. Labor and management relations were improved in order to avoid the downward spiral caused by inflation and wage increase and to secure their employment when the oil crises damaged the economy.

In fact, in the process of economic recovery in the 1950s and 1960s, the rate of changes in nominal wage rates relied on the previous year's inflation rate in terms of CPI (indexation) and rate of changes in labor productivity. This mechanism prevailed in the Japanese society in the decades after World War II.

Table 4.1:   Determinants of nominal wage rates in FY1970–2000.

	$ln\,W(t) = \alpha + \beta\,lnCPI(t-1) + \gamma\,lnLPI\,(t-1)$				
Period	α	β	γ	Adjusted R^2	DW
FY1970–1980	−3.23	0.7038	1.106	0.975	1.595
	(−2.72)	(3.17)	(2.41)		
FY1980–1990	−0.166	0.319	0.760	0.983	1.288
	(−0.32)	(1.06)	(7.26)		
FY1990–2000	−0.103	0.485	0.572	0.697	0.978
	(−0.10)	(1.76)	(1.73)		

Note: Values in parenthesis mean t-statistics. W: nominal wage rates; CPI: consumer price index; LPI: labor productivity.
Source: Estimated and compiled by the author.

Table 4.1 shows the relationship between rate of changes in nominal wage rates and previous year's inflation rate and rate of changes in labor productivity by decade during FY1970–2000. As shown in Table 4.1, the conventional wage rates determining system still remained significant in the 1970s, on a macro basis, while these causes were gradually insignificant in the 1980s and not recognized in the 1990s.

As noted earlier, income distribution plays a crucial role in determining the performance of the economy. This mechanism is one of the key issues in economics. In particular, wage income share and profit share are critical factors determining the demand-side and the supply-side economy since the larger wage income share results in increase in the household sector's expenditures.

Table 4.2 shows the averaged ratio of household income (Y_H) to nominal GDP and of corporate income (Y_C) to nominal GDP by five-year period from FY1980 to FY2008. As for the household income, the ratio to nominal GDP was declining period by period, in which the ratio was around 0.7, on average, in the FY1980s and in the first half of the FY1990s, while the ratio in the latter half of the FY1990s was declining to 0.68, on average, and to 0.64 in the first half of the FY2000s and to 0.63 in FY2005–2008.

On the other hand, the ratio of corporate income to nominal GDP rose to 0.091, on average, in the period of the first half of the FY2000s and to

Table 4.2: Ratio of household income (Y_H) and corporate income (Y_C) to GDP, and percentage share (%) of Y_H and Y_C, FY1980–2008.

Period	Y_H/GDPN	Y_C/GDPN	Y_H:Y_C	Y_H:Y_C(U.S.)
FY1980–1984	0.716	0.094	88.4:11.6	(89.8:10.2)
FY1985–1989	0.690	0.101	87.2:12.8	(90.1: 9.9)
FY1990–1994	0.706	0.068	91.2: 8.8	(89.7:10.3)
FY1995–1999	0.681	0.073	90.3: 9.7	(89.5:10.5)
FY2000–2004	0.643	0.091	87.6:12.4	(89.2:10.8)
FY2005–2008	0.629	0.090	87.5:12.5	(89.3:10.7)

Source: Calculated and compiled by the author, based on SNA93, ARNA, ESRI, Cabinet Office and US Bureau of Economic Analysis, Survey of Current Business for the US.

0.093, on average, in the period from FY2005 to FY2008, although the ratio declined to 0.068 in the first half of the FY1990s and 0.073 in the latter half of the FY1990s. Particularly, the ratio of corporate income was rising in the FY2000s and recorded the highest ratios of 0.110 in FY2004, at 0.101 in FY2005, was at 0.105 in FY2006 and at 0.109 in FY2007 and hence was at 0.105, on average, in FY2005–2007, although it declined to 0.068 in FY2008 during the world financial crisis and hence was 0.090, on average, in FY2005–2008.

As a result, as shown in the third column of Table 4.2, the percentage share of household income in total has been declining during the past decades. In the FY2000s, the share of household income declined to 87.5–87.6 per cent and hence the share of corporate income rose to 12.4–12.5 per cent. Thus, it could be seen that these declines in percentage share of household income describe the distorted income distribution structure which caused the structural deflationary economy of Japan, if we compare them to the fairly stable household income share of the US at 89–90 per cent, listed in the fourth column of Table 4.2.

In addition to that, asset accumulation has large effects on the demand-side (Tobin, 1951). As noted earlier, Ando (2002) and Ando *et al.* (2003) discussed, by utilizing Tobin's q ratio, the behaviors of the Japanese corporate sector to increase the position of assets to liabilities resulted in an over-investment and in constraints on the household income through distorting income distribution. This hypothesis, termed as the "over-investment hypothesis" by Hayashi, is very crucial to understanding the causes of the prolonged Japanese economic slump, considering the effects of not only household income flows but also asset and debt accumulation on the economy. It seems that the distorted income distribution may be one of the major causes of the Japanese deflation. Therefore, we examine the causes of the stagnation of household expenditures from the viewpoints of income distribution and asset and debt accumulation in the household sector in this study, as well as from the perspective of corporate sector behavior as proposed by Ando *et al.* (2003).

The profit share rose and household income share declined, and many corporations could employ their large profits for investment and R&D expenditure, which resulted in strengthening the supply-side economy. In particular, the corporate sector, which experienced severe competitive pressure in the world economy, accelerated capital accumulation and technical progress.

4.2.   Income Distribution Patterns and the Supply-Side

From the private sector perspective, corporations have taken a prudent attitude toward investment, but continued to implement large R&D expenditure, which led to an increase in their profit share despite the deflationary situation within the Japanese economy. As a result, the position of accumulated savings has increased. The behavior of the corporate sector to increase its accumulated savings may result from uncertainty of economic climates and the prevailing global accounting system. It seems that the corporate sector tends to save a lot of money for future investment opportunities as a precautionary motive. Indeed, the corporate income tax cut policy for inducing investments might have a positive effect, but it has not large impacts on the investment behaviors.[1]

Concerning the behaviors of the corporate sector as Ando (2002, 2003) and Hayashi (2006) discussed, as a matter of fact, the averaged Tobin's q ratio remained much lower than unity in the past two decade, as demonstrated in Figure 4.1. The averaged Tobin's q ratio is defined as the ratio of net financial liabilities (financial liabilities—financial assets) to non-financial assets in non-financial private corporate sector. Therefore, the

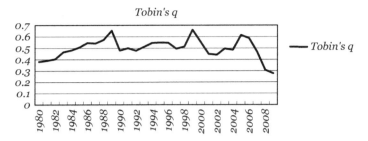

Figure 4.1: Averaged Tobin's q ((liabilities−financial assets)/non-financial assets) in FY1980–2009.
Source: Developed by the author, based on SNA93, ESRI, Cabinet Office.

ratio may be nearly unity theoretically to maintain consistency between corporate assets and liabilities. However, the ratio has been very low at 0.4–0.5, on average, although it was increasing in expansionary phase of the economy.

The lower Tobin's q ratio, which may result from the corporate sector's behaviors to increase accumulated savings, would be consistent with the consumer's behaviors in the household sector not to increase their consumption under the liquidity constraints in the deflationary economy. The private corporate sector, nevertheless, has continued vital investments in spite of the lower demand-side economy and Tobin's q ratio, which may be the reason Ando raised the issue of distorted income distribution in Japan as the over-investment hypothesis.

As noted, the ratio comprises three variables, including financial liabilities and financial assets in numerator and non-financial assets in denominator, in which the larger financial assets result in the lower q ratio as the distorted income distribution and the larger non-financial assets result in the lower q ratio as the over-investment hypothesis. In any case, the low q ratio and the behaviors of the corporate sector, particularly in the past two decades, could not be explained rationally by economic theories, particularly by neoclassical economic theories, as demonstrated in Figure 4.2.

As seen in the Tobin's q ratio and its components, the private corporate sector has made strong behaviors for investment and R&D expenditure in these decades. Therein, vital capital accumulation and technical progress have reinforced the supply-side economy.

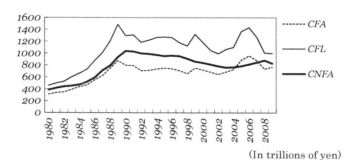

(In trillions of yen)

Figure 4.2:   Corporate financial assets (CFA), financial liabilities (CFL) and non-financial assets (CNFA) in a non-financial corporation.
Source: Developed by the author based on SNA93, ESRI, Cabinet Office.

Owing to the consistently implemented capital accumulation with technical progress even in the period after the bursting of the bubble economy, the GDP capacity increased, on average, at 3.80 per cent in FY1980–1990, at 2.13 per cent in FY1990–2000 and at 1.34 per cent in FY2000–2008, as discussed in Chapter 3. As demonstrated in Figure 4.3, the contribution of the Solow residual as TFP (RES) to GDP capacity growth might be remarkable as well as capital accumulation, in place of the limited increase in labor suply. In particular, the contribution of labor to GDP capacity has been stagnant with declines in labor and economic slump since the early 1990s, as shown in Figure 4.3.

In comparison with the performance of TFP changes in high-growth era after WWII, it seems that the TFP growth has been declining, particularly after the bursting of the bubble economy. However, its contribution to the GDP capacity growth might be relatively significant.

Table 4.3 shows the contribution rate of changes in factor of production, including TFP to GDP capacity growth in FY1980–2008. According to these estimates, it can be seen that the contribution rate of changes in TFP to the GDP capacity growth increased from 24.7 per cent, on average, in the FY1980s, to 28.6 per cent in the FY1990s and to 44.0 per cent in FY2000–2008. These contribution rates might be lower than the contribution rate at 68 per cent in 1956–1976 estimated by Minami (1981) based on Tinbergen (1942). However, it is understandable that technical

(In trillions of yen)

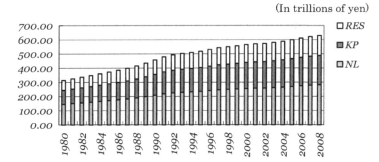

Figure 4.3: Contributions of labor (NL), capital stock (KP) and residual (RES) to GDP capacity (GDPC) in FY1980–2008.

Note: The residual including TFP has derived from the Cobb–Douglas function discussed in the previous chapter, as follows.

$\ln(\text{GDPC}) = A' + \alpha \ln(\text{KP}) + \beta \ln((1 - \text{UR}/100))^*\text{NL}^*1.099) + p_1((\text{IP} + \text{IP}(-1) + \text{IP}(-2))/\text{KP}) + p_2 \,(\text{TIME})$

$T' = A' + p_1((\text{IP} + \text{IP}(-1) + \text{IP}(-2))/\text{KP}) + p_2(\text{TIME})$
$\quad = \ln(\text{GDPC}) - (\alpha \ln(\text{KP}) + \beta \ln((1 - 2.00/100))^*\text{NL}^*1.099))$

Therefore, $T = \exp(T')$
where, $T =$ the Solow residual including technical progress as TFP, $A' = 0.268$, $\alpha = 0.301$, $\beta = 0.699$, $p_1 = 0.238$, $p_2 = 0.0041$.

Source: Estimated and compiled by the author.

Table 4.3: Growth of factor of production and its contribution rate to GDP capacity growth in FY1980–2008 (%).

% changes in	GDPC	KP	NL	(α)	TFP
FY1980–1990	3.80	6.61	1.24	(0.301)	0.94
	(100.0)	(52.4)	(22.9)		**(24.7)**
FY1990–2000	2.13	3.80	0.54	(0.301)	0.61
	(100.0)	(53.7)	(17.7)		**(28.6)**
FY2000–2008	1.34	3.01	−0.23	(0.301)	0.59
	(100.0)	(67.6)	(−11.6)		**(44.0)**

Note: Concerning these estimates, please see the note in Figure 4.3.
Source: Estimated and compiled by the author.

progress has played a significant role for strengthening the supply side of the economy, particularly in the deflationary economy.

With respect to causes of technical progress in the Japanese economy, Shishido and Nakamura (1992a, 1992b) analyzed the causes of technical progress, on a sectoral basis, employing the multi-sector econometric model of Japan. In their analysis, employing the 64-sectoral basis Keynes–Leontief-type econometric model, the causes of induced technical progress were examined, on a sectoral basis, based on the Hicksian technical progress. According to their analysis, as shown in Table 4.4, neutral technical progress and biased technical progress with labor-saving and capital-saving technical progress were observed in many sectors. Particularly, a number of manufacturing sectors facing severe competition in world markets, including metal products, general machinery, electric machinery and automobiles, experienced induced technical progress to reduce the costs, particularly through labor-saving technical progress, and to improve the qualities of products in the 1970s and the 1980s, as demonstrated in Table 4.5. In other words, the vital investment in R&D might be inevitable to some extent in Japan for strengthening price and non-price competitiveness and hence technical progress for competition in world markets, which resulted in the strong supply-side.

Table 4.4:   TFP functions: parameters with positive or negative values in terms of the numbers of sectors (out of 64 sectors, j:01–64).

$\ln(\text{TFP}_j) = c + \lambda \ln(P_{xj}/P_{zj}) + \alpha \ln(P_{wj}) + \beta \ln(P_{rj}) + (-(\alpha + \beta)) \ln P(k_j) + \gamma 1 V_j + \gamma 2 T$												
	λ			α			β			$-(\alpha + \beta)$			γ_1	γ_2
(sign)	+	−	0	+	−	0	+	−	0	+	−	0	+	+
Primary	7	1	1	5	3	1	3	4	2	5	3	1	5	2
Secondary	10	22	2	17	17	0	27	6	1	10	23	1	7	13
Tertiary	7	7	1	3	7	5	12	2	1	4	11	0	7	5
Total	24	30	4	25	27	6	42	12	4	19	37	2	19	20

Note: P_x, P_z, P_w, P_r, P_k, V and T denote output price, total input price, labor cost, intermediate input price, user cost of capital, vintage factor and time trend, respectively.
Source: Shishido and Nakamura (1992a).

Table 4.5: TFP functions: regression results (sample: 1960–1984).

$$\ln TFP_j = c + \lambda \ln(P_{xj}/P_{zj}) + \alpha \ln P_{wj} + \beta \ln P_{rj} + (-(\alpha+\beta))\ln P_{kj} + \gamma_1 V_j + \gamma_2 T$$

	c	λ	α	β	$-(\alpha+\beta)$	γ_1	γ_2	R^2	DW
01	−2.6	0.37 (3.7)	0.07 (0.9)	0.007 (0.5)	−0.8			0.60	1.72
02	−1.7	0.39 (3.7)	−0.02 (−0.3)	−0.01 (−0.5)	0.03			0.51	1.83
04	−22.94	0.67 (3.5)	0.07 (0.6)	−0.32 (2.0)	0.25	0.38 (1.9)	0.01 (0.9)	0.59	2.16
05	0.57	0.30t−1 (1.3)	−0.2 (0.4)	0.02 (0.4)	0.18			0.78	1.95
06	1.34	0.85 (3.2)	−0.52 (−6.2)		0.52			0.89	1.28
07	−3.76		0.41 (5.5)	−0.02 (−1.0)	−0.39	0.36t−2 (4.1)		0.71	1.60
08	−1.35	0.18 (1.4)	0.07 (2.0)	0.16 (5.2)	0.23	0.006 (0.3)		0.95	2.39
09	−3.68	−0.33 (−1.5)	0.53 (15.3)	−0.05 (−2.5)	−0.48	0.08 (3.7)		0.98	2.45
12	−32.45	0.64 (2.6)			0	0.26t−2 (3.6)	0.02 (3.8)	0.68	1.66
13	−38.92	1.33 (1.5)	−0.38 (−3.6)	0.26 (3.1)	0.12		0.02 (2.6)	0.59	2.78
14	−29.70	1.32t−1 (6.4)	−0.66 (−4.8)	1.18 (5.7)	−0.52	0.17t−2 (1.5)	0.01 (2.0)	0.94	2.04
15	−41.83		−0.54 (−2.9)	0.15 (0.8)	0.39		0.02 (3.4)	0.43	0.38
16	−1.89	0.07 (2.0)	−0.23 (−4.8)	0.51 (5.8)	−0.28			0.76	2.14
17	4.95	−1.18t−1 (−2.8)	0.16t−1 (2.7)	0.41t−1 (−2.3)	0.25			0.38	2.05
18	−83.21	−0.52 (−1.2)	−0.33 (−1.0)		0.33		0.05 (2.3)	0.47	0.46
19	−37.34	−1.09 (−2.6)	−0.20 (−1.4)	0.19 (2.8)	0.01			0.72	2.44
20	−19.18		0.06 (1.2)	0.15 (3.8)	−0.22		0.01 (1.7)	0.64	1.91

(Continued)

Table 4.5:   (Continued)

$$lnTFP_i = c + \lambda\, ln(P_{xi}/P_{zi}) + \alpha\, lnP_{wi} + \beta\, lnP_{ri} + (-(\alpha+\beta))\, lnP_{ki} + \gamma_1\, V_i + \gamma_2\, T$$

	c	λ	α	β	$-(\alpha+\beta)$	γ_1	γ_2	R^2	DW
21	−47.02	1.43 (3.6)	−0.29 (3.1)	0.41 (5.8)	−0.12		0.03 (4.9)	0.85	1.93
22	−18.64	−0.31 (−0.6)	−0.15 (−0.9)	0.17 (1.6)	−0.12			0.58	1.81
23	12.84	−2.81 (−2.6)	−0.02 (−4.4)	0.15 (1.5)	−0.13			0.31	1.45
24	3.23	−0.84 (−1.5)	0.03 (0.3)	0.20 (1.0)	−0.23			0.70	1.91
25	1.59	−0.22 (−1.5)	−0.11 (−6.7)	0.27 (7.4)	−0.16			0.81	1.98
26	−4.30	1.35 (4.5)	−0.23 (−3.3)	0.42 (6.3)	−0.19	0.11t−2 (2.0)		0.90	2.54
27	−10.03	−1.71 (−3.7)	−0.44 (−4.2)	0.31 (4.3)	0.15	0.12t−2 (1.4)	0.01 (1.1)	0.57	1.84
28	−1.13	−0.32 (0.8)	0.20 (3.9)	0.44 (3.9)	−0.66	0.08t−2 (1.6)		0.94	1.82
29	−0.92	−0.32t−1 (−1.3)	0.23t−1 (3.3)	−0.10t−1 (−1.1)	−0.13			0.75	1.51
30	−0.82	−0.28 (−1.5)	0.21 (3.1)	0.24 (3.1)	−0.45	0.04 (0.5)		0.98	1.52
31	−0.26	−0.13 (−1.6)	0.11 (1.0)	−0.11 (3.3)	0			0.55	1.04
32	3.27	−0.46t−1 (−6.6)	−0.09t−1 (−1.6)	−0.23t−1 (−4.5)	0.32			0.90	1.09
33	−4.47	0.44t−1 (3.2)	0.23 (2.8)	0.16 (6.7)	−0.39			0.94	1.06
34	−1.16	0.76 (2.6)	−0.37 (−5.4)	0.80 (3.8)	−0.43			0.79	1.06
35	−4.02	0.71t−1 (3.1)	0.12t−1 (2.5)	−0.26t−1 (−3.1)	0.14			0.69	1.75
36	−1.52	−0.20 (−0.6)	0.32t−1 (3.8)	−0.50t−1 (−2.8)	0.18			0.62	1.08
37	3.16	0.61 (1.2)	−0.64 (−9.7)	0.24t−1 (1.7)	0.40			0.90	2.47
38	0.95	−0.39t−1 (3.5)	0.06 (2.7)	0.16 (5.0)	−0.32			0.89	1.97

(Continued)

Table 4.5: (Continued)

$$lnTFP_i = c + \lambda \ln(P_{xi}/P_{zi}) + \alpha lnP_{wi} + \beta lnP_{ri} + (-(\alpha+\beta)) lnP_{ki} + \gamma_1 V_i + \gamma_2 T$$

	c	λ	α	β	$-(\alpha+\beta)$	γ_1	γ_2	R^2	DW
39	0.41	−0.29 (−1.8)	0.06(1.8)	0.23 (4.0)	−0.29			0.89	2.41
40	−24.03	−1.58 (4.9)	−0.19 (−2.8)	0.28 (3.8)	−0.09		0.02 (4.1)	0.96	1.72
41	−56.68	−0.22 (−1.3)	0.14†−1(3.6)	0.16(2.0)	−0.30		0.03 (9.7)	0.99	2.56
42	1.29	−0.85†−1 (−1.2)	0.19†−1 (3.2)	0.51 (2.6)	−0.70			0.60	0.98
43	2.08	−0.86†−1 (−2.3)	0.13 (1.6)	0.48 (10.5)	−0.61			0.97	1.18
44	−19.80	−1.42 (−2.4)	0.12†−1 (0.8)	0.47 (7.6)	−0.59		0.03 (2.1)	0.86	1.48
45	−114.25	0.63 (1.0)	−2.1 (−1.4)	0.30 (2.3)	−0.09		0.06 (4.1)	0.93	0.58
46	−4.28	0.37†−1(1.5)	0.27 (4.2)	0.11 (1.5)	−0.38	0.03 (1.7)		0.96	2.27
47	−3.53	0.79 (1.9)	−0.04 (−.8)	0.23 (4.6)	−0.19			0.72	1.53
48	−1.11	0.44 (1.1)	−0.13†−1 (−1.4)	0.34 (3.1)	−0.21	0.07†−1 (.8)		0.86	2.69
49	−43.20	0.46 (1.1)	−0.56 (3.6)	0.61 (5.7)	−0.05		0.02 (2.2)	0.73	2.06
50	10.10	−1.41†−1 (−1.1)	−0.41(−7.9)	0.16 (2.0)	0.25			0.87	2.02
51	0.33	0.12 (2.0)	−0.10 (−2.6)	−0.15 (−5.2)	0.25			0.92	1.90
52	−2.29	0.53 (2.9)		0.27 (4.3)	−0.27	0.13†−2 (2.0)		0.74	1.94
53	−51.47	−0.46†−1 (−3.5)	0.14 (1.0)		−0.14	0.03 (4.9)		0.90	2.13
54	−7.17	−0.59†−1 (−2.7)		0.38 (7.3)	−0.38	0.28†−2 (3.1)	0.005 (1.5)	0.90	1.82
55	4.19	−0.41 (−3.4)	−0.09 (.7)	0.20(4.3)	−0.11			0.82	1.43
56	6.94	−0.72 (−5.0)	−0.46 (3.5)	0.15(0.9)	0.31			0.93	1.87
57	−24.58	−0.06 (−0.8)		0.01 (0.4)	−0.01	0.20†−2 (3.6)	0.01 (2.1)	0.82	2.23

(Continued)

Table 4.5:   (Continued)

$$lnTFP_j = c + \lambda \ln(P_{xj}/P_{zj}) + \alpha \ln P_{wj} + \beta \ln P_{rj} + (-(\alpha+\beta)) \ln P_{kj} + \gamma_1 V_j + \gamma_2 T$$

	c	λ	α	β	$-(\alpha+\beta)$	γ_1	γ_2	R^2	DW
58	−1.40		0.12 (1.5)	0.20 (2.0)	−0.32			0.51	0.80
59	−4.32	−0.74 (1.9)	0.95 (2.3)	−0.05 (0.4)	−0.90	0.91†−2 (2.4)		0.27	1.10
60	−117.45	0.45 (2.5)		0.14 (3.2)	−0.14	0.37†−2 (3.1)	0.06 (6.3)	0.93	1.97
63	−0.004	0.54 (1.4)	−0.27 (−3.7)	0.25 (1.6)	0.02	0.20†−2 (1.6)		0.71	0.75

Source: Shishido and Nakamura (1992a).

TFP_j: total factor productivity in sector j; $TFP_j = X_j/Z_j$ in data base; X_j : total output in sector j; Z_j : total input in sector j.

Sectoral classification: 01. General crops, 02. Industrial crops, 03. Livestock for textile, 04. Other livestock and service, 05. Forestry. 06. Fisheries, 07. Coal mining, 08. Iron ores, 09. Non-ferrous metallic ores 10. Crude petroleum, 11. Natural gas, 12. Other mining, 13. Meat and dairy products, 14. Grain products, 15. Manufactured sea foods, 16. Other foods, 17. Beverage. 18. Tobacco, 19. Natural textile, 20. Chemical textile, 21. Other textile, 22. Wearing apparel, 23. Wood and wood products, 24. Furniture, 25. Pulp and paper, 26. Printing and publishing, 27. Leather products, 28. Rubber products, 29. Basic and intermediate chemicals, 30. Final chemicals, 31. Petroleum products, 32. Coal products, 33. Cement, 34. Other ceramic, 35. Iron products, 36. Rolling casting and forgings, 37. Alminum, 38. Other non-ferrous products, 39. Metal products, 40. Machinery, 41. Electrical machinery, 42. Automobile, 43. Aircraft, 44. Other transport equipment, 45. Instruments and related products, 46. Miscellaneous manufacturing, 47. Housing construction, 48. Industrial construction, 49. Public construction, 50. Other construction, 51. Electric power, 52. Gas, 53. Water and sanitary service, 54. Wholesale and retail trade, 55. Real estate, 56. Railways, 57. Truck and buses, 58. Other transportation, 59. Communication, 60. Finance and insurance, 61. Government services, 62. Public services, 63. Other services, 64. Unallocated.

Concerning the role of technical progress for growth, Sato and Morita (2009) emphasized the importance of embodied technical progress and hence labor-saving technical progress, for improving quality rather than increasing quantity for Japan in comparison with the US. Indeed, in Japan, growth has been achieved through capital augmenting technical progress in the decades after World War II, especially after oil crises period, although it has been advanced by labor. This kind of cost-price incentive technical progress has been recognized on a macro-basis from the 1980s onward, particularly since the Plaza Accord with yen appreciation, as follows.[2]

$$\ln(\text{TFP}) = c + \lambda \ln (P_x/P_z) + \alpha \ln (P_w/P_k) + \beta \ln (P_r/P_k)$$
$$+ \gamma_1 (\text{IP} + \text{IP}(-1) + \text{IP}(-2))/\text{KP} + \gamma_2 \text{ TIME}$$

Based on this theoretical model, we got the result.

$$\ln(\text{TFP}) = 2.464 + 0.01122 \ln(P_x/P_z) + 0.06712 \ln(P_w/P_k)$$
$$\quad (74.01) \quad (2.01) \quad\quad\quad\quad (9.03)$$
$$- 0.00395 \ln (P_r/P_k) + 0.02499 (\text{IP} + \text{IP}(-1) + \text{IP}(-2))/\text{KP}$$
$$\quad (-1.89) \quad\quad\quad\quad\quad (6.90)$$
$$+ 0.00511 \text{ TIME}$$
$$\quad (46.23)$$

C-O(1982–2008)   Adjusted $R^2 = 0.998$, $SD = 0.0011$, $DW = 1.224$

where TFP=total factor productivity derived from the Cobb–Douglas production function as the Solow residual, P_x = output price, P_z = input price, P_w = labor cost (nominal wage rate), P_k = user cost of capital, P_r = intermediate input price, $(\text{IP}+\text{IP}(-1)+\text{IP}(-2))/\text{KP}$ = vintage factor, TIME = time trend.

The causal relations between macro-variables are the same with the sectoral analysis by Shishido and Nakamura (1992a), in which the expected sign conditions are: λ, the coefficient of P_x/P_z, <0 for competitive sector and >0 for non-competitive sector, α, the coefficient of P_w/P_k, >0 or <0, β, the coefficient of P_r/P_k, >0 or <0, and γ_1 and γ_2, the coefficints of the vintage factor and time trend, >0. Therefore, α and β indicate biased price factors and the coefficient of P_k is implied to be $-(\alpha + \beta)$ since a homogeneity constraint of degree is imposed.

In this framework, TFP derived from the Cobb–Douglas production function as the Solow residual is decomposed into induced technical progress, with cost-price incentives, the Solow neutrality (vintage) and other technical progress including the Hicksian neutrality (time trend) within the Cobb–Douglass production function. It can be seen due to the regression result that the induced technical progress, especially labor-saving technical progress, seems very significant and effective, on a macro-basis, as well as sectoral analysis.

These causations can be explained in Figure 4.4. The indicators in the figure are indexed at 100 in FY1980 in order to examine the relations between these indicators and TFP in FY1980–2008. The total factor productivity (TFP), as the Solow residual, has been increasing consistently in FY1980–2008. In this period, on the other hand, relative labor cost (P_w/P_k) has been stagnant since the 1990s and declined in the 2000s, and vintage of capital stock (VIN) has also declined sharply since the bursting of the bubble and became stagnant in the 2000s. Therefore, it can be seen that labor-saving technical progress might have played a significant role to stimulate TFP, on a macro-basis, incorporated with the vintage of capital stock (embodied technical progress).

In addition to that, if we investigate the contribution of the components to rate of changes in total factor productivity (TFP), as shown in Figure 4.5,

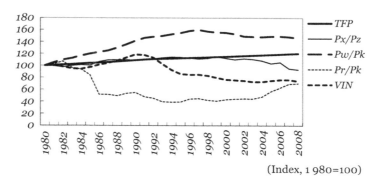

(Index, 1980=100)

Figure 4.4: Trend of TFP and its determinants, relative input price (P_x/P_z), labor-user cost (P_w/P_k), intermediate user cost (P_r/P_k) and vintage (VIN) in FY1980–2008.

Source: Estimated and developed by the author.

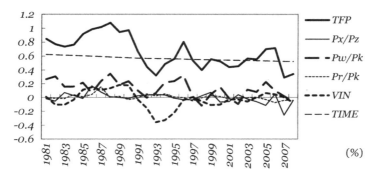

Figure 4.5: Changes in TFP (%) and contribution of each component to changes in TFP in FY1981–2008.
Note: Based on the TFP regression result discussed earlier, the contribution of each component to TFP changes is estimated.
Source: Estimated and developed by the author.

we could recognize very interesting causations between them. First of all, it can be seen that relative labor cost (Pw/Pk) has had strong influences to stimulating TFP as a cost-price incentive during whole period. However, second, except for the boom periods, the vintage effects have had negative contribution to TFP changes. Third, the Hicksian neutrality has had the highest positive influences to TFP changes during the whole period. Finally, relative output price to input price has fluctuated with the limited positive or negative impacts during the whole period. In other words, it can be seen due to these investigations that the corporate sector's behaviors to the productivities' improvement might be different based on the economic climate.

As discussed earlier, these causations would be introduced to a multi-equation structural model system, as follows.

$$GDP = TFP \, K^{\alpha} \, L^{\beta} \quad (\alpha + \beta = 1)$$

$$TFP = f \left(PX/PZ, WN, \left(\sum IP \right) / K, TIME \right)$$

However, we have not employed these equations in this study because TFP is too sensitive for scenario simulations within a multi-equation structural model system (Nakamura, 2008). Accordingly, this study has utilized the estimated GDP capacity derived from the Cobb–Douglas function with capital stock, labor, vintage factor and time trend discussed in Chapter 3.

4.3. Income Distribution, Asset Accumulation and the Demand-Side Economy

Income distribution patterns have crucial influences to both the demand-side as well as the supply-side. This section, therefore, examines the effects of income distribution patterns on the demand-side economy, with special focus on the asset and debt accumulation in the household sector.

As discussed earlier, household income share in GDP has declined in the past few decades from around 0.70 in the FY1980s to around 0.63 in the 2000s, as shown in Table 4.2. This downward trend that might result from the distorted income distribution by the private corporate sector has been crucial constraints on the household sector's expenditures, especially on the household consumption expenditure.

Within the prolonged economic stagnation and declines in the wage income share, the household sector expenditures have been impoverished since the collapse of the bubble. The growth performance of the household expenditures therefore has been falling, in which private consumption expenditure has declined from 4.05 per cent in the 1980 to 1.29 per cent in the 1990s and to 0.77 per cent in the 2000s, and housing investment has recorded the negative average growth at −2.38 per cent in the 1990s and −5.23 per cent in the 2000s, as shown in Table 4.6.

Furthermore, within such a situation, the contribution of private consumption (CP) to GDP growth percentage point in terms of percentage point(s) has been followed up by government consumption (CG) and exports of goods and services (EGS) in the 2000s, despite the largest share of the private consumption in GDP, as indicated in parentheses of Table 4.6.

In addition, asset and debt accumulation and its changes also have had crucial influences to the household expenditures through asset and debt effects as well as income effects, particularly in the deflationary economy. Figure 4.6 shows financial assets (HFA), non-financial assets (NHFA) and total financial liabilities (HTD) in the household sector, respectively. These assets and liabilities increased in the 1980s, particularly during the bubble period in the latter half of the 1980s. The non-financial assets in

Table 4.6: Annual average growth rate of major GDP components and its contribution to GDE growth by decade in FY1980–2009 (%).

	GDP	CP	CG	IP	IH	IG	EGS
FY1980–1990	4.67	4.05	3.80	8.82	3.46	0.98	5.59
		(2.31)	(0.58)	(1.21)	(0.20)	(0.07)	(0.44)
FY1990–2000	1.09	1.29	3.05	−0.36	−2.38	1.97	3.08
		(0.72)	(0.46)	(−0.05)	(−0.12)	(0.15)	(0.28)
FY2000–2009	0.46	0.77	1.80	−1.21	−5.23	−5.33	4.46
		(0.43)	(0.32)	(−0.18)	(−0.16)	(−0.26)	(0.58)

Source: Compiled by author based on SNA93, chain-linked, ARNA, ESRI.
Note: Value in parenthesis indicates the contribution of each component in terms of percentage point(s) to GDE growth.

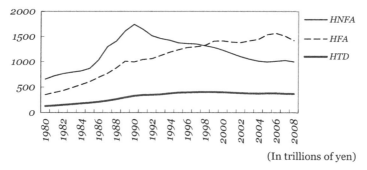

(In trillions of yen)

Figure 4.6: Financial assets (HFA), non-financial assets (HNFA) and total liabilities (HTD) in the household sector, FY1980–2008.
Source: Developed by the author, based on SNA93, ESRI, Cabinet Office.

the household sector, which were heavily dependent on the value of real estate, declined after the bursting of the bubble. With the depreciated value of the household non-financial assets, many households have extensively suffered from large debt burden since the bursting of the bubble economy.

Furthermore, household total liabilities have remained stable at a higher level since the mid-1990s since many households have had a difficulty in borrowing money from financial institutions for obtaining real estate and durable goods because of declines in the non-financial asset value, including real-estate asset value. The huge amounts of household financial assets, nevertheless, may have positive effects on the behavior related to household expenditures, which might sustain the domestic demand and thus preventing a hard landing of the economy in the period after the bursting of the bubble.

For many households, particularly for the low-income and middle-income class with liquidity constraints, the depreciation of non-financial asset value and the high position of liabilities might be critical. As shown in Figure 4.7, the ratio of the financial liabilities to the non-financial assets may explain this situation, particularly after the bursting of the bubble. Within the deflationary economy in Japan, it seems that most of the households may have experienced negative impacts in declines of nominal wage rates with real debt effect, as emphasized by Fisher (1933) as the "Fisher effect", which might be larger than the "real balance effect" or the "Pigou effect" (Pigou, 1943) because debtors' propensity to expend is larger than that of creditors. In the case of Japan, it seems that the households who obtained real-estate and durable goods have had a large burden of liabilities, with declines in nominal income under the deflationary economy.

As a result of distorted income distribution, the household sector's expenditure, in particular, the household consumption expenditure, has been stagnant during the past two decades. Figure 4.8 demonstrates the share of major real GDP components in real GDP. In the figure, the share of real household consumption expenditure (CH/GDP) was slightly

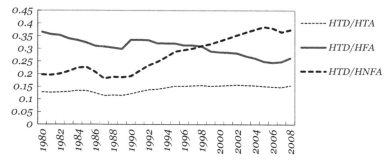

Figure 4.7:   Ratio of financial liabilities (HTD) to total assets (HTA), to financial assets (HFA) and to non-financial assets (HNFA).
Source: Developed by the author, based on SNA93, ESRI, Cabinet Office.

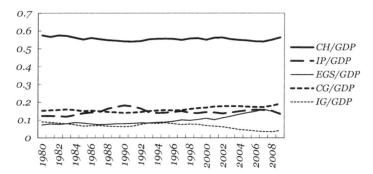

Figure 4.8: Share of major real GDP components in real GDP, FY1980–2009. *Source*: Developed by the author based on SNA93, chain-linked, ESRI, Cabinet Office.

decreasing up to FY2007 and increased in FY2008–2009, whereas the share of real government consumption (CG/GDP) and real exports of goods and services (EGS/GDP) were consistently increasing.

On the other hand, the share of real private non-housing investment (IP/GDP) fluctuated along with a business cycle, but remained at a higher share at 15 to 20 per cent. On the contrary, the real government investment share (IG/GDP) has drastically declined since the mid-1990s, under the central government policy of a reform of public finance and administration.

In general, the share of consumption may be stable or slightly declining in line with economic growth in the boom and may tend to increase in stagnation. In Japan, nonetheless, the share of real consumption expenditure in real GDP has been declining slightly in the long-term slump, which means that the household sector might seriously suffer from lower income and be damaged by the declines in income after the bursting of the bubble. On the other hand, export and investment demands might lead the demand-side economy. However, these components are dependent on the external demands and closely related to the supply-side. The figure may explain these situations.

4.4. Deflationary Gap and Deflation

As discussed in the previous sections, the structural deflationary economy has been attributable to distorted income distribution, especially since the bursting of the bubble, in which the supply-side has been strengthened and the demand-side has been stagnant. In addition, the prolonged stagnation has accelerated deflation with declines in prices and nominal wage rates during the past two decades.

The current deflationary economy is not a mere disinflation, but, in a sense, a structural deflation with a vicious circle between economic stagnation and deflation (declines in prices and wage rates). This logic can be seen in Figures 4.9 and 4.10. As demonstrated in Figure 4.9, the deflationary gap in terms of ratio to actual real GDP was declining in the 1980s within the bubble economy. In the peak of the bubble in 1990, the ratio of the gap declined to 1.9 per cent because of the vital demand-side GDP growth in the latter half of the 1980s. However, after the bursting of the bubble, the trend of its ratio was increasing except the period of the boon starting from 2002.

With large macro-imbalances and yen appreciation, prices and nominal wage rates also have been declining since the early 1990s, as shown in Figure 4.10. In the 1980s, the Japanese economy successfully achieved fairly high growth with creeping inflation, in which nominal wage rates increased sharply much more than deflators of GDP and personal consumption (PCP), as demonstrated in Figure 4.10. However, it can be seen in Figures 4.9 and 4.10 that the economy has suffered from the long-term deflation and prices (deflators) and nominal wage rates have been declining during the past couple of decades since the early 1990s.

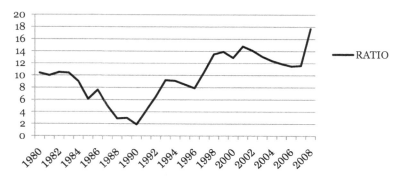

Figure 4.9: Ratio of deflationary gap to actual real GDP, (GDPC – GDP)/GDP × 100 (%), FY1980–2008.
Source: Estimated and compiled by the author.

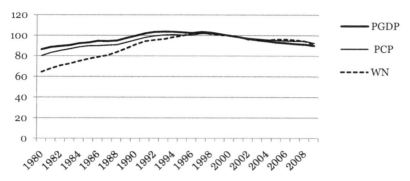

Figure 4.10: Deflators of GDP (PGDP) and private consumption (PCP), and nominal wage rates (WN), FY1980–2009. (Index: FY2000 = 100).
Source: Compiled by the author, based on SNA93, ESRI, Cabinet Office.

End Notes

[1] Due to the corporate income tax cut for inducing investment, indeed, corporate sector has positive effects. However, the effects are limited because the corporate income tax cut has been applied to the corporations with current surplus and its tax cut has substantially resulted in the household sector tax increase.

[2] This macro-TFP function is unstable for dynamic simulations, but useful for deciding the production function specification employed in the present study. But, we would like to introduce this Cobb–Douglas production function with TFP and to endogenize TFP explicitly in our multi-equation structural model system in the next stage. However, we endogenize TFP utilizing the Solow residual to examine the performance of technical progress in the future scenario forecasts, as follows.

$$\text{TFP} = \exp\left(0.2638 + 0.238((\text{IP} + \text{IP}(-1) + \text{IP}(-2))/\text{KP})\right.$$
$$+ 0.0041\,\text{TIME} = \exp\left(\ln(\text{GDPC}) - (0.301\,\ln(\text{KP})\right.$$
$$+ 0.699\ln((1 - 2.00/100))*\text{NL}*1.099))$$
$$\text{TFPI} = \text{TFP}/\text{TFP}.2000*100$$

CHAPTER 5

The Theoretical Model Framework

5.1. The Theoretical Model for Empirical Analyses

In this section, we discuss a theoretical model framework. As long as the supply-side economy is larger than the demand-side in Japan, the demand-side performance determines the actual economic growth, hence we basically employ a demand-side–oriented type model. However, the supply-side is also taken into account for analyzing the Japanese deflationary economy. Accordingly, in the present study, we develop a demand–supply integrated-type growth model. In addition, in the model framework, relationships between the demand-side and the supply-side economies are consistently taken into consideration.

There are several types of growth theories such as the Harrod–Domar model (Harrod, 1939; Domar 1947), neoclassical growth theory (Solow, 1956; Swan, 1956) and new growth theory (Romer, 1986; Lucas, 1988). However, these models, except for the Harrod–Domar model, rely on a supply-side approach for growth. On the other hand, the Harrod–Domar model is a very unique model to analyze equilibrium growth with IS balance, as an extension of Keynes's static equilibrium analysis, but still a theoretical model in a closed economic system.

These growth models are, however, too naïve and supply-oriented as a theoretical model in applying them to the actual economy. Therefore, we introduce a more realistic model for an empirical study on the Japanese economy so as to analyze the demand-side and supply-side structure and hence the deflationary economy, and to examine the major driving forces for growth in the Japanese economy.

As is well known, since Keynes (1936) has introduced the concept of the Keynes multiplier to the demand-side model in Chapter 10 of his book *The General Theory of Employment, Inerest and Money*, the concept of the multiplier has been employed as a fiscal stimulus in economic recession.

By extending this concept, we can develop a demand-side growth model incorporated with the supply-side growth model. Here, we discuss the theoretical framework of the demand-supply integrated growth model, as follows.

Supply-side model

$$Y_s = TK^\alpha L^\beta \quad (\alpha + \beta = 1) \tag{1}$$

$$K = K(-1) + I - D \quad (D = \delta K(-1)) \tag{2}$$

where $Y_s, K, L, T, I, D, \alpha, \beta$ and δ represent supply-side GDP, capital stock, labor, total factor productivity, investment, depreciation of capital, capital share, labor share and rate of depreciation, respectively.

If $Y_s > Y_d$, Y_s is depressed to the level of Y_d as $Y_s{'} (= Y_d)$ and if $Y_s < Y_d$, Y_d is depressed to the level of Y_s as $Y_d{'} (= Y_s)$, as discussed earlier. In the case of $Y_s > Y_d$, K and L are reduced to $K{'}$ and $L{'}$.

Demand-side model

$$Y_d = C + I + G^* + E^* - M \tag{3}$$

$$C = C_d(Y_w) + C^*(p, r, A, N) = \gamma Y_w + C^* \tag{4}$$

$$I = I_d(Y_c) + I^*(r, p, K(-1)) = \mu Y_c + I^* \tag{5}$$

$$M = M_d(Y_d) + M^*(p, e, \dots) = \lambda Y_d + M^* \tag{6}$$

$$Y_w = \theta Y_d \quad (Y_i = Y_w + Y_c = Y_d) \tag{7}$$

$$Y_c = (1 - \theta)Y_d \tag{8}$$

where $Y_d, Y_i, C, C_d, I, I_d, G, E, M, M_d, Y_w, Y_c, p, r, A, N, e$ and θ refer to demand-side GDP, overall distributed income (wage income plus corporate income), overall consumption expenditure, consumption expenditure dependent on Y_w, overall investment, investment dependent on Y_c, government expenditure, exports, imports, imports dependent on Y_d, wage income, corporate income, prices, rate of interest, net financial assets, number of population, foreign exchange rate and wage income share,[1] respectively. In addition, γ, μ, λ and * mean marginal propensity to consume out of Y_w, to invest out of Y_c, to import out of Y_d and variables independent of Y_d in the IS model, respectively.

From Equations (3) to (8) we get a reduced form equation, as follows:

$$Y_d = (1/(1 - \gamma\theta - \mu(1 - \theta) + \lambda) (C^* + G^* + I^* + E^* - M^*). \quad (9)$$

Therefore, the multiplier is defined, as follows.

$$\text{Multiplier} = 1/(1 - \gamma\theta - \mu(1 - \theta) + \lambda)$$

Then, taking a form of rate of changes,

$$\Delta Y_d/Y_d = (1 - \gamma\theta - \mu(1 - \theta) + \lambda)^{-1}(\Delta W/W) \quad (10)$$
$$(\Delta W/W = (\Delta C^*/C^*)(C^*/Y_d) + (\Delta G^*/G^*)(G^*/Y_d)$$
$$+ (\Delta I^*/I^*)(I^*/Y_d) + (\Delta E^*/E^*)(E^*/Y_d$$
$$- (\Delta M^*/M^*)(M^*/Y_d)).$$

If household financial asset effects are taken into account and the assets are determined simultaneously with consumption and wage income ($A = A(-1) + \Delta A = A(-1) + \eta Y_w + \Delta A^*$), the multiplier is more complicated, as follows.

$$\text{Multiplier} = 1/(1 - (\gamma + \varepsilon\eta)\theta - \mu(1 - \theta) + \lambda)$$

In both cases, nevertheless, the multiplier effects rely on not only the marginal propensity to consume (γ) and to invest (μ) but also the wage income share (θ).[2] (Please see Appendix C.)

Price model to integrate the Supply-side within the Demand-side

$$p = p \left((+) pm, (+) w, (-) \tau\right) \quad (11)$$
$$(w = Y_w/L, \tau = Y_s/L)$$

where pm, w and τ represent import price in terms of local currency, nominal wage per labor and the supply-side labor productivity, respectively.

Equation (11) is a price function to elucidate a quantity adjustment process (Marshallian adjustment process), in which prices rely on intermediate input costs, labor cost and technical progress. With a price adjustment process (Walrasian adjustment process) in Equations (4)–(6), Equation (11) integrates both the demand-side and the supply-side through an equilibrium process in a multi-equation structural model system, based on micro-foundation of macro-analysis. In addition the wage income share (θ) and profit share ($1 - \theta$) integrate both the demand-side and supply-side, and the model is closed, based on a principle of equivalent of three aspects.

As explained earlier, the demand–supply integrated growth model mainly consists of three equations: Equations (1), (10) and (11), as a growth model. Equation (1) is a conventional Cobb–Douglas production function, and Equation (10) is the dynamic analog of the Keynes–Harrod multiplier model, which consists of the multiplier and rate of changes in autonomous components of Y_d with the ratio of each component to Y_d as a weight. In short, the demand-side growth depends on these two factors, including the multiplier which is the "accelerator" for growth $((1 - \gamma\theta - \mu(1 - \theta) + \lambda)^{-1})$ and growth rate of autonomous demand-side components with their weights, which is the "generator" for growth ($\Delta W/W$). In this framework, Keynes emphasized the significant role of government sector, and Harrod studied the role of exports for growth in an open economy. In particular, in an open economic system, the growth of exports is dominant for economic growth as a major autonomous component (generator) through an accelerator (multiplier) in the demand-side growth model.

In addition, the accelerator is changing if θ, the wage income share, increases or decreases, which directly affects the economic growth. In other words, if γ is larger than μ in Equation (10), the increase in θ results in the larger multiplier and *vice versa*, which has the certain effects on the economic growth. This is one of the key points in the present study [see Equation (7)].

Accordingly, in this framework, both the price adjustment process and the quantity adjustment process play a significant role so as to integrate the demand-side with the supply-side economy. Furthermore, the distribution of income between profits and wages plays a key function for growth in this model framework, which was discussed by economists of the Keynesian

growth school in the 1950s and the 1960s with reference to the relations between the natural rate of growth and the warranted growth in the
Harrod–Domar model framework.[3]

In addition, we will introduce one more important consequence based
on this framework, which is the effect of fiscal policy on the economy.
The fiscal policy consists of two major policies, government investment
changes and direct income tax changes, as demand stimulus. The effect of
government investment changes on the economy is defined as follows.

$$\Delta Y_d = (1/(1 - \gamma\theta - \mu(1 - \theta) + \lambda))\Delta G^*$$

On the other hand, if we consider the effect of tax changes on the economy,
the consumption function (4) discussed earlier should be changed to Equation (4′) associated with personal income tax (T) behavioral equation, as
follows:

$$C = \gamma(Yw - T) + C^* \tag{4'}$$

$$(T = t\,Yw + T_w^*, \ t_w : \text{marginal income tax rate})$$

$$T = \mu(Y_c - T_c) + T^*$$

$$(T_c = t_c Y_c + T_c^*, t_c : \text{marginal corporate tax rate})$$

Therefore, the impacts of changes in the fixed tax (T_w^*) in personal income
tax on the economy can be examined by the following equation:

$$\Delta Y_d = (-\gamma/(1 - \gamma\,\theta(1 - t_w) - \mu(1 - \theta)(1 - t_c) + \lambda))\Delta T_w^*$$

And, the effects of government investment changes on the economy are
evaluated by the following equation:

$$\Delta Y_d = (1/(1 - \gamma\,\theta(1 - t_w) - \mu(1 - \theta)(1 - t_c) + \lambda))\Delta G^*$$

In macroeconomics textbooks, we employ marginal propensity to consume
out of national income $(\gamma\theta)$ in examining the effect of tax changes, not
out of wage income (γ). It is, therefore, noteworthy that the effect of
the tax cut in this framework may be larger than its effects discussed in
macroeconomics textbooks because $\gamma \geq \gamma\theta \ (0 \leq \theta \leq 1)$.

Furthermore, considering the effects of not only income effects but
also asset effects, the impacts of fiscal policy may be larger in terms
of magnitude and longer in terms of duration, which could track the

actual economy more precisely. These differentials of the effects of fiscal policy will be examined in the dynamic simulation tests, later on, in Chapter 8.

In the actual economy, however, the causations of economic growth are more complicated, so we develop a more realistic and plausible model that is able to explain the actual economy. In the next chapter, we discuss the demand–supply integrated macro-econometric model of Japan, based on the theoretical model framework, discussed earlier. Before discussing the integrated econometric model, we review the concept of neoclassical growth model approach and of demand-side oriented growth model, as discussed previously, focusing on the role of the Keynes multiplier and income distribution patterns for growth.

5.2.   Growth Model: A Supply-Side Approach

As discussed in the previous section, supply-side approach is, in a sense, dominant in growth theory. Even in the Harrod–Domar model, the growth (g) is determined by saving ratio (s) and capital-output ratio (c) as $g = s/c$, in which there is no demand-side components. Neo-classical growth model, including the Solow–Swan model being stimulated by the Harrod–Domar model, is a typical supply-side approach, in which the growth relies on changes in capital stock and labor within a production function, and investment is equal to savings. In other words, major actors in the neo-classical growth model are the factors of production including capital stock, labor and technology.

Let us review the mechanism for growth with a simple macro-growth model. Here, we employ three equations such as production function which is explained by capital stock (K) and labor (L) to determine the supply-side GDP (Y_s), the demand-side GDP (Y_d) equation, which depends on consumption (C) and Investment (I), and labor function in which labor grows at n, as follows.

$$Y_s = F(K, L) \tag{12}$$

$$Y_d = C + I \tag{13}$$

$$L = L_0 e^n \tag{14}$$

If we do not consider depreciation of capital, investment is defined as changes in capital stock in terms of time ($I = dK/dt$). As labor grows at n in this system, both equations of Y_s and Y_d are transformed to per-labor function based on the constant return to scale, as follows.

$$y_s = f(k) \qquad (15)$$

$$y_d = c + i \qquad (16)$$

where:

$y_s = Y_s/L$
$k = K/L$
$y_d = Y_d/L$
$c = C/L$
$i = I/L$

Based on $I = dK/dt$,

$$dk/dt = i - nk \qquad (17)$$

Then, we get a differential equation to explain the equilibrium path of capital accumulation, as follows.

$$dk/dt = f(k) - c - nk \quad (i = y_d - c, y_s = y_d) \qquad (18)$$

In this equation, if we employ a simple consumption function, $C = aY$, the equation is, as is well known, the Solow model and k is converged to a certain level at the steady state with the supply-side production function. Even if we employ the Solow–Swan model, the Ramsey model (1928) or the other supply-side oriented growth models, including new growth model, the GDP is defined by capital accumulation as the supply-side GDP, and consumption is determined by a certain ratio of the supply-side GDP. Accordingly, the supply-side approach might be unsuitable for an analysis on the Japanese economy, in which the supply-side GDP is larger than the demand-side GDP ($Y_s > Y_d$), as far as an analysis on the effects of income distribution patterns on the demand-side economy is concerned. We need to employ a demand-side economics rather than a supply-side economics for the Japanese economy.[4]

5.3.   Income Distribution and Keynes Multiplier in the Demand-side Model

On the other hand, economic growth in the demand-side approach depends on the Keynes multiplier as an accelerator and growth of independent components as a generator as discussed in Equation (10), so that the dimension of the multiplier is very important to determine the growth performance. Accordingly, we examine the role of the Keynes multiplier with reference to the distribution of income utilizing a simple demand-side model.

Here, we employ a simple demand-side model in a closed system comprising seven equations, which is the consistent demand-side model we discussed earlier, as follows.

$$Y_d = C + I \qquad (19)$$
$$C = C_d + C^* \qquad (20)$$
$$C_d = \gamma\, Y_w \qquad (21)$$
$$I = I_d + I^* \qquad (22)$$
$$I_d = \mu\, Y_c \qquad (23)$$
$$Y_w = \theta\, Y_d \qquad (24)$$
$$Y_c = (1 - \theta)\, Y_d \qquad (25)$$
$$(0 < \gamma < 1, \quad 0 < \mu < 1, \quad 0 \le \theta \le 1)$$

where $Y_d, C, C_d, C^*, I, I_d, I^*, Y_w, Y_c, \gamma, \mu$ and θ are demand-side national income, overall consumption, consumption dependent on Y_d, consumption independent of Y_d, overall investment, investment depending on Y_d, investment independent of Y_d, wage income, corporate income, marginal propensity to consume, marginal propensity to invest and wage income share, respectively

From Equations (19) to (25), we get a reduced form equation, as follows.

$$Y_d = 1/(1 - \gamma\,\theta - \mu(1 - \theta))\ (C^* + I^*) \qquad (26)$$

Thus, the multiplier (m) is defined, as

$$m = 1/(1 - \gamma\,\theta - \mu(1 - \theta))$$
$$= 1/(1 - \mu - (\gamma - \mu)\theta).$$

If $f(\theta) = (1 - \mu - (\gamma - \mu)\theta)$ and $df(\theta)/d\theta = -(\gamma - \mu) < 0$,

$$\gamma > \mu.$$

In addition, if $df(\theta)/d\theta = -(\gamma - \mu) > 0$,

$$\gamma < \mu.$$

Then, therefore, if $df(\theta)/d\theta = -(\gamma - \mu) = 0$,

$$\gamma = \mu.$$

Concerning the Keynes multiplier with changes in $\theta(0 \le \theta \le 1)$, the multiplier is illustrated by case in terms of γ and μ, as follows.

(1) The case of $\gamma > \mu$: the marginal propensity to consume (γ) is higher than the marginal propensity to invest (μ).

In this case, $\gamma > \mu$, the multiplier (m) is an increasing function of θ in between $1/(1 - \gamma)$ and $1/(1 - \mu)$, when θ is in between zero and unity in a closed system, as shown in Figure 5.1. If the denominator of the multiplier $(1 - \mu - (\gamma - \mu)\theta)$ is zero with a specific combination of γ, μ and θ, the multiplier gets larger infinitely in a closed system.

For example, if the wage income share (θ) is unity and the marginal propensity to consume to wage income (γ) is unity, or if the wage income share (θ) is zero and the marginal propensity to invest is unity, the multiplier is infinite. In other words, the multiplier is in between unity and infinity in a closed economic system.

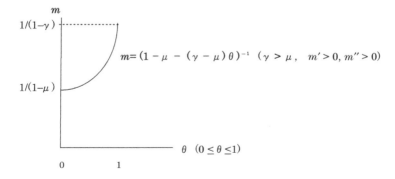

Figure 5.1: Multiplier and wage income share (θ) in $\gamma > \mu$.

However, if we extend this mechanism to an open economic system, the multiplier (m') is defined, as follows.

$$m' = (1 - \mu - (\gamma - \mu)\theta + \lambda)^{-1}$$

In an open economic system, the multiplier is defined above, which is the same as Equation (9) in the theoretical model framework discussed earlier. In an open economic system, the multiplier (m') is equal to an inverse of the marginal propensity to import $(1/\lambda)$ when $(1 - \mu - (\gamma - \mu)\theta)$ is zero. Thus, in this case, the economic growth relies on the multiplier $(1/\lambda)$ and on the changes in exports $(\Delta E^*/E^*)$ with the weight of exports to Y_d (E^*/Y_d) as a generator. In other words, when both γ and θ are unity, in which saving ratio (s) is zero, the multiplier results in the Harrod international multiplier (Harrod, 1933), as follows.

$$\Delta Y_d/Yd = (1/\lambda)(\Delta E^*/E^*)(E^*/Y_d)$$

Therefore, the multiplier is in between $1/(1-\mu+\lambda)$ and $1/(1-\gamma+\lambda)$ in an open economic system.

(2) The case of $\gamma < \mu$: the marginal propensity to consume (γ) is lower than the marginal propensity to invest (μ).

In the case of $\gamma < \mu$, the multiplier is a decreasing function of θ in between $1/(1 - \mu)$ and $1/(1 - \gamma)$, when θ is changing between zero and unity, as shown in Figure 5.2. Even in this case, it is assumed that the multiplier is infinitely larger when μ is unity and θ is zero or when γ is unity and θ is unity, as a specific case, in a closed economic system. In an open economic system, however, the multiplier cannot be infinite because of existence of the marginal propensity to import (λ), as discussed earlier.

(3) The case of $\gamma = \mu$.

On the contrary, when γ **is** equal to μ, the multiplier relies on only the propensity to invest and, hence, on $1/(1 - \mu)$ without any influences of changes in wage income share (θ). Therefore, the multiplier itself is stable, but the demand-side growth may be stagnant, whereas the propensity to consume is getting lower to the propensity to invest $(\gamma = \mu)$, as demonstrated in Figure 5.3.

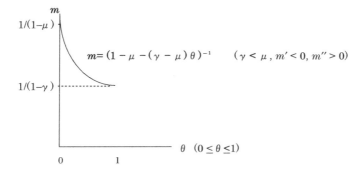

Figure 5.2: Multiplier and wage income share (θ) in $\gamma < \mu$.

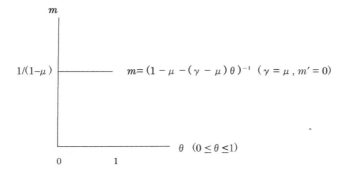

Figure 5.3: Multiplier and wage income share (θ) in $\gamma = \mu$.

Even in this case, when μ is unity, the multiplier is infinite in a closed system, but the multiplier relies on the propensity to import in an open economic system since saving ratio (s) is zero as well as in the other cases.

5.4. Simulations for Multiplier Effects on the Economy with Changes in Wage Income Share (θ)

Based on the demand-side model with reference to the Keynes multiplier, discussed earlier, based on Equations (19)–(27), we can examine the multiplier effects when the wage income share (θ) is changing. In order to simplify the calculation, we assume the initial values of Y, C, C_d, C^* and I are 100, 80, 60, 20 and 20, respectively and θ is changing in between 0.1

and 0.9. As the multiplier is defined in Equation (28), we can calculate the effects of changes in C^* on Y_d, C and I by employing the demand-side growth model incorporated with changes in wage income share (θ) and profit share ($1 - \theta$), as follows.

$$\Delta Y_d(t)/Y_d(t-1) = 1/(1 - \gamma\theta - \mu(1-\theta))(\Delta C^*(t)/C^*(t-1))$$
$$\times (C^*(t-1)/Y_d(t-1))$$
$$= 1/(1 - \mu - (\gamma - \mu)\theta)(\Delta C^*(t)/C^*(t-1))$$
$$\times (C^*(t-1)/Y_d(t-1))$$

As noted, the growth rate relies on the multiplier as an accelerator and rate of changes in C^* with the weight of C^* to Y_d. In other words, the growth rate of Y_d depends on γ, μ, θ, $\Delta C^*(t)/C^*(t-1)$ and $C^*(t-1)/Y_d(-1)$. For simulations, we assume that C^* increases by one unit from 20 to 21 (5 per cent increases in C^*) when γ is 0.6 and μ is 0.4 as Case A ($\gamma > \mu$), γ is 0.6 and μ is 0.8 as Case B ($\gamma < \mu$) and γ is 0.6 and μ is 0.6 ($\gamma = \mu$) as Case C.

Consequently, the multiplier in each case depends on γ, μ and θ, as summarized in Table 5.1. The multiplier is increasing in Case A, decreasing in Case B and not changing at 2.5 in Case C when θ is changing, as discussed earlier. If we assume a plausible value of the wage income share (θ) at 0.7 and, hence, the profit share ($1 - \theta$) at 0.3 in the economy without considering imports in a closed economic system, the multiplier is 2.17 in Case A, 2.94 in Case B and 2.5 in Case C. Hence, the demand-side economy (Y_d) increases by 2.17 per cent in Case A, by 2.94 per cent in Case B and by 2.5 per cent in Case C, when the independent consumption (C^*) increases by 5 per cent and hence the generator increases by 1 per cent.

As for the effects of the one unit change in the independent consumption (C^*), the demand-side economy (Y_d), the overall consumption (C) and the investment (I) are changing in terms of unit, as demonstrated in Figure 5.4, Figure 5.5 and Figure 5.6, by case. In all cases including Case A, Case B and Case C, these figures are consistent with Figures 5.1–5.3 and the demand-side components are relying on marginal propensity to consume (γ) and marginal propensity to invest (μ).

Table 5.1:   Keynes multiplier with changes in θ between 0.1 and 0.9.

θ	0.1	0.2	0.3	0.4	0.5	0.6	**0.7**	0.8	0.9
Case A $(\gamma > \mu)$ $(\gamma\ 0.6,\ \mu\ 0.4)$	1.72	1.79	1.85	1.92	2.00	2.08	**2.17**	2.27	2.38
Case B $(\gamma < \mu)$ $(\gamma\ 0.6,\ \mu\ 0.8)$	4.55	4.17	3.85	3.57	3.33	3.13	**2.94**	2.78	2.63
Case C $(\gamma = \mu)$ $(\gamma\ 0.6,\ \mu\ 0.6)$	2.50	2.50	2.50	2.50	2.50	2.50	**2.50**	2.50	2.50

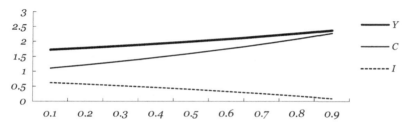

Figure 5.4:   Effects of the one unit change in C^* on Y, C and I with changes of θ in case A (γ:.60, μ:.40).

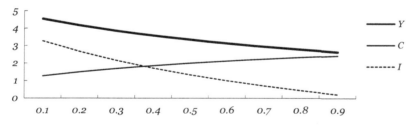

Figure 5.5:   Effects of the one unit change in C^* on Y, C and I with changes of θ in case B (γ:.60, μ:.80).

In addition, in all cases, the effects on consumption decrease and the effects on investment increase in line with the changes in both marginal propensities when the wage income share is declining. In particular, in Case A, decreases in the wage income share result in the lower effects on

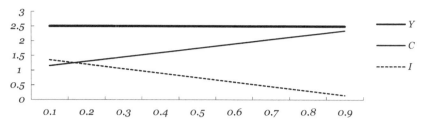

Figure 5.6:   Effects of the one unit change in C^* on Y, C and I with changes of θ in case C (γ:.60, μ:.60) (vertical: rate of changes in Y, C and I (%), horizontal: θ).

the consumption and hence on the demand-side economy (Y_d), but result in the higher effects on the investment.

In summary, this chapter discussed the simple theoretical model framework for empirical studies. However, the actual economy is more complicated, so we need to look into the actual economy and develop more plausible models for economic analyses. As Solow (1956, p. 65) mentioned, the theoretical model depends on some strict assumptions that cannot necessarily meet the workings of an actual economy.

On the contrary, in the case of empirical study, economists must look at our actual economy and examine the various causes for solving the problems seriously, so that experiments are indispensable irrespective of whether the model can explain the actual economy employing data, which is essential in econometric modeling and forecasting. In analyzing the deflationary economy of Japan, as long as we employ a supply-side approach, in which increases in consumption expenditures result in declines in savings and investments and, hence, result in declines in national income, we cannot solve the problems of the Japanese economy under deflation. In the next chapter, we discuss an econometric model that may be able to explain the actual economy, based on economic theories and empirical studies.

End Notes

[1]   In general, capital share (α) and labor share (β) are the same concept of profit share ($1 - \theta$) and wage income share (θ), theoretically. However,

we recognize the capital share and the labor share as a coefficient in the production function are a little bit different from wage income share (θ) and profit share ($1-\theta$) in the actual economy, especially in the Japanese economy. The differentials between labor share and wage income share cause the deflationary gap between actual GDP and GDP capacity, in which the wage income share gets lower than the labor share in the economy.

[2] Generally, a stock variable is calculated in an identity with net flows and the previous period stock. Therefore, if the households keep their assets in saving deposits, we can employ an identity of saving deposit (KS) as a financial asset, as follows.

$$KS(t) = KS(t-1) + S(t)$$
$$S(t) = Y(t) - C(t)$$

(Y: disposable income, C: consumption)

However, the households keep them in financial assets and non-financial assets. Therefore, we employ a behavioral equation to determine both assets which are substitutable between them depending on economic situations to increase their benefits and capital gains (losses). Accordingly, the assets are determined in a behavioral equation in the present study since the household sector holds the assets including financial assets (FA) and non-financial assets (NFA) within not only savings but also investment (speculation).

$$FA(t) = f((+)Y(t), \ (+) r(t), \quad (+) PSTOCK(t),$$
$$(+)FA(t-1), \ldots)$$
$$NFA(t) = f((+)Y(t), \ (-) r(t), \quad (+) PLAND(t),$$
$$(+) NFA(t-1), \ldots)$$

[3] Concerning this issue, both camps of the neo-classical growth school and the Keynesian growth school debated divergences of the natural rate of growth and the warranted growth in the Harrod–Domar model. Thirlwall (2002) precisely described this debate in terms of growth theory.

[4] In the early 1980s, the US government employed the supply-side policy to strengthen the supply-side of the economy, which was one of the pillars of the "Reganomics." Indeed, the supply-side of the US was relatively weak as compared to the demand-side. However, in the case of Japan, the supply-side is stronger than the demand-side economy.

CHAPTER 6

The Demand–Supply Integrated Econometric Model of Japan

6.1. Structure of the Demand–Supply Integrated Macro-Econometric Model

The Japanese macro-econometric model, which is a fiscal year base annual model, consists of nine blocks including (1) the real expenditure block, (2) the nominal expenditure block, (3) the prices and wage rates block, (4) the production block, (5) the population and labor force block, (6) the money and finance block, (7) the income distribution block, (8) the public finance block and (9) the international trade and balance of payment block. Based on the theoretical model framework discussed in the previous chapter, the Japanese macro-econometric model is designed and developed so as to examine the macro-economic structure of Japan, with special attention to the structural deflationary economy and its causations.

The model is basically a demand-side–oriented type model, a Keynesian-type model, but a supply-side model is incorporated with the demand-side model introducing GDP capacity explicitly so that the model is called a demand–supply integrated-type model. The total number of variables exceeds 160, with 131 endogenous and 37 exogenous variables including dummy and trend variables. This chapter discusses the structure of the demand–supply integrated macro-econometric model of Japan by block. (Please see the list of endogenous variables in Table 6.1 and exogenous variables in Table 6.2.)

Table 6.1:   List of endogenous variables.

Variable Name: Definition

CG: real government consumption expenditures (2000 constant prices, chain-linked)

CGN: nominal government consumption expenditures

CH: real household final consumption expenditure (2000 constant prices, chain-linked)

CHN: nominal household final consumption expenditure

CN: real non-profit organization consumption expenditure (2000 constant prices, chain-linked)

CNN: nominal non-profit organization consumption expenditure

CP: real private final consumption expenditures (2000 constant prices, chain-linked)

CPI: consumer price index (CPI.2005 = 100)

CPN: nominal private final consumption expenditures

DGAP: deflationary gap (GDPC − GDE)

DH: depreciation of real residential stock (2000 constant prices)

DIVC: corporate dividend paid

DP: depreciation of real private capital stock (2000 constant prices)

EG: real merchandise exports (2000 constant prices)

EGN: nominal merchandise exports

EGNB: nominal exports (f.o.b.)

EGNBS: nominal exports in terms of US$ (f.o.b.)

EGS: real exports of goods and services (2000 constant prices)

EGSN: nominal exports of goods and services

EINB: income transfers, credits in BOP

ES: real service exports (2000 constant prices)

ESC: employer's social contribution

ESN): nominal service exports

ESBNS: nominal service exports in terms of US$

EXR: exchange rate (yen/$)

EXRI: exchange rate index (EXRI.2000 = 100)

GDE: real gross domestic expenditures (2000 constant prices, chain-linked))

GDEN: nominal gross domestic expenditures

GDPC: real GDP capacity (2000 constant prices)

GEXDF: central government expenditure for defense

GEXEC: central government expenditure for economic corporation

---

(Continued)

Table 6.1: (*Continued*)

GEXED: central government expenditure for education

GEXFD: central government expenditure for foods

GEXGE: central government total expenditure in general accounts

GEXLF: central government expenditure for local finance

GEXLAB: central government expenditure for local allocation tax before an adjustment

GEXLA: central government expenditure for local allocation tax (LAT)

GEXLAD: supplementary budget for LAT

GEXND: central government expenditure for national debts

GEXPS: central government expenditure for public service

GEXPW: central government expenditure for public works

GEXSS: central government expenditure for social security

GEXTD: central government treasury disbursement

GRVGB: government bond revenue in general accounts

GRVGE: general accounts government revenue

GRVGEB: general government revenue without bond revenue

HFA: household financial assets

HNFA: household non-financial assets

HTA: household total assets

HTD: household total financial liabilities

INTCR: call rate

INTGB: government bond yield (10-year bond)

INTPR: prime rate

IG: real government investment (2000 constant prices, chain-linked)

IGN: nominal government investment

IH: real housing investment (2000 constant prices, chain-linked)

IHN: nominal housing investment

IP: real private non-residential investment (2000 constant prices, chain-linked)

IPN: nominal private non-residential investment

JG: real government inventory changes (2000 constant prices, chain-linked)

JGN: nominal government inventory changes

JP: real private inventory changes (2000 constant prices, chain-linked)

JPN: nominal private inventory changes

KH: real residential stock (2000 constant price)

KLGB: central government bonds outstanding

KLGBT: total national government debts outstanding

(*Continued*)

Table 6.1:   (*Continued*)

KP: real private capital stock (2000 constant prices)
KJP: real private inventory (2000 constant price)
LHL: legal working hours, per month
LHRAT: ratio of total working hours to legal working hours
LHT: total working hours, per month
MG: real merchandise imports (2000 constant prices)
MGN: nominal merchandise imports
MGNB: nominal imports (f.o.b.)
MGNS: nominal imports in US$ (f.o.b.)
MGOIL: real crude oil and oil products imports
MGOILN: nominal crude oil and oil products imports
MGOT: real merchandise imports excluding crude oil and oil products
MGOTN: nominal merchandise imports excluding oil and oil products
MGS: real imports of goods and services (2000 constant prices)
MGSN: nominal imports of goods and services
MINB: income transfers, debits in BOP
MS: real service imports (1994 constant prices)
MSN: nominal service imports
MSNBS: nominal service imports in terms of US$
M2CD: money supply, M2 plus CD
MB: monetary base
NL: number of labor
NLE: number of employed
NLW: number of waged and salaried employees
NP: total population
NP0014: population in the age group of 0 to 14 years
NP1564: population in the age group of 15 to 64 years
NP6500: population aged over 65 years
NU: number of unemployed
PCG: implicit deflator of CG
PCI: per-capita income in terms of US$
PCH: implicit deflator of CH
PCN: implicit deflator of CN
PCP: implicit deflator of CP
PEGS: implicit deflator of EGS
PEXY: export price in terms of local currency
PGDE: implicit deflator of GDE

(*Continued*)

Table 6.1: *(Continued)*

PIG: implicit deflator of IG
PIH: implicit deflator of IH
PIP: implicit deflator of IP
PJP: implicit deflator of JP
PLAND: real estate price
PMG: import price in local currency base
PMGS: implicit deflator of MGS
PMOTY: import price of non-oil and oil products in local currency base
POILY: crude oil price in local currency base (POILY.2000=100)
PSTOCK: stock prices (TOPIX base)
PX: output price
RKLG: ratio of accumulated government debt to nominal GDE
RNLF: female labor participation rate
ROTH: household other receipts
SH: savings in households
TAXCON: central government consumption tax revenue
TBG: trade balance in local currency
TBGS: trade balance in terms of US$
TBI: income balance in terms of local currency
TBS: service balance in local currency
TC: total corporate tax paid for central and local governments
TFP: total factor productivity (TFP index: TFPI.2000 = 100)
TP: total personal income tax paid for central and local governments
TXC: central government corporate income tax revenue
TXCL: local government corporate income tax revenue
TXG: central government total tax revenue
TXI: central government personal income tax revenue
TXIL: local government personal income tax revenue
UR: rate of unemployment
W: wages and salaries per employee
WN: nominal wage rates
YC: corporate income
YCB: corporate income (prior to dividend)
YDH: household disposable income
YDIV: household dividend income (including private unincorporated
    enterprises)
YE: compensation of employees

(Continued)

Table 6.1:   (*Continued*)

YHOT: other household income
YH: household income (including private unincorporated enterprises)
YIR: household interest income, receivable
YIP: household interest income, payable (consumer debt interest)
YRH: household property income
YROTH: household other property income
YU: income of private unincorporated enterprises
YW: wage and salaried income

Table 6.2:   List of exogenous variables.

Variable Name: Description

FA: foreign assets in terms of billion US$
FL: foreign liabilities in terms of billion US$
GEXOTH: central government other expenditures
GEXPWOR: central government expenditure for public works: budgetary base
GEXPWSU: supplementary for central government expenditure for public works
GRVOTH: other government revenue in the general accounts
INTOR: basic discount rate and basic loan rate (previously referred as official
    discount rate)
KLGOT: other national debts outstanding
NTOTH: household other net transfer
PJG: implicit deflator of JG
PMS: import price in terms of US$
POIL: crude oil price ($/barrel)
POTH: household other payments
PTW: world import deflator in dollar terms
RDIVC: ratio of dividend profits to corporate income
RTXC: effective corporate tax rate for central government
RTXCL: effective corporate tax rate for local government
RTXIL: effective personal income tax rate for local government
RTXCON: consumption tax rate
RTAXCON: rate of central government consumption tax revenue to total
    consumption tax
RYDIV: ratio of dividend income of household to corporate income
TBC: balance on current transfer in terms of local currency
TIME: time trend
TWM: real total world imports in US$

6.2. Model Structure and Specification by Block

6.2.1. Real expenditure block

In the real expenditure block, real gross domestic expenditure (GDE), and its components, including real household final consumption expenditure (CH), real non-profit institution final consumption expenditure (CN), real government consumption (CG), real housing investment (IH), real private non-housing investment (IP), real private inventory changes (JP), real exports of goods and services (EGS) and real imports of goods and services (MGS), are endogenously determined. In this block, in general, most of the expenditures are basically determined through income effects and price effects. Furthermore, the variables in the income distribution block and the money and finance block are employed to explain real household final consumption expenditure and real housing investment, through income effects and asymmetric effects of household assets and liabilities (Fisher, 1933), which is one of the key points in the present study.

The structure and specification of the real expenditure block are presented, as follows.

(1.1) *Real domestic expenditure*

$$GDE = CP + CG + IP + IH + IG + JP + JG$$
$$+ EGS - MGS + SD$$

(1.2) *Real household final consumption expenditure*

$$CH = f((+)YDH/PCH^*100, (+)PCH^*(1 + RTXC),$$
$$(+)HFA/PCH^*100), (+)HNFA/PCH^*100,$$
$$(-)\Delta HTD/PCH^*100, (-)INTOR(-1))$$

(1.3) *Real non-profit organization consumption expenditure*

$$CN = f((+)GDE, (+)CN(-1))$$

(1.4) *Real government final consumption expenditure*

$$CG = CGN/PCG^*100$$

(1.5) *Real housing investment expenditure*

$$IH = f((+)YDH/(PCP^*(1 + RTXC))^*100,$$
$$(-)INTOR(-1), (+)HTA/PIH^*100,$$
$$(-)\Delta HTD/PIH^*100, (-)KH(-1), (+)IH(-1))$$

(1.6) *Real non-housing investment*

$$IP = f((+)\Delta GDE, (+)(YC - TXC)/PIP^*100,$$
$$(+)CUR(-1), (+)IP(-1))$$

(1.7) *Real government investment*

$$IG = IGN/PIG^*100$$

(1.8) *Real private inventory changes*

$$JP = KJP - KJP(-1)$$

(1.9) *Real exports of goods and services*

$$EGS = (EG + ES)$$

(1.10) *Real imports of goods and services*

$$MGS = (MG + MS)$$

(1.11) *Real private final consumption expenditure*

$$CP = CH + CN$$

(1.12) *Real private inventory*

$$KJP = f((+)GDE, (+)PX/PCP, (+)KJP(-1), (+)D08)$$

(1.13) *Real housing stock*

$$KH = KH(-1) + IH - DH + SDH$$

(1.14) *Real depreciation of housing stock*

$$DH = f((+)KH, (+)GDE/GDE(-1), (+)DH(-1))$$

6.2.2. *Nominal expenditure block*

Regarding the nominal expenditure block, nominal GDE and nominal GDE components are endogenized. Nominal GDE and its components, except nominal government consumption (CGN) and nominal government investment (IGN), are determined in an identity. On the other hand, government consumption and government investment are endogenized in a behavioral equation [see Equations (2.5) and (2.7)], in which nominal government investment is endogenized by employing some central government expenditures, including public works expenditure (GEXPW), treasury disbursement (GEXTD) and disbursement of local allocation tax (GEXLA). This is also one of the key points in the present study [see Equation (2.7)].

(2.1) *Nominal gross domestic expenditure*

$$GDEN = CPN + CGN + IPN + IHN + IGN + JPN + JGN$$
$$+ EGSN - MGSN + SDN$$

(2.2) *Minimal private final consumption expenditure*

$$CPN = CHN + CNN$$

(2.3) *Nominal household final consumption expenditure*

$$CHN = CH*PCH/100$$

(2.4) *Nominal non-profit organization final consumption expenditure*

$$CNN = CN*PCN/100$$

(2.5) *Nominal government consumption expenditure*

$$CGN = f((+)WN, (+)GEXSS(-1), (+)CGN(-1))$$

(2.6) *Nominal non-housing investment*

$$IPN = IP*PIP/100$$

(2.7) *Nominal government expenditure*

$$IGN = f((+)GEXPW, (+)GEXTD,$$
$$(+)(GEXLA + GEXTT), (-)D98)$$

(2.8) *Nominal private inventory changes*

$$JPN = JP*PJP/100$$

(2.9) *Nominal government investment*

$$JGN = JG*PJG/100$$

(2.10) *Nominal exports of goods and services*

$$EGSN = EGSN*PEGS/100$$

(2.11) *Nominal imports of goods and services*

$$MGSN = MGS*PMGS/100$$

6.2.3. *Prices and wage rates block*

In the prices and wage rates block, the general deflator of GDE (PGDE), deflators of GDE components, output price (PX), exports price (PEXY), imports price (PMY), exchange rate (EXR), real estate price (PLAND) and nominal wage rates (WN) are determined endogenously. In determining output price and export price, labor productivity (GDPC/NL), which is the ratio of GDP capacity (GDPC) to the number of labor force (NL), is utilized as a proxy for technical progress [see Equations (3.8) and (3.10)]. In addition to that, the labor productivity with the demand-side GDP (GDE) is employed to determine nominal wage rates [see Equation (3.9)].

The exchange rate is also endogenized by purchasing power parity, the ratio of export price (PEXY) to US general deflator (PGDP <US>), and long-term interest rate parity between Japan and the US (INTGB/INTGB<US>) in this block [see Equation (3.14)].

(3.1) General deflator of GDE

$$PGDE = GDEN/GDE*100$$

(3.2) Deflator of final housing consumption

$$\ln(PCH) = f((+)\ln(PX), (+)\ln(WN, (+)\ln(PCH(-1)))$$

(3.3) Deflator of non-profit organization consumption

$$\ln(PCN) = f((+)\ln(PX), (+)\ln(WN), (+)\ln(PCN(-1)))$$

(3.4) Deflator of government consumption

$$\ln(PCG) = f((+)\ln(PX), (+)\ln(WN), (+)\ln(PCG(-1)))$$

(3.5) Deflator of non-housing investment

$$\ln(PIP) = f((+)\ln(PX), (+)\ln(WN),$$
$$(-)\ln(GDPC(-1)/NL(-1)), (+)\ln(PIP(-1)))$$

(3.6) Deflator of housing investment

$$\ln(PIH) = f((+)\ln(PX), (+)\ln(WN), (+)\ln(PIH(-1)))$$

(3.7) Deflator of government investment

$$\ln(PIG) = f((+)\ln(PX), (+)\ln(WN), \ln(PIG(-1)), (+)D08)$$

(3.8) Output price

$$\ln(\mathrm{PX}) = f((+)\ln(\mathrm{PMY}), (+)\ln(\mathrm{WN}),$$
$$(-)\ln(\mathrm{GDPC}(-1)/\mathrm{NL}(-1)), (+)\ln(\mathrm{PX}(-1)))$$

(3.9) Nominal wage rates

$$\mathrm{DOT}(\mathrm{WN}) = f((+)\mathrm{DOT}(\mathrm{PCP}), (-)\mathrm{UR}, (+)\mathrm{DOT}(\mathrm{GDE}/\mathrm{LW}))$$

(3.10) Export price in terms of local currency (merchandize: fob)

$$\ln(\mathrm{PEXY}) = f((+)\ln(\mathrm{PX}), (+)\ln(\mathrm{EXR}),$$
$$(-)\ln(\mathrm{GDPC}(-1)/\mathrm{NL}(-1)))$$

(3.11) Consumer price index

$$\ln(\mathrm{CPI}) = f((+)\ln(\mathrm{PX}), (+)\ln(\mathrm{WN}), (+)\ln(\mathrm{CPI}(-1)))$$

(3.12) Deflator of exports of goods and services

$$\ln(\mathrm{PEGS}) = f((+)\ln(\mathrm{PEXY}))$$

(3.13) Deflator of imports of goods and services

$$\ln(\mathrm{PMGS}) = f((+)\ln(\mathrm{PMY}))$$

(3.14) Exchange rate (Yen/$)

$$\mathrm{EXR} = f((+)\mathrm{PEXY}/\mathrm{PGDP{<}US{>}}, (-)\mathrm{INTGB}/\mathrm{INTGB{<}US{>}},$$
$$(+)\mathrm{EXR}(-1))$$

(3.15) Exchange rate index

$$\mathrm{EXRI} = \mathrm{EXR}/110.45{*}100$$

(3.16) Import price excluding crude oil and oil products

$$\mathrm{PMOTY} = \mathrm{PMOTS}{*}\mathrm{EXRI}/100$$

(3.17) Import price of crude oil and oil products

$$\mathrm{POILY} = (\mathrm{POIL}/28.23{*}100){*}\mathrm{EXRI}/100$$

(3.18) Import price (merchandize: fob)

$$\mathrm{PMY} = (\mathrm{POILY}{*}\mathrm{MGOIL} + \mathrm{PMOTY}{*}\mathrm{MGOT})/$$
$$(\mathrm{MGOIL} + \mathrm{MGOT})$$

(3.19) *Real estate price*

$$PLAND = f((+)GDE/GDE(-1), (+)PSTOCK,$$
$$(+)PLAND(-1))$$

6.2.4. Production block

As for the production block, factors such as GDP capacity (GDPC), capital stock (KP), capacity utilization rate of capital (CUR), depreciation of capital (DP) and deflationary gap (DGAP) are endogenously determined. In the present study, as noted, the supply-side GDP is endogenized as the GDP capacity, explicitly, adjusting capacity utilization rate of capital, unemployment rate (UR) and ratio of total working hours to legal working hours (LHRAT).

In addition, in the Cobb–Douglas production function, technical progress is taken into consideration while employing a vintage model as the Solow neutrality and time trend as the Hicksian-type neutral technical progress.

(4.1) *Real GDP capacity*

$$\ln(GDPC) = f((+)\ln(KP*CUR),$$
$$(+)\ln((1 - UR/100)*NL*LHRAT),$$
$$(+)(IP + IP(-1) + IP(-2))/KP, (+)TIME)$$

(4.2) *Private sector capital stock*

$$KP = KP(-1) + IP - DP$$

(4.3) *Depreciation of capital*

$$DP/KP(-1) = f((+)GDE/GDE(-1), (+)DP(-1)/KP(-2))$$

(4.4) *Capacity utilization rate of capital*

$$\ln(CUR*KP) = f(+)\ln(GDE))$$

(4.5) *Deflationary gap*

$$DGAP = GDPC - GDE$$

(4.6) *Total factor productivity (TFP) and TFP index (TFPI)*

$$\text{TFP} = \exp(0.263 + 0.238((\text{IP} + \text{IP}(-1) + \text{IP}(-2))/\text{KP})$$
$$+ 0.0041(\text{TIME}))$$
$$= \exp(\ln(\text{GDPC}) - 0.301\ln(\text{KP})$$
$$- 0.699\ln((1 - 2.00/100))*\text{NL}*1.099))$$
$$\text{TFPI} = \text{TFP}/\text{TFP}.2000*100$$

6.2.5. *Population and labor force block*

In the population and labor force block, total population (NP), number of labor (NL), number of employed (LNE), number of unemployed (NU), unemployment rate (UR) and number of wage and salaried employees (NLW) are endogenized.[1] The number of unemployed is determined by the rate of unemployment while the rate of unemployed relates to the labor market condition including labor supply, real wage rates, real GDE and Koyck-lag (UR(−1)) [see Equation (5.6)].

(5.1) *Total population*

$$\text{NP} = \text{NP0014} + \text{NP1564} + \text{NP6500}$$

(5.2) *Population, 0 to 14 years old*

$$\text{NP0014} = f((+)\text{NP0014}(-1), (+/-)\text{TIME},$$
$$(+/-)\text{TIME}*\text{TIME})$$

(5.3) *Population, 65 years old and over*

$$\text{NP6500} = f((+)\text{NP6500}(-1), (+)\text{TIME})$$

(5.4) *Number of active population, 15 to 64 years old*

$$\text{NP1564} = f((+)\text{NP1564}(-1), (+/-)\text{TIME},$$
$$(+/-)\text{TIME}*\text{TIME})$$

(5.5) *Number of labor*

$$\text{NL} = f((+)\text{WN}, (+)(\text{NP1564} + \text{NP6500}),$$
$$(+)\text{RNLF}, (+)\text{NL}(-1))$$

(5.6)   *Rate of unemployment*

$$UR = f((-)\ln(GDE), (+)\ln(WN(-1)/PGDE(-1)),$$
$$(+)\ln(NL), (+)UR(-1))$$

(5.7)   *Number of employed*

$$NLE = (1 - UR/100)*NL$$

(5.8)   *Number of unemployed*

$$NU = NL - NLE$$

(5.9)   *Number of wage and salaried employed*

$$NLW = f((+)GDE, (+)NLE, (-)WN(-1), (+)NLW(-1))$$

(5.10) *Ratio of total working hour to legal working hour*

$$LHRAT = f((+)GDE/GDE(-1), (-)NLE/NL,$$
$$(+)LHRAT(-1))$$

(5.11) *Female labor participation rate*

$$RNLF = f((+)GDE/GDE(-1), (+)WN/WN(-1),$$
$$(+)RNLF(-1))$$

6.2.6.   *Money and finance block*

With respect to the money and finance block, in this block, call rate (INTCR), prime rate (INTPR), long-term government bond yield (INTGB), money supply (M2+CD) and TOPIX base stock price (PSTOCK) are endogenously determined. In this block, there are two major control variables, monetary base (MB) and official discount rates (INTOR). Given both control variables, these endogenous variables are determined.

This block is also very important, since these variables determined in this block affect real household final consumption and real housing investment through changes of household assets and liabilities, as discussed earlier.

(6.1) *Call rate*

$$INTCR = f((+)INTOR, (-)M2CD)$$

(6.2) *Prime rate*

$$INTPR = f((-)M2CD/GDEN, (+)INTOR)$$

(6.3) *Government bond yield (10-year maturity)*

$$INTGB = f((+)INTPR, (+)INTGB<US>, (-)EXR)$$

(6.4) *Money supply, M2 + CD*

$$M2CD = f((+)GDE, (+)MB, (-)INTGB)$$

(6.5) *Stock price (TOPIX)*

$$PSTOCK = f((+)GDE/((GDE + GDE(-1))/2),$$
$$(-)INTOR - DOT(PGDE),$$
$$(+)PSTOCK(-1))$$

6.2.7. Income distribution block

In the income distribution block, private corporate income (YCB), private income (YP), household income (YH) and its components including compensation of employees (YE), wage and salaried income (YW), household property income (YRH), household dividend income (YDIVH) and unincorporated enterprises income (YU) are endogenized. In addition, household financial assets (HFA), household non-financial assets (HNFA) and household total liabilities (HTD) are also determined simultaneously with household income to examine not only income effects with flow variables but also the assets effects with stock variables on the household expenditures. This block is also very important to analyze the effects on the demand-side and the supply-side economy through changes of wage income share and profit share, as discussed in the theoretical framework.

(7.1) *Corporate income (before dividend)*

$$YCB = f((+)GDEN, (-)INTPR,$$
$$(+)PEXIY/PX, (-)YW, (-)D08)$$

(7.2) *Corporate income*

$$YC = YCB - DIVC$$

(7.3) *Corporate dividend paid*

$$DIVC = RDIVC^*YCB$$

(7.4) *Wages and salaries per employee*

$$W = f((+)WN, (+)GDE/GDE(-1), (+)W(-1))$$

(7.5) *Compensation of employees*

$$YE = YW + ESC$$

(7.6) *Wage and salaried income*

$$YW = W^*NLW/100$$

(7.7) *Household property income*

$$YRH = YIH + YDIV + YROTH$$

(7.8) *Household interest income*

$$YIH = YIR - YIP$$

(7.9) *Household interest income, receivable*

$$YIR = f((+)HFA, (+)INTGB, (+)YIR(-1))$$

(7.10) *Household interest income, payable (consumer debt interest)*

$$YIP = f((+)HTD, (+)INTGB, (+)YIP(-1))$$

(7.11) *Household dividend income*

$$YDIV = RYDIV^*YCB$$

(7.12) *Income of private unincorporated enterprises*

$$YU = f((+)GDEN, (-)INTORA, (-)WN/PCP)$$

(7.13) *Employer's social contribution*

$$ESC = f((+)YW, (+)ESC(-1))$$

(7.14) *Other household property income*

$$YROTH = f((+)GDEN/GDEN, (-)INTGB, (+)YHOT(-1))$$

(7.15) *Household income*

$$YH = YE + YRH + YU$$

(7.16) *Household disposable income*

$$YDH = YH + ROTH - TP - POTH$$

(7.17) *Household savings*

$$SH = YDH - CHN$$

(7.18) *Household financial assets*

$$\ln(HFA) = f((+)\ln(YDH), (+)\ln(PSTOCK),$$
$$(+)\ln(INTGB(-1)/INTOR(-1)),$$
$$(+)\ln(HFA(-1)))$$

(7.19) *Household non-financial assets*

$$HNFA/PLAND*100 = f((+)YDH/PLAND*100, (-)INTGB,$$
$$(+)PLAND/PLAND(-1),$$
$$(+)HNFA(-1)/PLAND(-1)*100)$$

(7.20) *Increment of household total liabilities*

$$\Delta HTD = f((+)YDH, (-)INTOR(-1), (+)PLAND,$$
$$(+)\Delta HTD(-1))$$

(7.21) *Household total assets*

$$HTA = HFA + HNFA$$

(7.22) *Household total liabilities*

$$HTD = \Delta HTD + HTD(-1)$$

6.2.8. *Public finance block*

As for the public finance block, central government revenue in general accounts (GRVGE) and its components, including individual income tax revenue (TXI), private corporation income tax revenue (TXC), consumption tax revenue (TAXCON) and the other revenues, are determined. In addition, central government expenditure in general accounts (GEXGE) and its components, including expenditure for social security (GEXSS), public works (GEXPW), national defense (GEXDF), economic corporation (GEXEC), local finance (GEXLA) and national debts (GEXND) are also determined. Furthermore, the financial source and disbursement of local allocation tax (LAT) to local governments are also determined in this block (Nakamura 2002, 2010).

(8.1) Central government household income tax revenue

$$TXI = f((+)YP, (+)GDEN/GDEN(-1), (+)TXI(-1))$$

(8.2) Central government corporate income tax revenue

$$TXC = RTXC*YCB$$

(8.3) Corporate tax rate for central government

$$RTXC = f((+)GDEN/GDEN(-1), (+)RTXC(-1))$$

(8.4) Total corporate income tax paid

$$TC = TXC + TXCL$$

(8.5) Total household income tax paid

$$TP = TXI + TXIL$$

(8.6) Total consumption tax paid

$$TXCON = RTXCON*CPN$$

(8.7) Central government consumption tax revenue

$$TAXCON = RTAXCON*TXCON$$

(8.8) Central government total tax revenue in general accounts

$$TXG = TXC + TXI + TAXCON + TXOTH$$

(8.9) Source of local allocation tax (LAT) system

$$GEXLAB = 0.32*TXI + 0.325*TXC$$
$$+ 0.295*TAXCON + TXLA$$

(8.10) *Central government expenditure for LAT*

$$GEXLA = GEXLAB + GEXLAD$$

(8.11) *Total central government expenditures in general accounts*

$$GEXGE = GEXSS + GEXLF + GEXED + GEXND$$
$$+ GEXPS + GEXDF + GEXEC + GEXFD$$
$$+ GEXPW + GEXOTH$$

(8.12) *Central government expenditure for social security in general accounts*

$$GEXSS = f((+)NP6500, (-)D8990, (+)D99)$$

(8.13) *Central government expenditure for social local finance*

$$GEXLF = f((+)GEXLAB)$$

(8.14) *Central government expenditure for education, science*

$$\ln(GEXED) = f((+)\ln(GRVGE), (+)\ln(GEXED(-1)))$$

(8.15) *Central government expenditure for public service*

$$\ln(GEXPS) = f((+)\ln(GRVGE), (+)\ln(GEXPS(-1)),$$
$$(-)TIME)$$

(8.16) *Central government expenditure for economic corporation*

$$GEXEC = f((+)GDEN, (+)U, (-)TIME)$$

(8.17) *Central government expenditure for national defense*

$$GEXDF = f((+)GDEN, (+)GEXDF(-1))$$

(8.18) *Central government expenditure for foods*

$$GEXFD = f((+)GRVGE/GDEN, (+/-)TIME,$$
$$(+/-)TIME*TIME)$$

(8.19) *Central government expenditure for public works*

$$GEXPW = f((+)(GEXPWOR + GEXPWSU))$$

(8.20) *Central government revenue prior to government bond revenue*

$$GRVGEB = TXG + GRVOTH$$

(8.21) *Central government bond issued*

$$GRVGB = GEXGE - GRVGEB$$

(8.22) *Central government revenue in general accounts*

$$GRVGE = TXG + GRVGB + GRVOTH$$

(8.23) *Local government household income tax revenue*

$$TXIL = RTXIL*YH(-1)$$

(8.24) *Local government corporate income tax revenue*

$$TXCL = RTXCL*YCB(-1)$$

(8.25) *Central government bonds outstanding*

$$KLGB = KLGB(-1) + GRVGEB - GEXED$$

(8.26) *Total national government debts outstanding*

$$KLGBT = KLGB + KLGOT$$

(8.27) *Ratio of accumulated government debt to nominal GDE*

$$RKLG = KLGB/GDEN*100$$

6.2.9. *International trade and balance of payment block*

In the international trade and balance of payment BOP block, real merchandise exports (EXG) and imports (MG), nominal merchandise exports (EXGN) and imports (MGN), real imports of crude oil and oil products (MGOIL), nominal imports of crude oil and oil products (MGOILN) and the other components of current balance of payments are endogenously determined. In addition, real merchandise exports and imports, and real service exports and imports endogenized in this block are linked to the real exports of goods and services, and real imports of goods and services in the real expenditure block.

In real merchandise exports function, the supply-side effects are also taken into account utilizing the supply-side labor productivity (GDPC/NL) [see Equation (9.1)].

(9.1) *Real merchandise exports*

$$\ln(\text{EXG}) = f((+)\ln(\text{TWM}), (-)\ln(\text{PEXIY}/\text{EXRI}/\text{PTW}),$$
$$(+)\ln(\text{GDPC}/\text{NL}))$$

(9.2) *Real imports of crude oil and oil products*

$$\ln(\text{MGOIL}) = f((+)\ln(\text{GDE})), (-)\ln(\text{POIL}^*\text{EXRI}/\text{PX}))$$

(9.3) *Real merchandise imports except crude oil and oil products*

$$\text{MGOT} = f((+)\text{GDE}/\text{GDE}(-1)), (-)\text{PMOTS}^*\text{EXRI}/\text{PX},$$
$$(+)\text{MGOT}(-1))$$

(9.4) *Nominal exports in BOP*

$$\text{EGNB} = f((+)\text{EGN})$$

(9.5) *Nominal imports in BOP*

$$\text{MGNB} = f((+)\text{MGN})$$

(9.6) *Service exports in BOP*

$$\text{ESNB} = f((+)(\text{EXCN}^*10 - \text{EGB}))$$

(9.7) *Service imports in BOP*

$$\text{MSNB} = f((+)(\text{MCN}^*10 - \text{MGB}))$$

(9.8) *Nominal merchandise exports*

$$\text{EGN} = \text{EXG}^*\text{PEXY}/100$$

(9.9) *Nominal merchandise imports*

$$\text{MG} = \text{MGOT} + \text{MGOIL}$$

(9.10) *Nominal merchandise imports excluding oil and oil products*

$$\text{MGOTN} = \text{MGOT}^*\text{PMOTY}/100$$

(9.11) *Nominal imports of oil and oil products*

$$\text{MGOILN} = \text{MGOIL}^*\text{POILY}/100$$

(9.12) *Nominal merchandise imports*

$$\text{MGN} = \text{MGOILN} + \text{MGOTN}$$

(9.13) Trade balance in terms of local currency

$$TBG = EGNB - MGNB$$

(9.14) Service balance in terms of local currency

$$TBS = ESNB - MSNB$$

(9.15) Income transfer, credits in local currency

$$EINB = f((+)FA(-1){*}EXR(-1), (+)INTGB/INTGB{<}US{>},$$
$$(-)EXR(-1), (-)D08)$$

(9.16) Income transfer, debits in local currency

$$MINB = f((+)FL(-1){*}EXR(-1), (+)INTGB{<}US{>},$$
$$(+)MINB(-1))$$

(9.17) Income balance in terms of local currency

$$TBI = EINB - MINB$$

(9.18) Current balance of payment in terms of local currency

$$CBP = TBG + TBS + TBI + TBC$$

(9.19) Nominal merchandise exports in US$

$$EGNBS = EGNB/EXR{*}1000$$

(9.20) Nominal merchandise imports in US$

$$MGNBS = MGNB/EXR{*}1000$$

(9.21) Trade balance in US$

$$TBGS = EGNBS - MGNBS$$

Concerning more detailed causations and model structure, we conduct regression analysis for major endogenous variables in the next section.

6.3. Unit Root Test

Before conducting a regression analysis, a unit root test is performed for all time series data employed in the model as discussed earlier. For the unit root test, in the present study, an Augmented Dickey–Fuller (ADF) test is employed to examine non-stationarity of all time series information, even in the case of annual data series. In order to examine the unit root problem with the ADF test, three basic equations, (1) without constant and trend,

Table 6.3: Unit root test with the augmented Dickey–Fuller test for major demand-side and supply-side variables: with trend and intercept.

Variable	Level	First Difference	Second Difference
GDE	−0.17	−3.37*	−6.34***
CH	0.02	−4.19***	−7.22***
IP	−1.03	−2.38	−4.73***
IH	−0.95	−5.27***	−8.70***
CG	−1.62	−3.68**	−4.92***
IG	−0.40	−2.80	−6.28***
EGS	−1.93	−3.17	−7.26***
MGS	−1.76	−2.36	−4.99***
PGDE	−0.70	−2.88	−5.92***
GDPC	−0.45	−2.08	−3.45*
KP	−1.20	−2.12	−3.44*
NL	−0.12	−2.34	−4.75***
UR	−0.95	−2.63	−4.85***

Note: *, ** and *** indicate the significance at 10%, 5% and 1%, respectively.

Level, First Difference and Second Difference with Trend and Intercept

Level: $\Delta Y = \alpha + \beta \, \text{Trend} + \delta Y(-1) + u$
First difference: $\Delta(\Delta Y) = \alpha + \beta \, \text{Trend} + \delta \Delta Y(-1) + u$
Second difference: $\Delta(\Delta(\Delta Y)) = \alpha + \beta \, \text{Trend} + \delta \Delta \, (\Delta Y(-1)) + u$

<ADF Critical Values in Level, First difference and Second difference>

	Level	First Difference	Second Difference
1%	4.324	4.339	4.356
5%	3.581	3.588	3.595
10%	3.225	3.229	3.233

Note: Sample: FY1980–2008.
Source: Estimated and compiled by the author.

(2) with constant and (3) with constant and trend are utilized in level, first difference and second difference case, respectively. These test results are very useful in recognizing the nature of time series in regression and in modeling and forecasting.

Table 6.3 shows the ADF test results for major demand-side and supply-side variables employed in the model within the level, the first difference and the second difference equation with intercept and trend. According to the ADF test results, as shown in Table 6.3, integrated orders are found to be different among data series. However, some series are stationary at first difference {I(1)} while the most of the time series are stationary at second difference {I(2)} except GDP capacity (GDPC) and capital stock (KP), which means non-stationarity of these series could not be rejected within the level equation with the above stated trend and intercept. Accordingly, we need to conduct our regression analysis carefully with evaluating various fundamental statistics and coefficients, based on economic theories. (See Appendix E for the other time series ADF test results.)

Endnote

[1] In the present study, total population relies on three cohort groups, in which interface between a demographic block and economic blocks is still weak in the model. We are now trying to integrate a cohort-type demographic model with the macro-model, as done by Shishido and Nakamura (1990).

CHAPTER 7

Regression Analysis

In the present study, we conducted a regression analysis employing a least square method to examine the structure of the Japanese macro-economy and to elucidate the causes of the deflationary economy.[1] In this section, we introduce some major regression results, with special emphasis on the endogenous variables related to the supply-side economy, the demand-side economy, the income distribution-side economy and prices.

7.1. Supply-Side

7.1.1. *Production function*

Based on the Cobb–Douglas production function, real GDP is explained by real capital stock in private sector (KP) with capacity utilization rate of capital (CUR), the number of employed (NL*(1−UR/100)*LHRAT) adjusted by labor working hour ratio (LHRAT), which is the ratio between overall working hours (LHT) to legal working hours (LHL), the ratio of sum of recent three-year real non-housing investment (IP+IP(−1)+IP(−2)) to real capital stock (KP), which is the Solow vintage model (Solow, 1960) with embodied technical progress, the Solow neutrality, and time trend (TIME) that represents the Hicksian neutral technical progress,[2] as follows.

$$\ln(\text{GDP}) = f((+)\ln(\text{KP*CUR}/100),$$
$$(+)\ln(\text{NL*}(1 - \text{UR}/100)\text{*LHRAT}),$$
$$(+)(\text{IP} + \text{IP}(-1) + \text{IP}(-2))/\text{KP}, \quad (+)\text{TIME})$$

According to the regression result with labor productivity function, the coefficient of capital stock, capital share, is 0.301759 and, hence, the coefficient of labor, labor share, is 0.698241(= 1−0.301759). In addition, the embodied technical progress and the Hicksian neutral technical progress are significantly represented in this regression result, which is consistent with the results of Shishido and Nakamura (1992a), emphasizing the role of labor-saving technical progress in Japan. The fundamental statistics such as t-value in parenthesis, Adjusted-R^2, standard error (SE) and Durbin–Watson ratio (DW) are also significant and performed well with the Cochrane–Orcutt procedure (C-O).

$$\ln (GDP/(1 - UR/100)*NL*LHRAT))$$
$$(12.03)$$
$$= 0.267797 + 0.301759 \ln (KP*CUR/100)$$
$$(5.63))$$
$$+ 0.238326 (IP + IP(-1) + IP(-2))/KP$$
$$(2.48)$$
$$+ 0.00412 \, TIME$$
$$(3.06)$$

C-O (1981–2008)   Adjusted-R^2 = 0.993   SE = 0.00955   DW=1.708

As discussed in Chapter 3, based on the regression result, the time series of GDP capacity (GDPC) is estimated from FY1981 to FY2008 by adjusting CUR, UR and LHRAT to employ the peak value at 100 (%) for CUR, at 2.09 (%) for UR and at 1.099 for LHRAT of FY1990, which is the final fiscal year of the bubble period, as follows.

$$\ln (GDPC) = 0.267797 + 0.301759 \ln (KP*100/100)$$
$$(12.08) \qquad (5.63)$$
$$+ (1 - 0.301759) \ln ((1 - 2.09/100)*NL*1.099)$$
$$(***)$$
$$+ 0.238326(IP + IP(-1) + IP(-2))/KP + 0.00412 \, TIME$$
$$(2.48) \qquad\qquad\qquad\qquad\qquad (3.06)$$

The estimated GDPC, which was demonstrated in Figure 3.2, was calculated based on this regression result. Furthermore, this estimated GDP capacity explicitly appears in the demand-supply integrated model as an endogenous and independent variable.

7.2. Demand-Side

As for the demand-side components regression results, we will discuss real household final consumption expenditure (CH), real housing investment (IH) and real private non-housing investment (IP) regression results, respectively. In principle, the demand-side GDP components are determined by income effects and price effects in the demand-side model. In addition, the supply-side effects also play a significant role in the demand-supply integrated model employed in the present study. Furthermore, the asset and debt effects are also taken into consideration for real household consumption and real housing investment, as discussed above.

7.2.1. *Household final consumption expenditure*

With respect to real final household consumption, which is one of the key endogenous variables in this model, real final household consumption (CH) relies on real household disposable income (YDH/PCH*100) as an income effect, deflator of household consumption considering the impacts of consumption tax rate (PCH*(1+RTXC)) as a price effect, real household financial asset (HFA/PCH*100), real household non-financial asset (HNFA/PCH*100) and the first difference of real household financial debt (ΔHTD/PCH*100), one year lagged official policy rate (INTOR(-1)) and Koyck-lag (CH(-1)), as follows.

$$CH = f((+) \text{ YDH/PCH*100}, \quad (-) \text{ PCH*}(1 + \text{RTXC}),$$
$$(+) \text{ HFA/PCH*100}, \quad (+) \text{ HNFA/PCH},$$
$$(+) \Delta(\text{HTD/PCH*100}), \quad (-) \text{ INTORA}(-1))$$

Basically, the consumption function depends on the absolute income hypothesis. In addition, we employ real household financial assets as the liquidity asset hypothesis (Tobin, 1951), real household non-financial assets and real household liabilities, so that these three variables are able to examine the real balance effect (Pigou effect) and the real debt effect (Fisher, 1933) when nominal wage rates and prices fall down.

According to the regression result, we can see very interesting causations between the dependent and independent variables. First, the coefficient of real disposable income is limited at 0.741, which is not the marginal propensity to consume to real GDE, but to real household disposable income. If we consider the ratio of household disposable income to nominal GDE at 0.58 as of FY2008, we can see that the marginal propensity to consume to real GDP is quite limited, at around 0.43 in FY2008. Recently, the marginal propensity to consume is declining with the higher autonomous consumption in Japan. Particularly, the propensity to consume in the rural districts of Japan is very low because of the large autonomous consumption and liquidity asset effects (Nakamura, 2010).

$$CH = 101{,}692.3 + 0.7412\ (YDH/PCH^*100)$$
$$\quad (5.66) \qquad (7.22)$$
$$\quad - 1{,}101.92.661\ PCH^*(1 + RTXC)$$
$$\quad (-3.38)$$
$$\quad + 0.04279\ (HFA/PCH^*100) + 0.00845\ (HNFA/PCH^*100)$$
$$\quad (4.57) \qquad\qquad\qquad\qquad (2.08)$$
$$\quad - 0.3887(\Delta HTD/PCH^*100) - 1{,}260.94\ INTOR(-1)$$
$$\quad (-3.96) \qquad\qquad\qquad\qquad (-2.05)$$

$$\text{OLS}(1981 - 2008) \quad \text{Adjusted-}R^2 = 0.997 \quad SE = 2{,}466.4 \quad DW = 1.723$$

In addition, price effects are also significant and effective in the result, in which the coefficient is 1,101.9, as a marginal effect. Therefore a 5 per cent point increase in consumption tax rate may result in declines in real consumption expenditure by around 5.0 trillion yen, on a static basis, since the level of PCH is 92.3 and consumption tax rate (RTXC) is 0.05 (5%) in FY2009. As for the effects of interest rate changes, the marginal effects of policy rate changes are very limited. The coefficient is 1,260.9 so that a 0.1 per cent point decline in policy rate may result in increase in real consumption by 0.1261 trillion yen, on a static basis, with one-year time-lag.

Furthermore, both the real asset effect and debt effect are significant. Though real household financial liabilities have the first difference form (Δ HTD/PCH*100), we can compare both the real asset effect and the real debt effect based on these coefficients with decomposing the real household financial assets (HFA/PCH*100) into the first difference (Δ HFA/PCH*100) and one-year lagged real household financial assets (HFA(-1)/PCH*100). The coefficients of the household financial assets, non-financial assets and financial liabilities are 0.0428, 0.0084 and 0.3887, respectively. Therefore, it can be seen that the real asset effect is smaller than the real debt effect, on a static basis,[3] as discussed earlier utilizing Fisher (1933).

7.2.2. *Housing investment*

Regarding real housing investment function, real housing investment depends on real disposable income with effects of changes in consumption tax rate incorporated with its deflator changes (YDH/(PCP*(1+RTXC))*100), one-year lagged official policy rate (INTOR(-1)), real household total assets (HTA/PCH*100), increments of real debts (Δ HTD/PCH*100), one-year lagged housing stock (KH(-1)) as a stock adjustment principle, and Koyck-lag variable (IH(-1)), as follows.

$$\text{IH} = f((+)\,\text{YDH}/(\text{PCP}^*(1+\text{RTXC}))^*100, \quad (-)\,\text{INTOR}(-1),$$
$$(+)\,\text{HTA}/\text{PIH}^*100, \quad (-)\Delta\,\text{HTD}/\text{PIH}^*100,$$
$$(-)\,\text{KH}(-1), \quad (+)\,\text{IH}(-1))$$

According to the regression result, the coefficient of real disposable income to induce housing investment is 0.196, which is relatively high considering the impacts of the coefficient of Koyck-lag (0.319), so the long-term marginal propensity to invest is around 0.288 (0.196/(1−0.319)). However, the stock adjustment effects may also be effective and significant since the housing investment was largely fluctuated in the regression sample period.

In addition, the effects of changes in official policy rate on the real housing investment are limited since the coefficient of official policy rate is 1,273.5. Furthermore, the real household asset effects and debt effects are also observed significantly as well as on the household consumption expenditure.

$$IH = 4{,}495.1 + 0.19633 \; YDH/(PCP^*(1+RTXC))^*100$$

(1.08)   (4.25)

$$- 1{,}273.5 \; INTOR(-1) + 0.00439 \; HTA/PIH^*100$$

(−3.71)   (2.94)

$$-0.10367\Delta \; HTD/PIH^*100 - 0.16296 \; KH(-1) + 0.31887 \; IH(-1)$$

(−2.02)   (−4.86)   (2.58)

OLS (1981–2008)   Adjusted-$R^2 = 0.886$ SE $= 1{,}142.1$ DW $= 1.766$

7.2.3. *Non-housing investment*

As is well known, non-housing investment is one of the most important endogenous variables in the demand–supply integrated model since
it affects both the demand-side and the supply-side of the economy as
the dual effect of investment. Real non-housing investment (IP) relies
on the conventional investment function with an acceleration principle
(Δ GDE), a profit principle employing real corporate disposable income
((YC−TXC)/PIP*100), a stock adjustment principle utilizing one-year
lagged capacity utilization rate (CUR(−1)) and Koyck-lag (IP(−1)), as
follows.

$$IP = f((+)\Delta \; GDE, \quad (+) \; (YC - TXC + YC(-1) - TXC(-1))/PIP^*100,$$

$$(+)CUR(-1), \quad (+) \; IP(-1))$$

In the regression analysis for real non-housing investment, we get a
very interesting result.

$$IP = -19367.0 + 0.3191\Delta \; GDE + 0.1998 \; (YC - TXC)/PIP^*100$$

(−2.76)   (5.63)   (2.72)

$$+ \; 20{,}794.1 \; CUR(-1) + 0.92226 \; IP(-1)$$

(2.20)   (19.73)

OLS (1981–2008)   Adjusted-$R^2 = 0.971$ SE $= 2.867$ DW $= 1.883$

In accordance with the regression result within the sample period from
FY1981 to FY2008, the first difference of real gross domestic expenditure

(Δ GDE) is significant, as a acceleration principle. In addition, real corporate disposable income, as a profit principle, is also significant.

With a liquidity trap in Japan, neither real nor nominal interest rates are significant during the sample period. However, interest rate effects to investment are considered through corporate income, in which prime rate is significant related to the corporate income. Recently, we can find these causations under the deflationary economy while we have continued our modeling and forecasting analysis for the Japanese and Hokkaido economy since the mid-1990s within the HEPCO–IUJ Project (Kido, Shimizu, Nagao and Nakamura, 1997–2010).

Furthermore, capacity utilization rate of capital is also crucial, as a capital adjustment principle, particularly under the deflationary economy. This causation is also very important to adjust the gap between the demand-side and the supply-side economy in a business cycle. The overall performance of the real non-housing investment regression result is quite well and significant in terms of fundamental statistics, including t-value in parenthesis, adjusted R^2, standard error (SE) and Durbin–Watson ratio (DW).

7.2.4. *Merchandise exports*

In the model, real exports of goods and services in the real expenditure block depend on real merchandise exports and real service exports in the international trade and BOP block. Here, we discuss the merchandise exports function and its regression result.

Basically, the specification of real merchandise exports is dependent on the Mundell–Flemming model framework, in which the real merchandise exports (EXG) are determined by real world trade (TWM) and the composed variable of export price in terms of local currency exchange rate index and deflator of world trade in terms of US\$ (PEXY/EXRI/PTW). In addition, the supply-side GDP labor productivity is taken into consideration as a supply side effect, as follows.

$$\ln{(EXG)} = f((+)\ln{(TWM)}, \quad (-)\ln{(PEXY/EXRI/PTW)},$$
$$(+)\ln{(GDPC/NL)})$$

The result of regression is quite interesting, in which the world demand impacts is not so large at 0.343 in terms of elasticity, and price effects are also very limited at 0.386 in terms of elasticity in spite of the large share of manufactured exports in total exports. It seems that the effects of exchange rate changes may be limited since the export-side Marshall–Lerner stable condition may be weak at 0.385. On the other hand, the supply-side effects may be larger at 1.32 in terms of elasticity, which means the real merchandise exports go up by 1.32 per cent when the labor productivity goes up by 1 per cent.[4]

$$\ln(EXG) = -0.2941 + 0.3429 \ln(TWM)$$
$$\quad (-0.73) \qquad (2.55)$$
$$\quad - 0.3853 \ln(PEXY/EXRI/PTW) + 1.3171 \ln(GDPC/NL)$$
$$\quad (-5.06) \qquad\qquad\qquad\qquad (3.67)$$

OLS (1980–2008)   Adjusted-R^2 = 0.988   SE = 0.044   DW = 1.523

7.2.5. *Merchandise imports*

For explaining merchandise imports for crude oil and the other natural resources (MGOIL), we employ real GDE as a income effect and composed variable (POIL*EXRI/PX) of crude oil price per barrel in terms US$ (POIL), exchange rate index (EXRI) and output price (PX), as a price effect, based on the Mundell–Flemming model framework as well as in real merchandise exports, as follows.

$$\ln(MGOIL) = f((+)\ln(GDE), \quad (-)\ln(POIL^*EXRI/PX))$$

The regression result is quite well and significant in terms of t-value and the other fundamental statistics. In addition, the coefficients are quite reasonable in terms of elasticity, in which the income effects are relatively high at 0.834, but the price effects are not so high at 0.200 in terms of elasticity.

$$\ln(MGOIL) = -1.90156 + 0.834229 \ln(GDE))$$
$$\quad (-2.33) \qquad (13.39)$$
$$\quad - 0.200364 \ln(POIL^*EXRI/PX) + 0.106251\ D08$$
$$\quad (-14.57) \qquad\qquad\qquad (3.79)$$

OLS (1980–2009)   Adjusted-R^2 = 0.912   SE = 0.024780   DW = 1.771

On the other hand, merchandise imports for other goods (MGOTH) are determined by changes in real GDE (GDE/GDE(−1)), relative imports price of the other goods (PMOTS*EXRI) to domestic output price (PX) and Koyck-lag (MGOT(−1)), as follows.

$$MGOT = f((+) \, GDE/GDE(-1), \, (-)PMOTS{*}EXRI/PX,$$

$$(+) \, MGOT(-1))$$

The regression result is fairly good in terms of fundamental statistics. The coefficient of Koyck-lag is fairly large since the changes in real GDE is employed as a income effect, in which when real GDE increases by one per cent point real merchandise imports for the other goods increase by 43,473 units (4,347.3 billion yen).

$$MGOT = -36037.3 + 43473.4 \, GDE/GDE(-1)$$
$$(-1.73) \qquad (2.17)$$
$$- 0.5614.67 \, PMOTS{*}EXRI/PX + 0.96918 \, MGOT(-1)$$
$$(-3.01) \qquad\qquad\qquad (18.68)$$

OLS (1981–2009)   Adjusted-R^2 = 0.960   SE = 2,107.03   DW = 1.903

7.3. Income Distribution

As we discussed, variables in the income distribution block play a significant role in linking the demand-side to the supply-side economy. Within the circle from production (supply-side) to income distribution (income distribution-side), from income distribution to expenditure (demand-side) and from expenditure to production, we examine the causations among these three-sided economies for analyzing the structural deflationary economy of Japan.

7.3.1. *Corporate income prior to dividend*

Concerning corporate sector income, corporate income before dividend (YCB) is a function of nominal GDE, nominal prime rate (INTPR) as a cost principle, wage and salaried income (YW) with an expected negative sign as a labor cost and ratio of export price to output price (PEXY/PX) that is related to pricing-to-market with pass-through mechanism, as follows.

$$YCB = f((+)\,GDEN, \quad (-)\,INTPR, \quad (-)\,YW,$$
$$(+)\,PEXY/PX\,(-)\,D08)$$

In accordance with the result of this regression analysis, four indepen-dent variables significantly explained corporate income, of which nominal GDE and wage income (YW) are dominant. The coefficient of YW at 0.973, around 1.00, demonstrates that one unit increase in YW may result in decrease in YCB by one unit, which explains the substitution relation between profit share and wage income share, as discussed in Equation (8), in Chapter 5. In addition, the relative price of exports price to output price is also related to corporate income, which explains the negative effects of pass-through mechanism on corporate income when the yen-dollar rate is appreciated.[5]

$$YCB = 13.400.0 + 0.562106\,GDEN - 3{,}164.34\,INTPR - 1.01206\,YW$$
$$\quad(0.77)\qquad\quad(13.03)\qquad\qquad(-8.96)\qquad\qquad\qquad(-14.12)$$
$$+\,2{,}5331.5\,PEXY/PX - 7{,}967.25\,D08$$
$$(2.35)\qquad\qquad\qquad(-2.79)$$

OLS (1981–2008)   Adjusted-$R^2 = 0.917$ SE $= 2{,}556.72$ DW $= 2.252$

7.3.2. *Wage and salaried income*

Wage and salaried income (YW), which has the largest share in the household income, relies on wages and salaries per employee (W) and the number of wage and salaried employees (NLW) within an iden-tity of YW=W*NLW. In addition, the wages and salaries per employee are dependent on nominal wage rates (WN). Therefore, these three regression results, including the wages and salaries per employee, nomi-nal wage rates and the number of wage and salaried employees, are dis-cussed here.

For determining wage and salaries per employee, nominal wage rates (WN), GDE growth rates (GDE/GDE(−1)) and Koyck-lag (W(−1)) are taken into account as explanatory variables since wages and salaries per employee fluctuate depending on the changes in economic climate, along with the changes in nominal wage rates because wages and salaries per employee include bonus and extra incomes for over time working.

$$\ln(W) = f((+)\ln(WN), \quad (+)\ln(GDE/GDE(-1)), \quad (+)\ln(W(-1)))$$

According to the regression result, these three independent variables are significant and the coefficients are quite reasonable at 0.52348 for WN, 0.2654 for GDE growth and 0.4198 for Koyck-lag $(W(-1))$ in terms of elasticity. In other words, it seems that wages and salaries per employee heavily depend on nominal wage rates, which rely on the labor demand–supply condition and the demand-side labor productivity and economic climates.

$$\ln(W) = 2.562 + 0.51348 \quad \ln(WN) + 0.2654$$
$$(3.62) \qquad (2.58) \qquad (2.20)$$
$$\ln(GDE/GDE(-1) + 0.4198 \quad \ln(W(-1))$$
$$(2.21)$$

OLS (1981–2008)   Adjusted-$R^2 = 0.988$,   SE $= 0.012$,   DW $= 1.654$

As discussed, nominal wage rates determine the wages and salaries per employee, so the nominal wage rates are one of the key variables for household income. In this study, percentage changes in the nominal wage rates are determined by percentage changes in deflator of household consumption expenditure (DOT(PCH), percentage changes in demand-side labor productivity (DOT(GDE/NLW) and unemployment rate (UR) with negative sign condition based on the Phillips–Lipsey curve, as follows.

$$DOT(WN) = f((+)DOT(PCH), \quad (-)UR, \quad (+)DOT(GDE/NLW))$$

The regression result of the nominal wage rates demonstrates very interesting implications, which may be consistent with our analyses in the previous chapters, As we discussed in Chapter 4 within Table 4.1, the coefficient of the percentage changes in deflator of household consumption is very low at 0.579, which means the indexation between nominal wage rates changes and inflation rate has collapsed in the regression tested period. As a result, real wage rates may be declining unless other independent variables are improved drastically.

Furthermore, the coefficient of the percentage changes in the demand-side labor productivity is also very low at 0.315, which means the realized labor productivity improvements have affected the nominal wage rates insufficiently and, as a result, the wage income has been stagnant with the lower wage income share. These lower coefficients might explain the current prolonged deflationary economy of Japan.

On the other hand, the coefficient of rate of unemployment is around 1.0, which explains nominal wage rates neutrally depend on labor demand-supply condition in labor markets, based on the Phillips–Lipsey curve theory. Thereby, a one percentage point increase in unemployment rate results in the decline in nominal wage rates by one per cent.

$$DOT(WN) = 4.1496 + 0.5786\ DOT(PCH) - 1.0473\ UR$$
$$((4.36) \quad (3.13) \qquad\qquad (-4.16)$$
$$+ 0.3154\ DOT(GDE/NLW)$$
$$(4.44)$$

OLS (1981–2009)　Adjusted-R^2 = 0.902　SE = 0.708　DW = 2.041

On the other hand, the number of wage and salaried employees is a function of economic climate (GDE), labor demand (NLE), one-year lagged nominal wage rates (WN(−1)) with negative expected sign and Koyck-lag, as follows.

$$NLW = f((+)\ GDE, \quad (+)\ NLE, \quad (-)\ WN(-1), \quad (+)\ NLW(-1))$$

The regression result shows these causations significantly. Within these causations, the one-year lagged nominal wage rates have significant effects on the number of employee because wage rates are the cost of labor in labor market.

$$NLW = -1{,}158.52 + 0.001178\ GDE + 0.4603\ NLE - 7.3576\ WN(-1)$$
$$(-4.70) \qquad (6.82) \qquad\quad (8.79) \qquad (-4.06)$$
$$+ 0.69617\ NLW(-1)$$
$$(18.41)$$

OLS (1981–2009)　Adjusted-R^2 = 0.999　SE = 15.007　DW = 1.648

7.3.3. *Household financial and non-financial assets and liabilities*

In the present study, we highlight the endogenization of household assets and liabilities and examine the impacts of these assets and liabilities on the economy. In this phase, the financial and non-financial assets and total liabilities in the household sector are discussed in a regression model.

Regarding household assets, household financial assets (HFA) are determined by household disposable income (YDH), TOPIX base stock price (PSTOCK), relative long-term (10-year) government bond yields (INTGB) to official policy rate (INTOR) and the Koyck-lag (HFA(-1)). The household financial assets are similar to accumulated household savings. However, the overall asset values may fluctuate along with the household financial asset values such as equity values and bond values. Accordingly, we employ a behavioral equation instead of an identity of determining an asset variable, as follows.

$$\text{HFA} = f((+)\,\text{YDH}, \quad (+)\,\text{PSTOCK},$$

$$(+)\,\text{INTGB}(-1)/\text{INTOR}(-1), (+)\,\text{HFA}(-1))$$

In accordance with the regression result, each independent variable is significant and, particularly, the Koyck-lag variable is very significant because HFA is a stock variable. In addition, stock price and government bond yield may have significant effects on the household financial asset values along with changes in economic climate.

$$\text{HFA} = -86,079.6 + 1.035\text{YDH} + 50.5204\,\text{PSTOCK}$$

$$(-1.76) \qquad (3.07) \qquad (4.26)$$

$$+\ 10,373.5\,\text{INTGB}(-1)/\text{INTOR}(-1) + .7567\,\text{HFA}(-1))$$

$$(4.59) \qquad\qquad\qquad (16.55)$$

OLS (1981–2008)   Adjusted-$R^2 = 0.995$ SE $= 27,436$ DW $= 1.930$

Concerning household non-financial assets, we employ the ratio function to real estate price (NHFA/PLAND), which is explained by the ratio of household disposable income to real estate price (YDH/PLAND), government bond yield (INTGB) with a negative correlation, changes in real estate price (PLAND/PLAND(−1)) and Koyck-lag variable (NHA(−1)). This is because the non-financial asset values comprise tangible assets, including real estate with over 80 per cent in total, so that declines in real estate price may directly affect non-financial asset values.

$$HNFA/PLAND^*100 = f((+)YDH/PLAND^*100,$$

$$(-)\,INTGB(+)PLAND/PLAND(-1),$$

$$(+)\,HNFA(-1)/PLAND(-1)^*100)$$

The regression result demonstrates these causations significantly. The real disposable income increase results in increases of non-financial asset possession, while declines in long-term interest rate result in the shift from financial assets to non-financial assets.

$$HNFA/PLAND^*100 = 256,195 + 0.1560\ YDH/PLAND^*100,$$
$$(1.79) \qquad (2.17)$$
$$-\,25,596.9\ INTGB$$
$$(-3.13)$$
$$+\,438,265.4\ PLAND/PLAND(-1)$$
$$(2.62)$$
$$+\,0.4122\ HNFA(-1)/PLAND(-1)^*100$$
$$(2.91)$$

OLS (1981–2008)   Adjusted-$R^2 = 0.912$ SE $= 34,994.5$ DW $= 1.720$

For household total liabilities, we employ the first difference function, in which the changes in household total liabilities (Δ HTD = HTD − HTD(−1)) rely on household disposable income (YDH), official policy rate (INTOR), real estate price (PLAND) and Koyck-lag (Δ HTD(−1)), as follows.

$$\Delta\,HTD = f((-)\,YDH, \quad (-)\,INTOR(-1),$$

$$(+)\,PLAND, \quad (+)\,\Delta\,HTD(-1))$$

According to the regression result, these causations are explained significantly. As well as seen in the household asset equations, an increase in household disposable income reduces household liabilities, while the lower interest rate stimulates purchases of durable goods and real estate, and the higher real estate price may result in increases of current expenditures.

$$\Delta\ \text{HTD} = 50{,}329.5 - 0.25858\ \text{YDH} - 3{,}152.12\ \text{INTOR}(-1)$$
$$(4.11) \qquad (-4.02) \qquad\qquad (-3.13)$$
$$+\ 288.07\ \text{PLAND} + 0.50922\Delta\ \text{HTD}(-1)$$
$$(2.80) \qquad\qquad (2.64)$$

OLS (1982–2008)   Adjusted-$R^2 = 0.836$,   SE $= 5050.93$,   DW $= 1.422$

By employing the real household consumption (CH) regression result together with these assets (HFA, HNFA) and liabilities (HTD) regression results, the static effects of YDP changes on the household financial and non-financial assets, liabilities and on the consumption expenditure can be calculated. In accordance with the regression result of real household final consumption, the coefficient of real disposable income is 0.742 so that one trillion yen increase in nominal disposable income stimulates real household consumption by 0.785 trillion yen (0.785 = 0.742*1000/PCH*100) in FY2008, on a static basis, with employing the single equation since PCH is 0.945 in FY2008.

By integrating these three equations, including two assets and one liability equations, with the real household consumption equation, however, a one trillion yen increase in nominal household disposable income results in increase of real household consumption by 0.864 trillion yen in FY2008, on a static basis, even without taking account of multiplier effects and other indirect effects. This consequence is because it is expected that the household financial and non-financial asset values also increase and the values of liabilities decrease when the disposable income increases.

7.4. Prices

As we discussed, the prices and wage rates block also play a very significant role in integrating both the demand-side and the supply-side economy, through a price adjustment process and a quantity adjustment process in the demand–supply integrated model. Here, we examine the determinants of prices based on the regression results.

7.4.1.   *Output price*

As is well known, output price is a key price in the model because the output price affects the other prices and deflators of GDE components. Output price (PX) is a function of import price (PMY = PM\$*EXRI/100) in local currency base, which reflects the prices of raw materials and intermediate goods imported from the rest of the world, nominal wage rates (WN), one-year lagged supply-side labor productivity (GDPC(−1)/NL(−1)), and Koyck-lag (PX(−1)), as follows.

$$\ln{(PX)} = f((+)\ln{(PMY)}, \quad (+)\ln{(WN)},$$
$$(-)\ln{(GDPC(-1)/NL(-1))}, \quad (+)\ln{(PX(-1))}$$

In accordance with the regression result, these causes are observed significantly. In particular, the supply-side labor productivity plays a significant role in determining the output price, in which the output price goes down by around 0.2 per cent when the labor productivity goes up by one per cent with a one-year time lag.

$$\ln{(PX)} = 1.76137 + 0.120073\ln{(PMY)} + 0.247875\ln{(WN)}$$
$$\quad (2.22) \qquad (5.82) \qquad\qquad (2.88)$$
$$\quad - 0.198535\ln{(GDPC(-1)/NL(-1))} + 0.441172\ln{(PX(-1))}$$
$$\quad (-3.56) \qquad\qquad\qquad\qquad (3.74)$$

C-O (1981–2009)   Adjusted-R^2 = 0.955,   SE = 0.012157,   DW = 2.047

7.4.2.   *Deflator of household consumption expenditure*

In principle, real GDE components, including real household final consumption expenditure, are determined by income effects and price effects, as discussed earlier, and the price effects play a significant role in determining the components of the demand-side model through the price adjustment process. At the same time, prices rely on the quantity adjustment process, so that the supply-side plays an important role in the demand-supply integrated model. Here, we discuss a household consumption deflator function that is one of the major deflators of the GDE components.

In the household consumption deflator function, deflator of household consumption (PCH) relies on output price (PX), nominal wage rates (WN) and Koyck-lag (PCH(−1)) within a logarithm function, and the effects of the supply-side is incorporated through output price (PX), as follows.

$$\ln{(PCH)} = f((+)\ln{(PX)}, \quad (+)\ln{(WN)}, \quad (+)\ln{(PCH(-1))}$$

In accordance with the regression result, each independent variable is very significant, and the overall performance is quite well in terms of fundamental statistics within the Cochrane–Orcutt procedure (C-O). As output price is influenced by the supply-side labor productivity, the productivity indirectly affects the household consumption deflator through output price.

$$\ln{(PCH)} = -0.0560 + 0.189596\ln{(PX)} + 0.285576\ln{(WN)}$$
$$\quad\quad (-0.08) \quad\quad (4.16) \quad\quad\quad\quad\quad\quad (4.85)$$
$$\quad + 0.512058\ln{(PCH(-1))}$$
$$\quad (5.91)$$

C-O (1981–2009)   Adjusted-$R^2 = 0.989$,   SE $= 0.004024$,   DW $= 1.955$

7.4.3. *Export price*

Export price also plays a very important role in deciding the demand for exports through price effects and stimulating domestic effective demand through multiplier effects. Even after the Plaza Accord in September 1985, the share of exports in GDP was increasing, and in the longest boom period from FY2002, exports led Japanese economic growth.

In the export price function, we employ three independent variables such as output price (PX), exchange rate (EXR) and one-year lagged supply-side base labor productivity (GDPC(−1)/NL(−1)), as follows.

$$\ln{(PEXY)} = f((+)\ln{(PX)}, \quad (+)\ln{(EXR)},$$
$$(-)\ln{(GDPC(-1)/NL(-1))}$$

According to the regression result, export price is mainly determined by output price with the high coefficient at 0.908 in terms of elasticity, and influenced by exchange rate and the supply-side productivity. As for the effects of the exchange rate, the coefficient of exchange rate indicates the extent to which yen fluctuations are "passed-through" to dollar base export prices in the mechanism based on pricing-to-market behaviors, which may rely on a strong supply-side economy. The performance of the result is quite well and very significant in terms of t-value and the other fundamental statistics within the C-O procedure.

$$\ln(\text{PEXY}) = 0.086566 + 0.908030 \ln(\text{PX}) + 0.305964 \ln(\text{EXR})$$

$$(0.07) \qquad (4.40) \qquad\qquad (7.26)$$

$$- 0.239279 \ln(\text{GDPC}(-1)/\text{NL}(-1))$$

$$(-2.27)$$

C-O (1981–2009)   Adjusted-$R^2 = 0.988$ SE $= 0.019577$ DW $= 1.437$

In summary, in this section, we examine the macroeconomic structure of Japan, with special emphasis on the major endogenous variables in relation to the causes of the structural deflation of the Japanese economy with a regression analysis. Based on these regression results, we may, to some extent, clarify the causes of the structural deflation, on a static basis. (All of the behavioral equation regression results and identities are listed in Appendix A.)

In addition, the regression analysis represents the effects of supply-side labor productivity on many endogenous variables, particularly prices and deflators, and on the overall economy. Table 7.1 demonstrates the direct and indirect effects of the labor productivity changes on some endogenous variables, on a static basis. For example, output price (PX) has the direct effects of productivity changes while exports price (PEXY) and deflator of non-housing investment (PIP) have both the direct and indirect effects of the supply-side productivity changes, and consumer price (CPI), deflator of household consumption (PCH), deflator of housing investment (PIH), deflator of government consumption (PCG) and deflator of government investment (PIG) also have the indirect effects through output price (PX). These effects are fairly large, particularly in export price (PEXY). In the case of export price, a one per cent increase in supply-side labor productivity (GDPC/NL) improvement may result in declines in export price by 0.32

Table 7.1: Direct and indirect effects of changes in supply-side productivity on prices and real merchandise exports, in terms of elasticity.

Variables	Direct Effects	Indirect Effects
PX	−0.199	
PEXY	−0.239	−0.180 (−0.908*0.199 through PX)
CPI		−0.037 (−0.187*0.199 through PX)
PCP		−0.038 (−0.189*0.199 through PX)
PCG		−0.051 (−0.2592*0.1985 through PX)
PIP	−0.242	−0.084 (−0.424*0.199 through PX)
PIH		−0.038 (−0.192*0.199 through PX)
PIG		−0.092 (−0.461*0.199 through PX)
EXG	+1.317	+0.076 (0.385*0.239 through PEXY)

Source: Estimated and compiled by the author.

per cent, by 0.24 per cent with direct effects and by 0.18 per cent with indirect effects through output price changes.

Furthermore, real merchandise exports (EXG) are directly influenced by changes in supply-side productivity and its positive indirect effect through changes in export price (PEXY). These indirect and indirect effects on the real merchandise exports are also remarkable. Table 7.1 demonstrates that the real merchandise exports increase by 1.393 per cent, including 1.317 per cent with direct supply-side effects, and by 0.076 per cent with indirect effects through price effects when the supply-side productivity increases by 1 per cent.

End Notes

[1] In the present study we employ OLS instead of 2SLS since the model is complicated with many endogenous and exogenous variables. Therefore, we examine the results of OLS carefully based on some fundamental statistics in regression and utilize them in simulation analyses.

As for the method of estimation, as discussed earlier, we employ OLS carefully considering fundamental statistics and select the better results for a multi-equation structural model system with the Gauss–Seidel method and step-wise procedure as many econometric modeling projects utilize, as follows.

Estimation Method for Econometric Modeling of Major Projects in Japan:

Econometric Model of Japan

Project	Type of Model	Number of Equations	Method
NIRA-LINK	Multi-Sector Model (Annual Model)	4,000	OLS
CRIEPI	Macro Model (Annual)	130	OLS
Cabinet Office, Japanese Gov.	Macro Model (Annual)	120 (core model) 1,000 (public sector)	OLS
ICSEAD	Macro Model (Annual)	120	OLS
JETRO World Model	Macro Model (Annual)	120	OLS
IUJ – HEPCO	Macro Model (Annual)	130 (Japan) 70 (each prefecture)	OLS

Note: NIRA-LINK Project: Multi-sectoral world model project by Japan–US World Model Center and University of Pennsylvania; ICSEAD: International Centre for the Study of East Asia Development; CRIEPI: Central Research Institute of Electric Power Industry; JETRO: Japan External Trade Organization; IUJ: the International University of Japan; HEPCO: Hokkaido Electric Power Co. Ltd.

Indeed, concerning bias of OLS estimates in a simultaneous system, the possibilities of reducing the bias of OLS estimators were discussed by Maddala (1988) utilizing Working (1927), in which the OLS estimates could be utilized in the simultaneously determined equation system, improving the fundamental statistics, in particular variance of an error term with a better specification in each behavioral equation. Nevertheless, bias of the OLS estimates should be carefully considered and therefore we need to make a double check on this issue in the process of model reliability tests and so on, as well as in regression analysis.

[2] As noted, TFP heavily relies on the Solow vintage (Solow-neutral) and time trend (Hicks-neutral). See Nakamura (2008).

[3] Interestingly, Ando (2002) assumed the coefficient of financial assets at 0.05 in consumption function when he estimated the losses of the household sector's welfare during the past decades utilizing the Ando measure. The estimated coefficient in this study at 0.04279 may be consistent with the Ando's assumption.

[4] Krugman (1989) discussed the effects of labor productivity changes on merchandise exports with the 45° rule, in which there are strong relations between output growth and exports growth.

[5] In the present study, we have tried to link capital transfers, credits and investment income in BOP to corporate income. Interestingly, however, both the income transfers and the investment income could not explain corporate income significantly. As far as I know, there is no evidence of explaining this causation in empirical studies for the Japanese economy.

CHAPTER 8

Dynamic Simulation Tests

This chapter performs some dynamic simulation tests, including a model reliability test with Goldberger Tests, a dynamic Keynes multiplier test, a monetary and financial policy simulation test and a yen appreciation simulation test. In particular, the dynamic multiplier test is indispensable in examining the macro demand-side economic structure. As noted, these dynamic simulation tests are very important to reveal the biased estimates in a multi-equation structural model system and to improve the structure of the model.

In the present study, we employ the software system named SYMSYS (Sato and Nakamura, 1996) in dynamic simulation tests and scenario forecasts. In solving a multi-equation structural model system, we employ a step-wise solving procedure with the Gauss–Seidel iterative solution method and 0.1 per cent convergent criteria for the dynamic simulation tests and future forecasts.

8.1. Model Reliability Test: Final Test in Goldberger Tests

Before conducting the dynamic simulation tests and future forecasts, we perform the model reliability test utilizing the final test that is the most severe among the Goldberger tests. In the final test, all of the endogenous variables in the model are interpolated and compared to the actual value by variable during the regression sample period from FY1981 to FY2008.

Table 8.1 demonstrates the final test results for major endogenous variables with MAPE (Mean Absolute Percentage Error). According to the final test results, real GDE is interpolated within a 2.32 per cent error range in MAPE. The real GDE is calculated by totaling its components, including

Table 8.1: Final test results for major variables with MAPE, FY1981–2008 (%).

GDE	2.32	CH	2.18	CG	2.52	IP	6.11	IH	6.13
EGS	4.96	MGS	4.74	PGDE	1.27	GDPC	2.01	UR	4.31
WN	1.94	YC	8.43	YW	2.86	EXR	6.74	M2CD	3.73
EG	4.25	MG	4.04	KP	3.97	CUR	5.01	PX	1.56
HFA	3.78	HNFA	4.37	HTD	3.44	TOPIX	3.71	PLAND	2.84

Note: MAPE: $\Sigma((|\text{Estimated}-\text{Actual}|)/\text{Actual})/N * 100$.
Source: Estimated by the author.

real household consumption (CH), real government consumption (CG), real private non-housing investment (IP), real government investment (IG), real private (JP) and government inventory changes (JG), real exports of goods and services (EGS) and real imports of goods and services (MGS), so that errors in these components affect the error of real GDE. In the test, these GDE components are also accurately interpolated within a 2.18 per cent error range for CH, a 6.11 per cent error range for IP, and so on, as shown in Table 8.1.

On the other hand, the supply-side GDP capacity is interpolated quite well in the final test within a 2.01 per cent error range in MAPE and other endogenous variables in the production block are also well interpolated within a 3.97 per cent error range for KP and a 5.01 per cent error range for CUR, as shown in Table 8.1. Endogenous variables in the income distribution block are also fairly accurately interpolated in the final test. For example, wage and salaried income (YW) and private corporate income (YC) are also interpolated within a 2.83 per cent error range and within a 8.43 per cent error range, respectively while household financial assets (HFA), non-financial assets (HNFA) and total liabilities (HTD) are also well performed in interpolation within a 3.78 per cent error range, a 4.37 per cent error range and a 3.44 per cent error range, respectively.

In accordance with the final test results, it seems that the model is fairly reliable in performing scenario simulations and future forecasts within 97.68 per cent accuracy in terms of real GDE. In other words, it seems that overall performance of this model is fairly powerful and we can utilize this model for dynamic simulation tests and future scenario forecasts.

8.2. Dynamic Keynes Multiplier Tests

The dynamic Keynes multiplier tests are essential in examining not only the macro demand-side economic structure but also the sensitivity of causations among variables within the macro-model. At the same time, as we discussed in the theoretical frame work, the Keynes multiplier is one of the key function for growth as an accelerator in the demand-side growth model. This dynamic multiplier is now being re-evaluated globally since many countries are employing large-scale fiscal policies after the 2008 World Financial Crisis. However, the multiplier itself depends on the macroeconomic structure of a country model variety so that there are various ranges of multipliers applicable to each model and country.

This section performs the dynamic Keynes multiplier tests assuming two cases of fiscal policy including: (1) Government investment increases by one trillion yen and (2) Personal income tax cut by one trillion yen from FY2001 to FY2008. The purpose is to examine the multiplier effects of both fiscal policies as compared to the final test simulation. In these multiplier tests, we assume that the increased government expenditure and personal income tax cuts are made up by issuing government bonds during the tested period.

8.2.1. *Effects of government investment increase*

As noted earlier, this section performs government investment increase scenario simulation and examines its impacts on the Japanese economy. Table 8.2 shows the results of the impacts of unceasing government investment initiatives by one trillion yen on the economy over the tested period. According to the results of this simulation, real GDE goes up by 1.56 trillion yen in FY2001, by 1.94 trillion yen in FY2002, by 2.10 trillion yen in FY2003, by 2.19 trillion yen in FY2004 and by 2.18 trillion yen in FY2005, and thereafter its impacts decline to 1.61 trillion yen in FY2008. In addition, the real GDE components have positive effects. For example, real household consumption expenditure (CH) increases by 0.28 trillion yen in FY2001, by 0.49 trillion in FY2002, by 0.63 trillion in FY2003, by 0.76 trillion in FY2004, by 0.86 trillion yen in FY2005 and by 0.86 trillion yen in FY2008, reaching the peak of 0.91 in the sixth-year, and thereafter its impacts decline. The other components also have positive effects along

Table 8.2: The impacts of government investment increase by 1 trillion yen on the economy, FY2001–2008: dynamic keynes multiplier test, deviation and % deviation, as compared to the final test.

(In trillions of yen)

FY	2001	2002	2003	2004	2005	2006	2007	2008
GDE	1.56	1.94	2.10	2.15	2.18	2.03	1.86	1.61
% dev.	(0.3)	(0.3)	(0.4)	(0.4)	(0.4)	(0.4)	(0.3)	(0.3)
GDPC	0.09	0.22	0.34	0.44	0.53	0.59	0.63	0.64
% dev.	(0.0)	(0.0)	(0.1)	(0.1)	(0.1)	(0.1)	(0.1)	(0.1)
DGAP	−1.48	−1.70	−1.75	−1.74	−1.64	−1.46	−1.22	−0.93
% dev.	(−1.7)	(−2.0)	(−2.2)	(−2.2)	(−2.2)	(−2.0)	(−1.8)	(−1.4)
CP	0.29	0.50	0.65	0.78	0.90	0.93	0.90	0.87
% dev.	(0.1)	(0.2)	(0.2)	(0.3)	(0.3)	(0.3)	(0.3)	(0.2)
CH	0.28	0.49	0.63	0.76	0.88	0.91	0.88	0.86
% dev.	(0.1)	(0.2)	(0.2)	(0.3)	(0.3)	(0.3)	(0.3)	(0.2)
CN	0.01	0.01	0.02	0.02	0.02	0.02	0.02	0.01
% dev.	(0.1)	(0.1)	(0.2)	(0.3)	(0.3)	(0.4)	(0.4)	(0.3)
IP	0.33	0.50	0.54	0.56	0.52	0.41	0.36	0.25
% dev.	(0.4)	(0.7)	(0.7)	(0.7)	(0.7)	(0.6)	(0.4)	(0.3)
IH	0.10	0.18	0.23	0.25	0.27	0.26	0.23	0.19
% dev.	(0.8)	(1.2)	(1.6)	(1.8)	(1.9)	(1.9)	(1.7)	(1.4)

(Continued)

Table 8.2:   (Continued)

FY	2001	2002	2003	2004	2005	2006	2007	2008
CG	-0.01	-0.01	-0.02	-0.05	-0.07	-0.10	-0.13	-0.14
% dev.	(-0.0)	(-0.0)	(-0.0)	(-0.1)	(-0.1)	(-0.1)	(-0.1)	(-0.1)
IG	0.99	0.99	0.98	0.98	0.98	0.97	0.97	0.96
% dev.	(3.0)	(3.2)	(3.2)	(3.3)	(3.5)	(3.7)	(4.1)	(4.4)
JP	0.09	0.06	0.05	0.03	0.01	-0.01	-0.02	-0.03
% dev.	(8.4)	(6.7)	(5.4)	(3.5)	(1.2)	(-1.3)	(-3.2)	(-4.4)
EGS	-0.02	-0.03	-0.04	-0.05	-0.06	-0.06	-0.06	-0.07
% dev.	(-0.0)	(-0.0)	(-0.0)	(-0.0)	(-0.1)	(-0.1)	(-0.1)	(-0.1)
MGS	0.21	0.24	0.29	0.34	0.36	0.38	0.40	0.42
% dev.	(0.3)	(0.4)	(0.4)	(0.5)	(0.5)	(0.6)	(0.6)	(0.6)
GDEN	1.61	2.18	2.47	2.87	3.18	3.41	3.50	3.40
% dev.	(0.3)	(0.4)	(0.5)	(0.6)	(0.6)	(0.7)	(0.7)	(0.7)
CPN	0.28	0.55	0.76	1.07	1.30	1.48	1.58	1.60
% dev.	(0.1)	(0.2)	(0.3)	(0.4)	(0.5)	(0.6)	(0.6)	(0.6)
CHN	0.28	0.54	0.74	1.05	1.27	1.44	1.54	1.56
% dev.	(0.1)	(0.2)	(0.3)	(0.4)	(0.5)	(0.6)	(0.6)	(0.6)
CNN	0.00	0.01	0.02	0.02	0.03	0.04	0.04	0.04
% dev.	(0.1)	(0.2)	(0.2)	(0.3)	(0.3)	(0.4)	(0.4)	(0.5)

(Continued)

Table 8.2: (Continued)

FY	2001	2002	2003	2004	2005	2006	2007	2008
CGN	0.01	0.04	0.08	0.13	0.18	0.24	0.29	0.33
% dev.	(0.0)	(0.0)	(0.1)	(0.1)	(0.2)	(0.2)	(0.3)	(0.3)
IPN	0.31	0.51	0.57	0.60	0.61	0.59	0.56	0.50
% dev.	(0.5)	(0.7)	(0.8)	(0.8)	(0.8)	(0.8)	(0.7)	(0.7)
IHN	0.11	0.19	0.26	0.31	0.34	0.34	0.32	0.26
% dev.	(0.8)	(1.3)	(1.7)	(2.1)	(2.3)	(2.3)	(2.2)	(1.9)
IGN	1.00	1.00	1.00	1.00	1.00	1.00	1.00	1.00
% dev.	(4.3)	(4.4)	(4.4)	(4.4)	(4.3)	(4.3)	(4.3)	(4.2)
JPN	0.06	0.07	0.04	0.02	0.01	−0.01	−0.02	−0.02
% dev.	(8.2)	(7.7)	(5.4)	(3.5)	(1.2)	(−1.3)	(−3.2)	(−3.6)
EGSN	−0.09	−0.15	−0.19	−0.21	−0.20	−0.18	−0.16	−0.15
% dev.	(−0.1)	(−0.2)	(−0.2)	(−0.2)	(−0.2)	(−0.2)	(−0.2)	(−0.1)
MGN	0.06	0.04	0.04	0.04	0.05	0.06	0.08	0.13
% dev.	(0.1)	(0.1)	(0.0)	(0.0)	(0.1)	(0.1)	(0.1)	(0.1)

(Continued)

Table 8.2: (Continued)

(Index: 2000 × 100)

FY	2001	2002	2003	2004	2005	2006	2007	2008
PGDE	0.03	0.06	0.11	0.16	0.22	0.27	0.32	0.35
% dev.	(0.1)	(0.1)	(0.2)	(0.2)	(0.3)	(0.4)	(0.4)	(0.4)
PCH	0.01	0.03	0.07	0.11	0.16	0.21	0.25	0.28
% dev.	(0.0)	(0.0)	(0.1)	(0.1)	(0.2)	(0.2)	(0.3)	(0.3)
PCG	0.01	0.04	0.10	0.16	0.24	0.31	0.38	0.43
% dev.	(0.0)	(0.0)	(0.1)	(0.2)	(0.2)	(0.3)	(0.4)	(0.5)
PIP	0.01	0.03	0.06	0.11	0.17	0.23	0.29	0.34
% dev.	(0.0)	(0.0)	(0.1)	(0.1)	(0.2)	(0.3)	(0.3)	(0.4)
PIH	0.01	0.03	0.08	0.14	0.21	0.29	0.36	0.42
% dev.	(0.0)	(0.0)	(0.1)	(0.1)	(0.2)	(0.3)	(0.4)	(0.4)
PIG	0.01	0.04	0.09	0.15	0.22	0.29	0.35	0.39
% dev.	(0.0)	(0.0)	(0.1)	(0.2)	(0.2)	(0.3)	(0.4)	(0.4)
PEGS	−0.09	−0.14	−0.16	−0.16	−0.15	−0.13	−0.11	−0.08
% dev.	(−0.1)	(−0.1)	(−0.2)	(−0.2)	(−0.1)	(−0.1)	(−0.1)	(−0.1)
PMGS	−0.28	−0.43	−0.52	−0.59	−0.64	−0.66	−0.66	−0.64
% dev.	(−0.2)	(−0.3)	(−0.4)	(−0.4)	(−0.5)	(−0.5)	(−0.5)	(−0.5)
PMY	−0.36	−0.54	−0.66	−0.74	−0.81	−0.84	−0.84	−0.81
% dev.	(−0.3)	(−0.4)	(−0.5)	(−0.5)	(−0.6)	(−0.6)	(−0.6)	(−0.5)
PX	−0.02	−0.03	−0.02	0.01	0.03	0.06	0.09	0.11
% dev.	(−0.0)	(−0.0)	(−0.0)	(0.0)	(0.0)	(0.1)	(0.1)	(0.1)

(Continued)

Table 8.2: (Continued)

FY	2001	2002	2003	2004	2005	2006	2007	2008
PEXY	-0.10	-0.14	-0.16	-0.16	-0.15	-0.13	-0.11	-0.08
% dev.	(-0.1)	(-0.1)	(-0.2)	(-0.2)	(-0.1)	(-0.1)	(-0.1)	(-0.1)
CPI	0.01	0.36	0.08	0.14	0.21	0.28	0.34	0.40
% dev.	(0.0)	(0.0)	(0.1)	(0.1)	(0.2)	(0.3)	(0.4)	(0.4)
EXR	-0.23	-0.34	-0.40	-0.45	-0.47	-0.47	-0.46	-0.43
% dev.	(-0.3)	(-0.4)	(-0.5)	(-0.5)	(-0.5)	(-0.5)	(-0.5)	(-0.5)
NLE	3.44	5.95	7.39	8.00	7.94	7.27	6.14	4.74
% dev.	(0.1)	(0.1)	(0.1)	(0.1)	(0.1)	(0.1)	(0.1)	(0.1)
UR	-0.05	-0.09	-0.10	-0.12	-0.11	-0.11	-0.09	-0.07
% dev.	(-1.0)	(-1.5)	(-1.9)	(-2.1)	(-2.0)	(-1.9)	(-1.6)	(-1.2)
M2CD	0.36	0.75	1.14	1.50	1.81	2.06	2.23	2.31
% dev.	(0.0)	(0.1)	(0.1)	(0.2)	(0.2)	(0.2)	(0.3)	(0.3)
INTPR	0.01	0.01	0.02	0.02	0.02	0.02	0.02	0.02
% dev.	(0.7)	(0.8)	(0.9)	(1.0)	(1.1)	(1.2)	(1.2)	(1.2)
TXG	0.41	0.43	0.43	0.43	0.41	0.39	0.34	0.28
% dev.	(0.8)	(0.8)	(0.8)	(0.8)	(0.8)	(0.8)	(0.7)	(0.6)
TXC	0.24	0.24	0.21	0.19	0.16	0.12	0.07	0.03
% dev.	(1.9)	(1.7)	(1.5)	(1.3)	(1.1)	(0.8)	(0.5)	(0.2)
TXI	0.16	0.18	0.20	0.21	0.22	0.21	0.19	0.17
% dev.	(1.2)	(1.3)	(1.4)	(1.5)	(1.6)	(1.6)	(1.6)	(1.4)

(Continued)

Table 8.2: (*Continued*)

FY	2001	2002	2003	2004	2005	2006	2007	2008
KLGBT	0.84	1.72	2.62	3.52	4.44	5.40	6.41	7.47
% dev.	(0.1)	(0.2)	(0.3)	(0.4)	(0.4)	(0.5)	(0.6)	(0.7)
YDH	0.66	0.81	1.16	1.49	1.76	1.96	2.06	2.09
% dev.	(0.3)	(0.3)	(0.5)	(0.6)	(0.7)	(0.8)	(0.9)	(0.9)
YE	0.45	0.62	0.97	1.33	1.62	1.84	1.97	2.02
% dev.	(0.2)	(0.3)	(0.4)	(0.6)	(0.7)	(0.8)	(0.9)	(0.9)
YC	0.22	0.17	0.12	0.08	0.03	−0.02	−0.05	−0.09
% dev.	(0.4)	(0.3)	(0.2)	(0.1)	(−0.0)	(−0.1)	(−0.2)	(−0.3)
HFA	1.95	3.44	4.59	5.53	6.26	6.73	6.90	6.76
% dev.	(0.1)	(0.2)	(0.3)	(0.4)	(0.4)	(0.5)	(0.5)	(0.5)
HNFA	0.81	1.08	1.26	1.40	1.48	1.49	1.43	1.30
% dev.	(0.1)	(0.1)	(0.1)	(0.1)	(0.2)	(0.2)	(0.2)	(0.1)
HTD	0.06	0.08	0.12	0.15	0.16	0.16	0.12	0.06
% dev.	(0.0)	(0.0)	(0.0)	(0.0)	(0.0)	(0.0)	(0.0)	(0.0)
PSTOCK	31.0	31.0	30.4	30.4	29.6	26.9	22.4	16.4
% dev.	(2.7)	(2.5)	(2.4)	(2.4)	(2.4)	(2.1)	(1.8)	(1.3)

Note: Deviation: (Scenario − Final Test). % deviation: (Scenario − Final Test) / Final Test * 100 (%).
Source: Simulated and compiled by the author.

with the rise in real GDE and achieve the peak impacts in the fourth and the sixth year during the tested period except for imports of goods and services (MGS). In the case of MGS, due to the increase of real GDE and the rise in PGDE, real imports of goods and services unceasingly rise when real government investment is boosted.

On the other hand, the supply-side GDP (GDPC) is also stimulated during the tested period. However, the impacts on the supply-side GDP are very limited at 0.1 per cent, in per cent deviation, from FY2003 to FY2008. As for the impacts on prices, when real government investment unceasingly rises, general deflator (PGDP) has fairly large effects at 0.1 per cent in FY2001 and in FY2002, at 0.2 per cent in FY2003 and FY2004, at 0.3 per cent in FY2005 and at 0.4 per cent in FY2006–2008, in per cent deviation, in comparison with the final test. As a result, most of the nominal value variables have large effects, in which household disposable income, for example, increases by 0.9 per cent in FY2008 in per cent deviation, as compared to the final test.

As a result of the stimulated demand-side economy, nominal GDE (GDEN) is increasing by 1.61 trillion yen in FY2001, by 2.18 trillion yen in FY2002, by 3.18 trillion yen in FY2005 and by 3.40 trillion yen in FY2008, in deviation, and by 0.3 per cent in FY2001, by 0.4 per cent in FY2002, by 0.6 per cent in FY2005 and 0.7 per cent in FY2008, in per cent deviation, as compared to the final test. At the same time, the central government overall tax revenues are also increasing, along with the stimulated nominal GDE, by 0.8 per cent in FY2001, 0.8 per cent in FY2002, 0.8 per cent in FY2005 and 0.6 per cent in FY2008, in per cent deviation, as compared to the final test, in which the marginal effects of the nominal GDE increase on the tax revenue may be fairly large through natural increases the revenue.

With respect to the impacts on prices and deflators, in this scenario simulation, the effects of the one trillion yen increase in government investment have a limited effect on prices since the supply-side economic expansion contributes to improving labor productivity and restraining price inflation. Accordingly, the prices and deflators slightly rise as a whole in spite of fairly large impacts on the economy. As a result, the general deflator of GDE, which is composed of deflators of GDE components, rises by 0.1 per cent in FY2001, by 0.3 per cent in FY2005 and by 0.4 per cent in FY2008, in per cent deviation, in comparison with the final test projection.

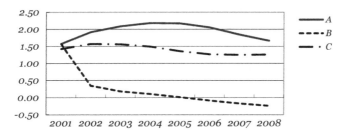

Figure 8.1: Dynamic Keynes multiplier: unceasing fiscal policy (A) and one year fiscal policy (B), and unceasing fiscal policy (C) without effects of assets and liabilities.
Source: Simulated by the author.

Concerning the Keynes multiplier, we have fairly large multiplier effects utilizing this model. Although the multiplier in the initial period is 1.57, it exceeds 2.0 from the third year to the sixth year achieving 2.21 in the fifth year, as the peak value, as demonstrated in Figure 8.1. This higher multiplier may result from the asset effects with both the household financial and non-financial assets endogenized in the demand-side model, as discussed in the theoretical framework.[1]

In accordance with our recent analysis (Nakamura, 2010), the dynamic Keynes multiplier is around 1.86 as the peak value in the fourth year, in which there is no assets effects on the household expenditures in the model. In the ESRI model analysis, however, the multiplier is around 1.0 in the initial year and thereafter it declines from the second year (Hida *et al.*, 2009). It seems that the lower multiplier in the ESRI relies on the structure of price equations, in which decreases in the deflationary gap by fiscal policy might raise the price level and result in declines of the demand components through price effects because the deflationary gap might be directly employed, as an explanatory variable, in price and deflator functions.

On the other hand, Shishido *et al.* (2011) realized the fairly high multiplier at 2.57 as a peak value in the seventh year. It seems that this model is a Keynes–Leontief type multi-sector model. Hence, each sector's supply-side is flexibly changing when the demand-side of the economy including both the final demand and the intermediate demand is enhanced by fiscal policy, thereby stimulating the demand-side through the forward I-O linkage effects.

In order to clarify the causes of the relatively higher multiplier during the tested period in the present study, we conduct a hypothetical one-year demand stimulus, in which the central government investment increases by one trillion yen only for the initial year, as Case B. According to this dynamic multiplier test, the multiplier in the initial year, FY2001, is the same with the previous case at 1.57, while, thereafter, the positive multiplier effects continue to the fifth year at 0.35 in FY2002, at 0.18 in FY2003, at 0.11 in FY2004 and 0.02 in FY2005, as shown in Figure 8.1. In other words, it can be seen that the one-year demand stimulus with government investment increase has fairly long-term effects on the economy.

In addition, we perform one more dynamic multiplier simulation as Case C, keeping assets effects and debt effects exogenous in this model and assuming that the one trillion yen government investment increase continues unceasingly from FY2001 to FY2008, as well as in Case A. Figure 8.1 also demonstrates the dynamic multiplier of Case C. As the household financial assets (HFA), household non-financial assets (HNFA) and household total liabilities (HTD) are given as the same values as the final test projection, the multiplier is a little bit lower at 1.42 in the initial year and thereafter increasing to 1.57 in the second year while it declines to 1.56 from the third year. In other words, with given household assets and liabilities exogenously, the dynamic multiplier effects may be lower in magnitude and shorter in duration.[2]

These differences between Case A and Case C present very important implications, in which the stock variables such as household assets and liabilities play a significant role for stimulating the demand-side economy including real final consumption expenditure and housing investment expenditure as asset effects, as well as household disposable income as income effects, as discussed in the theoretical framework section.

Moreover, we conduct one more experiment for examining the impacts of fiscal policy to examine the changes of the initial year's multiplier effects. In the fiscal policy of Case A and Case B started from FY2001 we obtained the Keynes multiplier of 1.572 in the initial year of FY2001. In this experiment, we change the initial year for the fiscal policy year by year in FY2001–2008 and examine the changes of the initial year's Keynes multiplier since the Keynes multiplier depends on not only marginal propensity to consume,

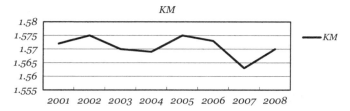

Figure 8.2: Changes in the initial year's Keynes multiplier simulated by the model in FY2001–2008.
Source: Simulated by the author.

to invest and to import but also the wage income share and hence the profit share and so on, as discussed in Chapter 5.

Figure 8.2 demonstrates the Keynes multiplier of the initial year from FY2001 to FY2008. As noted, the initial year's multiplier is changing based on the economic condition, particularly based on some factors in determining the Keynes multiplier as discussed in Chapter 5. The initial year's multiplier in FY2001 is the same as Case A and B, which rises to 1.575 in FY2002, declines to 1.570 in FY2003 and to 1.568 in FY2004 and rises to 1.575 in FY2005, but declines to 1.563 in FY2007 because the income distribution pattern between wages (household disposable income) and profits (corporate income) are changing in the tested period. By and large, as demonstrated in the figure, the trend of the multiplier was declining.

8.2.2. *Effects of personal income tax cut*

As discussed in the theoretical model framework, the multiplier effects in the case of income tax cut in utilizing this integrated model may be larger since we introduce not only the income effects but also the asset effects in the real household consumption function and housing investment function. Therefore, we perform the personal income tax cut scenario simulation in this section to experiment on the effects of personal income tax cut on the economy. In the simulation, a one trillion yen income tax cut is assumed to be continued during the tested period and the personal income tax is exogenized as a control variable in order to make both the government investment increase and personal income tax cut policy simulations comparable.[3]

Table 8.3 demonstrates the effects of personal income tax cut by one trillion yen on the Japanese economy from FY2001 to FY2008. In the case of the government investment demand stimulus, the increased government investment indirectly stimulates the demand-side components, which are determined simultaneously with GDE. On the other hand, in the case of the personal income tax cut, the enhanced household disposable income by tax cut directly stimulates household consumption and housing investment expenditures through income effects and indirectly stimulates them through assets effects, which ultimately drive GDE and the other components of GDE.

In accordance with the simulation results, we can see the different impacts of the income tax cut on the economy in comparison with those of the increased government investment simulation. Particularly, the effects on the household consumption and housing investment expenditures are fairly larger than those of the case of government investment. Moreover, the duration for the effects is, to some extent, longer than the government investment case, improving the positions of household financial and non-financial assets and of overall liabilities, as discussed in the theoretical model framework.

As a result, the real household final consumption expenditure increases by 0.54 trillion yen in FY2001, by 0.91 trillion yen in FY2002 and by 1.19 trillion yen in FY2003 and attains the highest increase by 1.61 trillion yen in the seventh year, in terms of deviation, as compared to the final test projection. The other GDE components also have positive impacts indirectly. Consequently, real GDE increases by 0.99 trillion yen in FY2001, by 1.65 trillion yen in FY2002, by 1.99 trillion yen in FY2003, by 2.05 trillion yen in FY2004 and by 2.06 trillion yen in FY2005 as the peak value, in comparison with the final test, and, thereafter, the impacts on real GDE are declining.

As discussed, the effects of the personal income tax cut on the economy are smaller than that of the government investment increase because initial effects are dependent on the household disposable income increase by the marginal propensity to consume out of disposable income. However, it can be seen that household assets and liabilities play a significant role to simultaneously stimulate the economy through asset effects.

Table 8.3: The impacts of personal income tax cut by one trillion yen on the economy, FY2001–2008: dynamic Keynes multiplier test, deviation and % deviation, as compared to the final test.

(In trillions of yen)

FY	2001	2002	2003	2004	2005	2006	2007	2008
GDE	0.99	1.65	1.99	2.05	2.06	1.98	1.79	1.49
% dev.	(0.2)	(0.3)	(0.4)	(0.4)	(0.4)	(0.4)	(0.3)	(0.3)
GDPC	0.06	0.15	0.28	0.40	0.50	0.56	0.61	0.62
% dev.	(0.0)	(0.0)	(0.0)	(0.1)	(0.1)	(0.1)	(0.1)	(0.1)
DGAP	−0.94	−1.49	−1.74	−1.78	−1.69	−1.49	−1.21	−0.89
% dev.	(−1.1)	(−1.8)	(−2.1)	(−2.3)	(−2.2)	(−2.1)	(−1.8)	(−1.4)
CP	0.54	0.92	1.20	1.38	1.50	1.61	1.63	1.59
% dev.	(0.2)	(0.3)	(0.4)	(0.5)	(0.5)	(0.5)	(0.5)	(0.5)
CH	0.54	0.91	1.19	1.36	1.48	1.59	1.61	1.56
% dev.	(0.2)	(0.3)	(0.4)	(0.5)	(0.5)	(0.5)	(0.5)	(0.5)
CN	0.00	0.01	0.01	0.02	0.02	0.02	0.02	0.02
% dev.	(0.0)	(0.1)	(0.2)	(0.3)	(0.3)	(0.3)	(0.4)	(0.4)
IP	0.25	0.46	0.55	0.56	0.52	0.47	0.37	0.25
% dev.	(0.3)	(0.6)	(0.7)	(0.7)	(0.7)	(0.6)	(0.4)	(0.3)
IH	0.25	0.39	0.47	0.48	0.48	0.44	0.40	0.32
% dev.	(1.8)	(2.7)	(3.2)	(3.5)	(3.4)	(3.2)	(2.8)	(2.2)

(Continued)

Table 8.3:   (Continued)

FY	2001	2002	2003	2004	2005	2006	2007	2008
CG	-0.00	-0.01	-0.02	-0.05	-0.06	-0.09	-0.12	-0.14
% dev.	(-0.0)	(-0.0)	(-0.0)	(-0.1)	(-0.1)	(-0.1)	(-0.1)	(-0.1)
IG	-0.00	0.03	0.03	0.01	0.01	-0.01	-0.02	-0.04
% dev.	(-0.0)	(0.1)	(0.2)	(0.0)	(0.0)	(-0.0)	(-0.1)	(-0.2)
JP	0.07	0.08	0.06	0.03	0.02	-0.01	-0.02	-0.04
% dev.	(7.3)	(8.1)	(7.3)	(4.0)	(2.3)	(-0.9)	(-3.3)	(-4.8)
EGS	-0.01	-0.02	-0.03	-0.04	-0.05	-0.06	-0.06	-0.06
% dev.	(-0.0)	(-0.0)	(-0.0)	(-0.0)	(-0.0)	(-0.1)	(-0.1)	(-0.1)
MGS	0.12	0.20	0.27	0.32	0.35	0.36	0.38	0.38
% dev.	(0.2)	(0.3)	(0.4)	(0.5)	(0.5)	(0.5)	(0.5)	(0.5)
GDEN	0.96	1.68	2.21	2.62	2.92	3.11	3.18	3.13
% dev.	(0.2)	(0.3)	(0.5)	(0.5)	(0.6)	(0.6)	(0.6)	(0.6)
CPN	0.50	0.88	1.22	1.54	1.81	2.01	2.14	2.19
% dev.	(0.2)	(0.3)	(0.5)	(0.6)	(0.7)	(0.8)	(0.8)	(0.8)
CHN	0.49	0.87	1.21	1.51	1.78	1.97	2.10	2.14
% dev.	(0.2)	(0.3)	(0.5)	(0.6)	(0.7)	(0.8)	(0.8)	(0.8)
CNN	0.01	0.01	0.01	0.03	0.03	0.04	0.04	0.05
% dev.	(0.1)	(0.2)	(0.2)	(0.3)	(0.3)	(0.4)	(0.4)	(0.5)

(Continued)

Table 8.3: *(Continued)*

FY	2001	2002	2003	2004	2005	2006	2007	2008
CGN	0.01	0.03	0.06	0.11	0.16	0.21	0.27	0.31
% dev.	(0.0)	(0.0)	(0.1)	(0.1)	(0.2)	(0.2)	(0.3)	(0.3)
IPN	0.23	0.43	0.55	0.60	0.61	0.59	0.55	0.48
% dev.	(0.3)	(0.6)	(0.8)	(0.8)	(0.8)	(0.8)	(0.7)	(0.6)
IHN	0.26	0.41	0.49	0.53	0.54	0.51	0.46	0.39
% dev.	(1.8)	(2.7)	(3.3)	(3.6)	(3.6)	(3.5)	(3.1)	(2.6)
IGN	0.03	0.04	0.05	0.05	0.05	0.04	0.04	0.03
% dev.	(0.2)	(0.2)	(0.2)	(0.2)	(0.2)	(0.2)	(0.2)	(0.2)
JPN	0.06	0.07	0.05	0.03	0.01	−0.01	−0.02	−0.03
% dev.	(7.8)	(8.1)	(7.3)	(5.3)	(2.3)	(−0.9)	(−3.3)	(−4.8)
EGSN	−0.06	−0.12	−0.17	−0.19	−0.20	−0.20	−0.17	−0.14
% dev.	(−0.1)	(−0.1)	(−0.1)	(−0.1)	(−0.1)	(−0.1)	(−0.1)	(−0.1)
MGN	0.04	0.05	0.05	0.05	0.05	0.06	0.08	0.10
% dev.	(0.1)	(0.1)	(0.1)	(0.1)	(0.1)	(0.1)	(0.1)	(0.1)

(Continued)

Table 8.3:   (Continued)

(Index: 2000 = 100)

FY	2001	2002	2003	2004	2005	2006	2007	2008
PGDE	0.02	0.04	0.08	0.13	0.18	0.24	0.28	0.32
% dev.	(0.0)	(0.0)	(0.1)	(0.1)	(0.2)	(0.3)	(0.3)	(0.4)
PCP	0.01	0.02	0.05	0.09	0.14	0.19	0.23	0.26
% dev.	(0.0)	(0.0)	(0.1)	(0.1)	(0.2)	(0.2)	(0.3)	(0.3)
PCH	0.01	0.02	0.05	0.09	0.14	0.19	0.23	0.26
% dev.	(0.0)	(0.0)	(0.1)	(0.1)	(0.2)	(0.2)	(0.3)	(0.3)
PCG	0.01	0.03	0.07	0.14	0.21	0.28	0.35	0.40
% dev.	(0.0)	(0.0)	(0.1)	(0.1)	(0.2)	(0.3)	(0.4)	(0.4)
PIP	0.00	0.02	0.05	0.09	0.15	0.21	0.27	0.31
% dev.	(0.0)	(0.0)	(0.1)	(0.1)	(0.2)	(0.2)	(0.3)	(0.4)
PIH	0.01	0.02	0.06	0.12	0.18	0.26	0.33	0.39
% dev.	(0.0)	(0.0)	(0.0)	(0.1)	(0.1)	(0.2)	(0.2)	(0.3)
PIG	0.01	0.03	0.07	0.13	0.20	0.26	0.32	0.37
% dev.	(0.0)	(0.0)	(0.1)	(0.1)	(0.2)	(0.3)	(0.3)	(0.4)
PEGS	-0.06	-0.11	-0.14	-0.15	-0.15	-0.13	-0.10	-0.07
% dev.	(-0.0)	(-0.1)	(-0.1)	(-0.1)	(-0.1)	(-0.1)	(-0.1)	(-0.1)
PMGS	-0.17	-0.34	-0.45	-0.55	-0.60	-0.63	-0.62	-0.59
% dev.	(-0.1)	(-0.3)	(-0.4)	(-0.4)	(-0.5)	(-0.5)	(-0.5)	(-0.6)
PMY	-0.22	-0.43	-0.59	-0.70	-0.76	-0.79	-0.78	-0.74
% dev.	(-0.2)	(-0.3)	(-0.4)	(-0.5)	(-0.5)	(-0.5)	(-0.5)	(-0.5)

(Continued)

Table 8.3: (Continued)

FY	2001	2002	2003	2004	2005	2006	2007	2008
PX	−0.01	−0.02	−0.02	0.00	0.02	0.05	0.08	0.11
% dev.	(−0.0)	(−0.0)	(−0.0)	(0.0)	(0.0)	(0.0)	(0.1)	(0.1)
PEXY	−0.06	−0.11	−0.14	−0.15	−0.15	−0.13	−0.10	−0.07
% dev.	(−0.1)	(−0.1)	(−0.1)	(−0.1)	(−0.1)	(−0.1)	(−0.1)	(−0.1)
CPI	0.01	0.03	0.06	0.12	0.18	0.25	0.31	0.37
% dev.	(0.0)	(0.0)	(0.1)	(0.1)	(0.2)	(0.3)	(0.3)	(0.4)
EXR	−0.14	−0.27	−0.36	−0.42	−0.45	−0.45	−0.43	−0.39
% dev.	(−0.2)	(−0.3)	(−0.4)	(−0.5)	(−0.5)	(−0.5)	(−0.5)	(−0.5)
NLE	2.18	4.74	6.70	7.78	7.99	7.42	6.26	4.75
% dev.	(0.0)	(0.1)	(0.1)	(0.1)	(0.1)	(0.1)	(0.1)	(0.1)
UR	−0.03	−0.07	−0.10	−0.12	−0.12	−0.11	−0.10	−0.07
% dev.	(−0.6)	(−1.3)	(−1.8)	(−2.1)	(−2.2)	(−2.0)	(−1.7)	(−1.3)
M2CD	0.23	0.58	0.97	1.35	1.68	1.95	2.12	2.20
% dev.	(0.0)	(0.1)	(0.1)	(0.2)	(0.2)	(0.2)	(0.2)	(0.3)
INTPR	0.01	0.01	0.01	0.02	0.02	0.02	0.02	0.02
% dev.	(0.5)	(0.7)	(0.8)	(1.0)	(1.1)	(1.1)	(1.1)	(1.1)
TXG	−0.79	−0.72	−0.68	−0.66	−0.64	−0.64	−0.64	−0.64
% dev.	(−1.5)	(−1.3)	(−1.2)	(−1.1)	(−1.1)	(−1.1)	(−1.1)	(−1.1)
TXC	0.15	0.22	0.22	0.20	0.17	0.12	0.08	0.03
% dev.	(1.2)	(1.6)	(1.6)	(1.4)	(1.2)	(0.9)	(0.5)	(0.2)

(Continued)

Table 8.3:   (Continued)

FY	2001	2002	2003	2004	2005	2006	2007	2008
TXI	-1.00	-1.00	-1.00	-1.00	-1.00	-1.00	-1.00	-1.00
% dev.	(-5.1)	(-5.1)	(-5.1)	(-5.0)	(-5.0)	(-5.0)	(-5.0)	(-5.0)
KLGBT	0.99	1.92	2.82	3.82	4.77	5.69	6.75	7.64
% dev.	(0.1)	(0.2)	(0.3)	(0.4)	(0.4)	(0.5)	(0.6)	(0.7)
YDH	1.41	1.69	2.03	2.35	2.64	2.84	2.95	2.97
% dev.	(0.6)	(0.7)	(0.8)	(1.0)	(1.1)	(1.2)	(1.3)	(1.3)
YE	0.28	0.52	0.84	1.19	1.50	1.73	1.88	1.93
% dev.	(0.1)	(0.2)	(0.4)	(0.5)	(0.6)	(0.7)	(0.8)	(0.8)
YC	0.27	0.33	0.29	0.20	0.10	-0.00	-0.10	-0.20
% dev.	(0.6)	(0.7)	(0.6)	(0.4)	(0.2)	(-0.0)	(-0.2)	(-0.4)
HFA	1.19	2.63	3.95	5.03	5.84	6.34	6.52	6.37
% dev.	(0.1)	(0.2)	(0.3)	(0.4)	(0.4)	(0.5)	(0.5)	(0.5)
HNFA	0.70	1.00	1.11	1.14	1.38	1.23	1.15	1.05
% dev.	(0.0)	(0.1)	(0.1)	(0.1)	(0.2)	(0.2)	(0.1)	(0.1)
HTD	-0.08	-0.19	-0.31	-0.44	-0.59	-0.75	-0.92	-1.09
% dev.	(-0.0)	(-0.1)	(-0.1)	(-0.1)	(-0.2)	(-0.2)	(-0.2)	(-0.3)
PSTOCK	18.8	27.3	30.1	29.4	26.5	21.8	16.6	11.9
% dev.	(1.6)	(2.2)	(2.4)	(2.4)	(2.4)	(2.1)	(1.7)	(1.2)

Note: Deviation: (Scenario − Final Test); % deviation: (Scenario − Final Test)/Final Test * 100 (%).
Source: Simulated and compiled by author.

Concerning the effects on the household assets and liabilities, the household financial assets have fairly large impacts, increasing by 1.19 trillion yen in FY2001, by 5.84 trillion yen in FY2005 and by 6.37 trillion yen in FY2008 and the non-financial assets increase by 1.35 trillion yen in FY2005 and by 1.03 trillion yen in FY2008, in deviation, as compared to the final test projection. In addition, the total household liabilities are also improved by 0.59 trillion yen in FY2005 and by 1.09 trillion yen in FY2008 as compared to the final test. These improvements of the household assets and liabilities contribute to the expansion of the demand-side economy through asset effects.

Furthermore, in comparison to the government investment demand stimulus, we can see very interesting implications within these scenario simulations. Figure 8.3 demonstrates the Keynes dynamic multiplier of the personal income tax cut and the government investment increase in nominal and real terms in FY2001–2008, respectively. In the case of the personal income tax cut, the multiplier in the initial year is lower than that of the government investment increase scenario at 0.99, but from the second year, the multiplier is getting higher at 1.60 in FY2002, at 1.91 in FY2003, at 2.02 in FY2004 and at 2.04 in FY2005, as the peak value, and thereafter declining to 1.51 in FY2008, in real terms, narrowing the gap in comparison with the multiplier of the government investment increase case. Especially in the fourth to the fifth year, the multiplier of the personal income tax cut realizes the high value exceeding 2.0, in real terms, which is around 92 per cent of the government investment multiplier in FY2005,

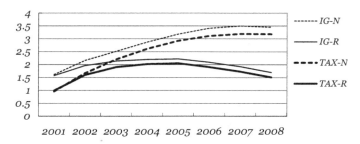

Figure 8.3: Personal income tax cut (TAX) and government investment (IG) multiplier in nominal (-N) and in real terms (-R), FY2001–2008.
Source: Simulated and developed by the author.

although the multiplier in the initial year is only 63 per cent as compared to the government investment multiplier. It seems that we may underestimate the dynamic effects of the personal income tax cut policy on the whole economy, particularly on the welfare of the household sector, including consumption expenditure, household investment and assets.

As for the impacts on the other endogenous variables, the effects of the income tax cut on the economy are limited as compared to the government investment increase case, as discussed earlier. However, it can be seen that increases in fiscal deficit are, to some extent, restrained because declines in overall tax revenues are canceled to some extent by the increase in consumption tax revenue with enhanced household consumption expenditure. As a result, the overall central government fiscal debt outstanding (KLGBT) increases by 4.77 trillion yen in FY2005 and by 7.64 trillion yen in FY2008, as compared to the final test projection, which is almost the same as the case of the government investment increase scenario in spite of the smaller multiplier in both nominal and real terms in comparison with the government investment increase scenario simulation.

8.3. Monetary and Financial Policy Simulation Test

The current Japanese economy suffers from twin traps including a fiscal deficit trap and a liquidity trap, in which we, to some extent, lose the degree of freedom in economic policy, particularly in fiscal policy, and monetary and financial policy. In this section, we perform a monetary and financial policy dynamic simulation test to evaluate its effects on the Japanese economy.

In this dynamic simulation test, we assume the Bank of Japan expands monetary base (high-powered money), which is one of the major exogenous variables in the model, by five trillion yen from FY2001 to FY2008 as compared to the final test. In accordance with the monetary policy test result with a five trillion yen increase in monetary base, the economy has positive impacts, as shown in Table 8.4. However, the effects on the economy are very limited. With the five trillion yen increase in monetary base, money supply (M2CD) increases by 8.83 trillion yen in FY2001, while the increase in M2CD gradually declines from FY2002 onward. It means that the marginal money multiplier is very low at around 1.77 since the

Table 8.4: The impacts of monetary base increase by five trillion yen on the economy, FY2001–2008: deviation and % deviation, as compared to the final test (baseline).

(In trillions of yen)

FY	2001	2002	2003	2004	2005	2006	2007	2008
GDE	0.85	0.94	0.98	1.03	1.07	1.07	1.02	0.93
% dev.	(0.2)	(0.2)	(0.2)	(0.2)	(0.2)	(0.2)	(0.2)	(0.2)
GDPC	0.22	0.40	0.53	0.92	0.68	0.72	0.74	0.73
% dev.	(0.0)	(0.1)	(0.1)	(0.1)	(0.1)	(0.1)	(0.1)	(0.1)
DGAP	−0.63	−0.54	−0.45	−0.41	−0.38	−0.35	−0.28	−0.19
% dev.	(−0.7)	(−0.7)	(−0.6)	(−0.5)	(−0.5)	(−0.5)	(−0.4)	(−0.3)
CP	0.08	0.18	0.29	0.39	0.48	0.54	0.57	0.57
% dev.	(0.0)	(0.1)	(0.1)	(0.1)	(0.2)	(0.2)	(0.2)	(0.2)
CH	0.08	0.17	0.28	0.38	0.46	0.52	0.56	0.56
% dev.	(0.0)	(0.1)	(0.1)	(0.1)	(0.2)	(0.2)	(0.2)	(0.2)
CN	0.00	0.01	0.01	0.01	0.02	0.02	0.01	0.01
% dev.	(0.0)	(0.1)	(0.1)	(0.1)	(0.1)	(0.2)	(0.2)	(0.2)
IH	0.01	0.04	0.07	0.10	0.13	0.14	0.15	0.14
% dev.	(0.1)	(0.2)	(0.5)	(0.7)	(0.9)	(1.0)	(1.0)	(1.0)

(Continued)

Table 8.4: (Continued)

FY	2001	2002	2003	2004	2005	2006	2007	2008
IP	0.71	0.66	0.56	0.49	0.42	0.36	0.29	0.22
% dev.	(0.9)	(0.8)	(0.7)	(0.6)	(0.5)	(0.4)	(0.4)	(0.3)
CG	−0.03	−0.07	−0.11	−0.14	−0.16	−0.17	−0.18	−0.19
% dev.	(−0.0)	(−0.1)	(−0.1)	(−0.1)	(−0.1)	(−0.2)	(−0.2)	(−0.2)
IG	−0.01	0.00	−0.01	−0.02	−0.02	−0.03	−0.03	−0.04
% dev.	(−0.1)	(0.0)	(−0.0)	(−0.1)	(−0.1)	(−0.1)	(−0.2)	(−0.2)
EGS	0.04	0.07	0.08	0.08	0.07	0.06	0.05	0.04
% dev.	(0.0)	(0.1)	(0.1)	(0.1)	(0.1)	(0.1)	(0.1)	(0.0)
MGS	0.02	0.03	−0.08	−0.12	−0.15	−0.17	−0.19	−0.20
% dev.	(0.0)	(−0.1)	(−0.1)	(−0.2)	(−0.2)	(−0.2)	(−0.3)	(−0.3)
GDEN	0.68	0.97	1.27	1.58	1.84	2.06	2.20	2.27
% dev.	(0.1)	(0.2)	(0.3)	(0.3)	(0.4)	(0.4)	(0.4)	(0.5)
CPN	0.14	0.33	0.53	0.71	0.87	1.00	1.09	1.14
% dev.	(0.1)	(0.1)	(0.2)	(0.3)	(0.3)	(0.4)	(0.4)	(0.4)
CHN	0.14	0.32	0.51	0.69	0.85	0.97	1.06	1.11
% dev.	(0.1)	(0.1)	(0.2)	(0.3)	(0.3)	(0.4)	(0.4)	(0.4)

(Continued)

Table 8.4: (Continued)

FY	2001	2002	2003	2004	2005	2006	2007	2008
CNN	0.00	0.01	0.02	0.02	0.02	0.03	0.03	0.03
% dev.	(0.1)	(0.1)	(0.2)	(0.3)	(0.3)	(0.4)	(0.4)	(0.4)
CGN	0.01	0.02	0.04	0.07	0.10	0.13	0.16	0.19
% dev.	(0.0)	(0.0)	(0.0)	(0.1)	(0.1)	(0.1)	(0.2)	(0.2)
IPN	0.68	0.68	0.64	0.60	0.57	0.53	0.49	0.45
% dev.	(1.0)	(1.0)	(0.9)	(0.8)	(0.8)	(0.7)	(0.7)	(0.6)
IHN	0.02	0.05	0.09	0.13	0.16	0.19	0.20	0.19
% dev.	(0.1)	(0.3)	(0.7)	(0.9)	(1.1)	(0.3)	(1.3)	(1.3)
IGN	0.03	0.03	0.03	0.03	0.03	0.04	0.04	0.04
% dev.	(0.1)	(0.1)	(0.2)	(0.2)	(0.2)	(0.3)	(0.3)	(0.2)
EGSN	0.36	0.50	0.54	0.52	0.47	0.41	0.36	0.31
% dev.	(0.4)	(0.5)	(0.6)	(0.5)	(0.5)	(0.4)	(0.3)	(0.3)
MGN	0.59	0.67	0.61	0.49	0.37	0.24	0.13	0.03
% dev.	(0.8)	(0.8)	(0.7)	(0.6)	(0.4)	(0.3)	(0.1)	(0.0)

(Continued)

Table 8.4: (Continued)

(Index: 2000 = 100)

FY	2001	2002	2003	2004	2005	2006	2007	2008
PGDE	0.01	0.03	0.07	0.12	0.16	0.20	0.23	0.26
% dev.	(0.0)	(0.0)	(0.1)	(0.1)	(0.2)	(0.2)	(0.3)	(0.3)
PCP	0.02	0.06	0.08	0.12	0.15	0.17	0.19	0.21
% dev.	(0.0)	(0.1)	(0.1)	(0.1)	(0.2)	(0.2)	(0.2)	(0.2)
PCH	0.02	0.06	0.08	0.12	0.15	0.17	0.19	0.21
% dev.	(0.0)	(0.1)	(0.1)	(0.1)	(0.2)	(0.2)	(0.2)	(0.2)
PCG	0.04	0.09	0.14	0.19	0.23	0.27	0.31	0.34
% dev.	(0.0)	(0.1)	(0.1)	(0.2)	(0.2)	(0.3)	(0.3)	(0.4)
PIP	0.05	0.11	0.16	0.20	0.23	0.26	0.28	0.30
% dev.	(0.1)	(0.1)	(0.2)	(0.2)	(0.2)	(0.3)	(0.3)	(0.3)
PIH	0.03	0.07	0.12	0.17	0.22	0.27	0.31	0.34
% dev.	(0.0)	(0.1)	(0.1)	(0.2)	(0.2)	(0.3)	(0.3)	(0.3)
PIG	0.06	0.13	0.19	0.24	0.27	0.30	0.32	0.34
% dev.	(0.1)	(0.1)	(0.2)	(0.2)	(0.3)	(0.3)	(0.3)	(0.3)
PEGS	0.36	0.47	0.47	0.43	0.38	0.33	0.28	0.24
% dev.	(0.4)	(0.5)	(0.5)	(0.4)	(0.4)	(0.3)	(0.3)	(0.2)
PMGS	0.93	1.15	1.12	1.00	0.84	0.69	055	0.43
% dev.	(0.8)	(0.9)	(0.9)	(0.8)	(0.6)	(0.5)	(0.4)	(0.3)

(Continued)

Table 8.4: (Continued)

FY	2001	2002	2003	2004	2005	2006	2007	2008
PMY	1.18	1.45	1.41	1.26	1.07	0.87	0.70	0.55
% dev.	(0.9)	(1.1)	(1.0)	(0.9)	(0.7)	(0.6)	(0.5)	(0.4)
PX	0.11	0.19	0.22	0.23	0.23	0.23	0.22	0.21
% dev.	(0.1)	(0.2)	(0.2)	(0.2)	(0.2)	(0.29)	(0.2)	(0.2)
PEXY	0.37	0.48	0.48	0.44	0.39	0.34	0.29	0.25
% dev.	(0.4)	(0.5)	(0.5)	(0.4)	(0.4)	(0.3)	(0.3)	(0.2)
CPI	0.03	0.07	0.11	0.16	0.20	0.24	0.28	0.31
% dev.	(0.0)	(0.1)	(0.1)	(0.2)	(0.2)	(0.3)	(0.3)	(0.3)
PSTOCK	11.7	15.6	19.1	21.3	21.8	20.8	18.4	15.0
% dev.	(1.0)	(1.3)	(1.5)	(1.7)	(1.7)	(1.7)	(1.4)	(1.1)
EXR	0.79	0.94	0.88	0.76	0.62	0.48	0.37	0.27
% dev.	(0.9)	(1.0)	(1.0)	(0.8)	(0.7)	(0.6)	(0.4)	(0.3)
NLE	1.86	3.16	3.96	4.41	4.58	4.45	4.05	3.43
% dev.	(0.0)	(0.1)	(0.1)	(0.1)	(0.1)	(0.1)	(0.1)	(0.1)
UR(%)	−0.23	−0.44	0.52	−0.61	−0.67	−0.64	−0.60	−0.51
% dev.	(−0.5)	(−0.8)	(−1.1)	(−1.2)	(−1.2)	(−1.2)	(−1.1)	(−1.1)
M2CD	8.83	7.97	7.22	6.58	6.02	5.53	5.09	4.69
% dev.	(1.1)	(1.0)	(0.9)	(0.8)	(0.7)	(0.7)	(0.6)	(0.6)
INTPR	−0.04	−0.04	−0.03	−0.02	−0.02	−0.01	−0.01	−0.00
% dev.	(−2.6)	(−1.9)	(−1.6)	(−1.3)	(−0.9)	(−0.7)	(−0.4)	(−0.2)

(Continued)

Table 8.4: (Continued)

FY	2001	2002	2003	2004	2005	2006	2007	2008
INTGB	-0.04	-0.03	-0.03	-0.02	-0.02	-0.01	-0.01	-0.01
% dev.	(-0.7)	(-0.2)	(-1.8)	(-1.5)	(-1.1)	(-0.8)	(-0.6)	(-0.4)
WN	0.03	0.07	0.12	0.17	0.23	0.28	0.32	0.35
% dev.	(0.0)	(0.1)	(0.1)	(0.2)	(0.2)	(0.3)	(0.3)	(0.4)
YDH	0.14	0.31	0.54	0.76	0.95	1.10	1.20	1.27
% dev.	(0.1)	(0.1)	(0.2)	(0.3)	(0.4)	(0.5)	(0.5)	(0.5)
YE	0.21	0.31	0.49	0.67	0.84	0.99	1.10	1.17
% dev.	(0.1)	(0.1)	(0.2)	(0.3)	(0.4)	(0.4)	(0.5)	(0.5)
YC	0.31	0.29	0.25	0.22	0.18	0.13	0.09	0.04
% dev.	(0.7)	(0.6)	(0.5)	(0.4)	(0.3)	(0.3)	(0.2)	(0.1)
TXG	0.21	0.24	0.26	0.29	0.30	0.30	0.28	0.25
% dev.	(0.4)	(0.5)	(0.5)	(0.6)	(0.6)	(0.6)	(0.6)	(0.5)
TXI	0.07	0.08	0.10	0.12	0.13	0.14	0.14	0.14
% dev.	(0.5)	(0.6)	(0.7)	(0.9)	(1.0)	(1.0)	(1.0)	(1.0)
TXC	0.14	0.15	0.15	0.15	0.14	0.13	0.11	0.08
% dev.	(1.1)	(1.1)	(1.1)	(1.1)	(1.0)	(0.9)	(0.7)	(0.6)

Note: Deviation: (Scenario − Final Test); % deviation: (Scenario − Final Test)/Final Test * 100 (%).
Source: Forecasted and compiled by the author.

averaged money multiplier was around 6 to 7 in the 2000s, while the averaged multiplier in the 1980s was 11 to 12, which indicates that the Japanese economy is suffering from severe and prolonged stagnation with the liquidity trap. The effects on the demand-side economy are also limited at 0.85 trillion yen for real GDE, at 0.08 trillion yen for real household consumption and at 0.71 trillion yen for real private non-housing invest-ment, respectively, in FY2001, in terms of deviation, as compared to the final test projection.

As for the impacts on interest rates, the prime rate declines by 0.04 per cent point in FY2001, in deviation, as compared to the final test, which may stimulate some demand-side components. However, due to the limited impacts on financial variables, both the demand-side and supply-side of the economy may not have large effects within the five trillion yen monetary base increase policy. The limited effects of the monetary policy under the situation of the liquidity trap are explained by the IS-LM model framework. As well known, IS locus is determined by three equations, as follows.

$$S = f_1 (Y) (f_1' > 0)$$
$$I = f_2 (r) (f_2' < 0)$$
$$I = S$$

where Y, S, I and r refer to national income, saving, investment and interest rate, respectively.

In Japan, the saving ratio of Japan to Y is relatively high as compared to that of other countries, while investment is very inelastic to the changes in interest rates. Therefore, the investment curve may, to some extent, be steeper to the horizontal axis in (I, r) space, as shown in the right-hand-side of Figure 8.4.

As the IS locus depends on these three equations, the IS locus illus-trated in traditional (Y, r) space may also be steeper, to some extent, to the horizontal axis because it mainly relies on the investment curve, as shown in the left-hand side of Figure 8.3. Accordingly, if the LM locus shifts to right, interest rate (r) goes down sufficiently from r to r' while national income (Y) increases slightly from Y to Y' because of the steeper locus of IS, which explains the situation of limited effects of monetary and financial policies in Japan as demonstrated in this dynamic policy simulation test.

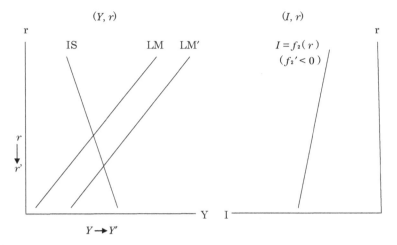

Figure 8.4: IS and LM loci in (Y, r) space and investment curve in (I, r) space within a liquidity trap in Japan.

8.4. Yen Appreciation Dynamic Simulation Test

Since Japan has introduced the floating system, the yen–dollar exchange rate has fluctuated drastically. In particular, just after the Plaza Accord, the yen rates to the other currencies sharply appreciated, which resulted in decreases of real exports and increases of real imports through price effects. Moreover, yen appreciation makes export industries' profits lower as producers have no choice to compete based on price factors in order to maintain their market share with pass-through as discussed in Chapter 7, through regression analysis. At the same time, yen appreciation has resulted in increases in FDI to the rest of the world, and many private corporations, including their sub-contractors, have shifted their production bases to the rest of the world.

Accordingly, this section conducts a yen appreciation scenario simulation and examines the impacts of yen appreciation on the Japanese economy. In this scenario, we assume the yen rate against the US dollar is appreciated by 5 yen as compared to the final test result. Therefore, the yen rate endogenized in the model is exogenized and controlled to be appreciated by 5 yen as compared to the level of the yen rate against the US dollar in the final test.

Based on this scenario assumption, the yen appreciation dynamic simulation was conducted and interesting results were shown in Table 8.4. According to the results of the dynamic simulation test, the 5 per cent yen appreciation has negative effects, as a whole, on the Japanese economy through direct and indirect effects.

As for the impacts on the variables in the real expenditure block, including real GDE and its components, real GDE has negative impacts through direct effects of real merchandise exports declines and imports increases, which are negative effects, and indirect effects of prices falls on real GDE as positive effects, as shown in Table 8.5. With these indirect and indirect effects, real GDE declines by 0.31 trillion yen in FY2001, by 1.45 trillion yen in FY 2005 and by 2.91 trillion yen in FY2008, in terms of deviation, as compared to the final test.

The negative impacts on real GDE mainly result from the changes in real exports and imports, in which the real exports of goods and services decrease by 0.18 trillion yen in FY2001, by 0.27 trillion yen in FY2002, by 0.32 trillion yen in FY2003, by 0.35 trillion yen in FY2005 and by 0.31 trillion yen in FY2008, while real imports increase by 0.30 trillion yen in FY2001, by 1.16 trillion yen in FY2005 and by 1.73 trillion yen in FY2009, in deviation terms, in comparison with the final test. It is worth noting that the effects of the 5 yen appreciation on the real exports are fairly small in comparison with that on the imports since the price effects through yen appreciation on real exports are recently declining with increases in non-price competitiveness, which may result in the limited Marshall–Lerner stable condition, and with a pass-through mechanism in the export side, as discussed in Chapter 5.

On the other hand, the positive impacts could be seen in the domestic demand variables in the first two or three years during the tested period. For example, private final consumption expenditures, in which the positive impacts are larger than the negative impacts in the first three years, increase by 0.15 trillion yen in FY2001, 0.14 trillion yen in FY2002 and by 0.09 trillion yen in FY2003, but thereafter the negative impacts exceed the positive impacts. As a result, the consumption expenditures falls by 0.22 trillion yen in FY2005 and by 0.94 trillion yen in FY2008, in terms of deviation, as compared to the final test that is the baseline for this scenario simulation, as demonstrated in Figure 8.5.

Table 8.5: The impacts of yen appreciation by 5 yen against US dollar on the economy, FY2001–2008: deviation and % deviation, as compared to the final test.

(In trillions of yen)

FY	2001	2002	2003	2004	2005	2006	2007	2008
GDE	−0.31	−0.47	−0.66	−1.00	−1.45	−1.95	−2.46	−2.91
% dev.	(−0.1)	(−0.1)	(−0.1)	(−0.2)	(−0.3)	(−0.3)	(−0.4)	(−0.5)
GDPC	−0.04	−0.06	−0.07	−0.09	−0.12	−0.16	−0.22	−0.28
% dev.	(−0.0)	(−0.0)	(−0.0)	(−0.0)	(−0.0)	(−0.0)	(−0.0)	(−0.0)
DGAP	0.27	0.41	0.59	0.91	1.33	1.79	2.24	2.64
% dev.	(0.3)	(0.5)	(0.7)	(1.1)	(1.7)	(2.5)	(3.3)	(4.3)
CP	0.15	0.14	0.09	−0.03	−0.22	−0.45	−0.70	−0.94
% dev.	(0.0)	(0.0)	(0.0)	(−0.0)	(−0.1)	(−0.2)	(−0.2)	(−0.3)
CH	0.15	0.15	0.10	−0.03	−0.21	−0.44	−0.68	−0.92
% dev.	(0.0)	(0.0)	(0.0)	(−0.0)	(−0.1)	(−0.1)	(−0.2)	(−0.3)
CN	−0.00	−0.01	−0.01	−0.01	−0.01	−0.01	−0.02	−0.02
% dev.	(−0.0)	(−0.0)	(−0.1)	(−0.1)	(−0.1)	(−0.2)	(−0.3)	(−0.4)
IH	0.04	0.01	−0.01	−0.06	−0.13	−0.21	−0.29	−0.36
% dev.	(0.3)	(0.1)	(−0.1)	(−0.4)	(−0.9)	(−1.5)	(−2.0)	(−2.4)
IP	−0.13	−0.11	−0.10	−0.15	−0.22	−0.32	−0.40	−0.47
% dev.	(−0.2)	(−0.1)	(−0.1)	(−0.2)	(−0.3)	(−0.4)	(−0.5)	(−0.5)

(Continued)

Table 8.5: (Continued)

FY	2001	2002	2003	2004	2005	2006	2007	2008
CG	0.13	0.27	0.38	0.48	0.56	0.64	0.71	0.79
% dev.	(0.1)	(0.3)	(0.4)	(0.5)	(0.5)	(0.6)	(0.7)	(0.7)
EGS	-0.18	-0.27	-0.32	-0.34	-0.35	-0.34	-0.32	-0.31
% dev.	(-0.2)	(-0.3)	(-0.3)	(-0.3)	(-0.3)	(-0.3)	(-0.3)	(-0.3)
MGS	0.30	0.54	0.76	0.97	1.16	1.35	1.54	1.73
% dev.	(0.5)	(0.9)	(1.2)	(1.5)	(1.8)	(2.1)	(2.3)	(2.6)
GDEN	0.28	-0.66	-1.47	-2.32	-3.26	-4.29	-5.40	-6.55
% dev.	(0.1)	(-0.1)	(-0.3)	(-0.5)	(-0.7)	(-0.9)	(-1.1)	(-1.3)
CPN	-0.12	-0.37	-0.63	-0.92	-1.28	-1.68	-2.13	-2.59
% dev.	(-0.0)	(-0.1)	(-0.2)	(-0.4)	(-0.5)	(-0.6)	(-0.8)	(-1.0)
CHN	-0.11	-0.35	-0.60	-0.89	-1.24	-1.63	-2.06	-2.51
% dev.	(-0.0)	(-0.1)	(-0.2)	(-0.3)	(-0.5)	(-0.6)	(-0.8)	(-1.0)
CNN	-0.00	-0.02	-0.03	-0.03	-0.04	-0.05	-0.07	-0.08
% dev.	(-0.0)	(-0.2)	(-0.2)	(-0.4)	(-0.5)	(-0.6)	(-0.8)	(-1.0)
CGN	-0.00	-0.01	-0.03	-0.05	-0.09	-0.15	-0.22	-0.30
% dev.	(-0.0)	(-0.0)	(-0.0)	(-0.1)	(-0.1)	(-0.1)	(-0.2)	(-0.3)
IPN	-0.27	-0.40	-0.53	-0.88	-0.86	-1.05	-1.24	-1.42
% dev.	(-0.4)	(-0.6)	(-0.7)	(-0.9)	(-1.2)	(-1.4)	(-1.6)	(-1.8)

(Continued)

Table 8.5: (Continued)

FY	2001	2002	2003	2004	2005	2006	2007	2008
IHN	0.03	-0.02	-0.06	-0.12	-0.21	-0.31	-0.41	-0.51
% dev.	(0.2)	(-0.1)	(-0.4)	(-0.9)	(-1.5)	(-2.1)	(-2.8)	(-3.4)
IGN	-0.01	-0.02	-0.02	-0.03	-0.05	-0.06	-0.07	-0.08
% dev.	(-0.0)	(-0.1)	(-0.1)	(-0.1)	(-0.2)	(-0.3)	(-0.4)	(-0.4)
EGSN	-1.73	-2.11	-2.36	-2.53	-2.67	-2.80	-2.94	-3.07
% dev.	(-2.1)	(-2.4)	(-2.6)	(-2.6)	(-2.7)	(-2.7)	(-2.8)	(-2.8)
MGN	-2.42	-2.31	-2.19	-2.06	-1.94	-1.80	-1.65	-1.23
% dev.	(-3.1)	(-2.8)	(-2.6)	(-2.3)	(-2.1)	(-1.9)	(-1.9)	(-1.6)
PGDE	0.10	-0.05	-0.16	-0.26	-0.36	-0.47	-0.58	-0.71
% dev.	(0.1)	(-0.1)	(-0.2)	(-0.3)	(-0.4)	(-0.6)	(-0.7)	(-0.8)
PCP	-0.08	-0.17	-0.24	-0.30	-0.36	-0.43	-0.51	-0.59
% dev.	(-0.1)	(-0.2)	(-0.3)	(-0.3)	(-0.4)	(-0.5)	(-0.6)	(-0.7)
PCH	-0.08	-0.17	-0.24	-0.03	-0.36	-0.43	-0.51	-0.59
% dev.	(-0.1)	(-0.2)	(-0.3)	(-0.3)	(-0.4)	(-0.5)	(-0.6)	(-0.7)
PCG	-0.13	-0.26	-0.38	-0.49	-0.59	-0.70	-0.83	-0.96
% dev.	(-0.1)	(-0.3)	(-0.4)	(-0.5)	(-0.6)	(-0.7)	(-0.9)	(-1.0)
PIP	-0.19	-0.29	-0.56	-0.69	-0.81	-0.93	-1.05	-1.13
% dev.	(-0.2)	(-0.4)	(-0.6)	(-0.8)	(-0.9)	(-1.0)	(-1.2)	(-1.3)
PIH	-0.10	-0.22	-0.34	-0.45	-0.57	-0.69	-0.82	-0.96
% dev.	(-0.1)	(-0.2)	(-0.3)	(-0.4)	(-0.6)	(-0.7)	(-0.8)	(-0.9)

(Continued)

Table 8.5: (Continued)

FY	2001	2002	2003	2004	2005	2006	2007	2008
PIG	-0.24	-0.44	-0.59	-0.71	-0.81	-0.92	-1.04	-1.17
% dev.	(-0.2)	(-0.4)	(-0.6)	(-0.7)	(-0.8)	(-0.9)	(-1.0)	(-1.2)
PEGS	-1.76	-1.98	-2.09	-2.15	-2.21	-2.26	-2.32	-2.38
% dev.	(-1.9)	(-2.1)	(-2.2)	(-2.3)	(-2.4)	(-2.4)	(-2.5)	(-2.5)
PMGS	-4.76	-4.94	-5.11	-5.28	-5.45	-5.63	-5.81	-5.99
% dev.	(-4.6)	(-4.7)	(-4.7)	(-4.8)	(-4.8)	(-4.9)	(-4.9)	(-4.9)
PMY	-6.02	-6.25	-6.46	-6.68	-6.89	-7.11	-7.34	-7.57
% dev.	(-4.2)	(-4.3)	(-4.3)	(-4.4)	(-4.4)	(-4.4)	(-4.5)	(-4.5)
PX	-0.53	-0.77	-0.90	-0.98	-1.04	-1.11	-1.18	-1.25
% dev.	(-0.6)	(-0.7)	(-0.8)	(-0.9)	(-1.0)	(-1.0)	(-1.1)	(-1.2)
PEXY	-1.79	-2.01	-2.12	-2.19	-2.25	-2.30	-2.36	-2.43
% dev.	(-1.8)	(-2.0)	(-2.1)	(-2.1)	(-2.2)	(-2.2)	(-2.3)	(-2.3)
PEX$	3.04	2.81	2.69	2.61	2.55	2.49	2.42	2.36
% dev.	(2.6)	(2.3)	(2.2)	(2.2)	(2.1)	(2.1)	(2.0)	(2.0)
CPI	-0.09	-0.20	-0.30	-0.40	-0.50	-0.60	-0.72	-0.84
% dev.	(-0.1)	(-0.2)	(-0.3)	(-0.4)	(-0.5)	(-0.6)	(-0.8)	(-1.0)
EXR	-5.00	-5.00	-5.00	-5.00	-5.00	-5.00	-5.00	-5.00
% dev.	(-4.0)	(-4.1)	(-4.4)	(-4.7)	(-4.4)	(-4.3)	(-4.4)	(-5.0)
NLE	-0.68	-1.99	-3.65	-5.54	-7.55	-9.43	-11.02	-12.19
% dev.	(-0.0)	(-0.0)	(-0.1)	(-0.1)	(-0.1)	(-0.2)	(-0.2)	(-0.2)

(Continued)

Table 8.5:   (Continued)

FY	2001	2002	2003	2004	2005	2006	2007	2008
UR	0.01	0.03	0.06	0.08	0.12	0.14	0.17	0.19
% dev.	(0.2)	(0.5)	(1.0)	(1.5)	(2.1)	(2.6)	(3.2)	(3.6)
M2CD	-0.07	-0.17	-0.30	-0.49	-0.76	-1.11	-1.54	-2.02
% dev.	(-0.0)	(-0.0)	(-0.0)	(-0.1)	(-0.1)	(-0.1)	(-0.2)	(-0.2)
INTPR	0.00	-0.01	-0.01	-0.02	-0.03	-0.04	-0.04	-0.05
% dev.	(0.2)	(-0.3)	(-0.7)	(-1.2)	(-1.7)	(-2.3)	(-2.9)	(-3.4)
TXG	0.03	-0.17	-0.31	-0.44	-0.58	-0.71	-0.83	-0.93
% dev.	(0.1)	(-0.4)	(-0.6)	(-0.9)	(-1.2)	(-1.4)	(-1.6)	(-1.8)
KLGBT	0.00	0.01	0.11	0.19	0.29	0.42	0.56	0.72
% dev.	(0.0)	(0.0)	(0.0)	(0.0)	(0.0)	(0.0)	(0.0)	(0.1)
YDH	-0.00	-0.46	-0.72	-1.08	-1.52	-2.03	-2.57	-3.12
% dev.	(-0.0)	(-0.2)	(-0.3)	(-0.4)	(-0.5)	(-0.7)	(-0.9)	(-1.1)
YE	0.10	-0.19	-0.31	-0.54	-0.88	-1.29	-1.74	-2.21
% dev.	(0.0)	(-0.1)	(-0.1)	(-0.2)	(-0.4)	(-0.6)	(-0.8)	(-1.0)
YC	-0.09	-0.09	-0.09	-0.12	-0.15	-0.17	-0.16	-0.12
% dev.	(-0.2)	(-0.2)	(-0.2)	(-0.2)	(-0.3)	(-0.3)	(-0.3)	(-0.2)
HFA	-0.06	-1.85	-4.08	-6.34	-8.59	-10.84	-13.09	-15.03
% dev.	(-0.0)	(-0.1)	(-0.3)	(-0.5)	(-0.6)	(-0.8)	(-0.9)	(-1.1)

(Continued)

Table 8.5: (Continued)

FY	2001	2002	2003	2004	2005	2006	2007	2008
HNFA	-0.02	-0.22	-0.55	-0.98	-1.46	-1.97	-2.48	-2.95
% dev.	(-0.0)	(-0.0)	(-0.1)	(-0.1)	(-0.2)	(-0.3)	(-0.3)	(-0.4)
HTD	0.22	-0.08	-0.29	-0.45	-0.58	-0.71	-0.82	-0.96
% dev.	(0.1)	(-0.0)	(-0.1)	(-0.1)	(-0.1)	(-0.2)	(-0.2)	(-0.2)
TB	1.09	0.70	0.41	0.18	-0.03	-0.24	-0.47	-0.74
% dev.	(23.5)	(11.2)	(6.0)	(2.6)	(-0.4)	(-3.5)	(-6.9)	(-10.6)
TB$ (b.$)	14.17	10.60	7.75	5.28	2.93	0.53	-2.05	-4.87
% dev.	(27.5)	(16.1)	(10.7)	(7.1)	(4.0)	(0.7)	(-2.9)	(-6.7)
CBP	0.57	-0.60	-1.01	-1.36	-1.69	-2.02	-2.38	-2.77
% dev.	(3.6)	(-3.2)	(-4.8)	(-6.4)	(-7.8)	(-9.3)	(-10.7)	(-13.4)

Note: Deviation: (Scenario − Final Test); % deviation: (Scenario − Final Test)/Final Test * 100 (%)
Source: Simulated and compiled by author.

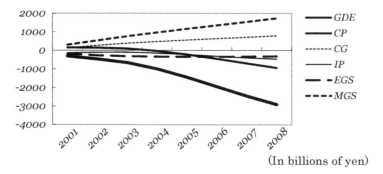

(In billions of yen)

Figure 8.5: Deviation of real GDE and its major components from the final test, FY2001–2008.
Source: Simulated and developed by the author.

However, the impacts of the 5 yen appreciation on the nominal economy are somewhat different from the impacts on the real value economy. Due to the declines in prices and deflators through yen appreciation, most nominal GDE components have negative impacts from the initial year of the simulation, and the negative impacts are larger than real values over the period because of declines in both real values and deflators. As a result, nominal GDE declines by 3.26 trillion yen in FY2005 and by 6.55 trillion yen in FY2008, in deviation, as compared to the baseline simulation, although it increases by 0.28 trillion yen in FY2001.

The large negative impacts on the nominal GDE are mainly dependent on the decreases in nominal exports since export prices in terms of yen (PEXY) fall with pass-through, in which the export prices decline by 1.8 per cent in FY2001, by 2.2 per cent in FY2005 and by 2.3 per cent in FY2008, in per cent deviation, as compared to the baseline simulation, while output price (PX) declines only by 0.6 per cent in FY2001, by 1.0 per cent in FY2005 and by 1.2 per cent in FY2008 in comparison with the baseline simulation. As a result, general deflator, PGDE, also declines by 0.4 per cent in FY2005 and by 0.8 per cent in FY2008 in comparison with the baseline simulation, as illustrated in Figure 8.6. Thus, the yen appreciation accelerates the spiral between the deflation and the yen appreciation.

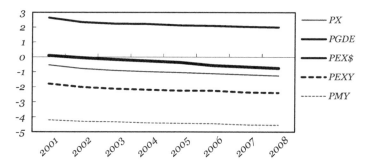

Figure 8.6: Per cent deviation of output price (PX), PGDE, export prices (PEXY) and export prices in US$ (PEX$) and import prices (PMY) from the final test, FY2001–2008.
Source: Simulated and developed by the author.

Moreover, the effects on export prices in terms of US$ (PEX$) is absorbed by the pass-through mechanism, so that the export prices in terms of US dollar rise by only 2.6 per cent in FY2001, by 2.1 per cent in FY2005 and by 2.0 per cent in FY2008, in terms of per cent deviation, as compared to the baseline simulation, which may be smaller than the impacts on import prices (PMY). As noted earlier, the pass-through mechanism distorts the effects of exchange rate changes on trade and trade balance. In the case of Japan, the pass-through coefficient is over 0.3 in terms of elasticity, which is fairly large because the changes in the yen rate to the US dollar is absorbed by changes in yen base export prices by over 30 per cent as a direct effect[6] [see Equation (3.10) in Appendix A].

In addition, we can see that trade imbalance could not be adjusted efficiently by the yen appreciation in this simulation. That is due to the weak Marshall–Lerner stable condition as discussed in Chapter 7. As a result, trade balance in terms of yen increases in the initial four years and thereafter decreases, but the extent of the adjustment may be very limited. On the contrary, the impacts on current accounts are fairly larger than on the trade balance because service balance and income balance are more sensitive to changes in exchange rates. Therefore, the current accounts are adjusted from the second year and decline by 1.69 trillion yen in FY2005 and by 277 trillion yen in FY2008, in terms of deviation, in comparison with the final test.

End Notes

[1] As we performed Keynes multiplier tests by changing nominal government expenditures and nominal personal income tax, the multiplier in terms of real value is calculated as follows.

Multiplier $= \Delta GDE/\Delta IG$ for the government investment increase case

Multiplier $= \Delta GDE/\Delta(TXI/PGDP*100)$ for the income tax cut case

[2] Hori *et al.* (1998) summarized Keynes multiplier of Japan conducted by the EPA (Economic Planning Agency) in the past, employing the EPA models. Interestingly, the multiplier was fairly different by model and by period developed, despite the same institute developed the models, as follows.

Multiplier of Government Expenditure Increases Implemented by the EPA.

Model Project (Tested Year)	Multiplier			Notes Real/ Nominal
	1st year	2nd year	3rd year	
Pilot model (1967)	2.17	4.27	5.01	Nominal
Master model (1970)	2.02	4.14	4.51	Nominal
Pilot model SP-15 (1974)	2.27	4.77	4.42	Nominal
Pilot model SP-17 (1976)	1.85	3.34	—	Nominal
Pilot model SP-18 (1977)	1.34	2.32	2.77	Nominal
EPA world model 1st version (1981)	1.27	2.25	2.72	Nominal
EPA world model 2nd version (1985)	1.47	2.25	2.72	Nominal
5th Econometric committee (1977)	1.81	3.29	3.66	Real
6th Econometric committee (1980)	1.50	1.57	1.25	Real
8th Econometric committee (1989)	1.18	1.50	1.56	Real
10th Econometric committee (1996)	1.30	1.45 ·	1.24	Real

As demonstrated, by and large, the multiplier was getting lower over time and drastically declined after the oil crises, which explains the wage income share's decline during the oil crises in the 1970s.

[3] In the actual economy, personal income tax cut policy stimulates the economy, and the income tax revenue may increase by natural increase in the revenue along with the economic expansion. However, in this scenario simulation, one trillion yen income tax is cut as compared to the final test projection in order to make comparison with the nominal government investment increase scenario.

[4] Interestingly, the extent of pass-through is drastically different on a sectoral basis and its impacts on sectoral real exports are also different among sectors, which heavily depend on sectoral capacity utilization rate and hence the supply capacity. See Adams, Gangnes and Shishido (1993).

CHAPTER 9

Long-Term Economic Forecasts up to FY2030

With the large structural deflationary gap and the other macro-imbalances, the Japanese economy will be facing an uncertain future. This chapter, therefore, performs some long-term scenario forecasts. Four scenario forecasts are conducted, including one baseline and three alternative policy scenario forecasts. One of the advantages to utilize econometric models is to evaluate the impacts of policy changes on various dimensions of the economy. Accordingly, this chapter examines the impacts of policy changes on the economy through conducting scenario simulations and forecasting the Japanese economy up to FY2030.

9.1. Baseline Forecast: A Most-Likely Scenario

The baseline forecast is performed as a most-likely scenario. In the baseline scenario, we assume that the world economic environment and the current Japanese trends, including economic policies and major exogenous variables of the Japanese economy in the model, will not change drastically in the future. (See exogenous variable set for the baseline in Appendix D.)

In accordance with the baseline forecast, as shown in Table 9.1, the Japanese economy will continue its impoverished growth in the future, in which it is expected that annual growth rate of real GDE will be 2.7 per cent in FY2010, following which the real growth rate will be declining to 1.0 per cent in FY2011, 0.9 per cent in FY2012 and thereafter 0.6 per cent in FY2014 and 0.7 per cent in FY2015. The annual average growth rates are, however, expected to be a little bit higher in the latter half of the 2010s. Thereafter, the economy will probably achieve 1.0 to 1.5 per cent annual growth rate in the 2020s. As a result, it is expected that the annual average growth rate of real GDE will be 0.91 per cent in the 2010s and 1.45 per cent in the 2020s, respectively, and the level of real GDE will

161

Table 9.1:   The baseline forecast FY2010–2030.

(in trillions yen, %).

FY	2010	2011	2012	2013	2014	2015	2020	2025	2030
				Estimated-Forecasts					
GDE	541.0	546.6	551.2	554.7	558.1	561.9	592.3	636.0	684.0
%	(2.7)	(1.0)	(0.9)	(0.6)	(0.6)	(0.7)	(1.3)	(1.5)	(1.5)
GDPC	635.1	636.5	637.9	639.2	640.4	641.6	647.5	673.9	704.6
%	(−0.3)	(0.2)	(0.2)	(0.2)	(0.2)	(0.2)	(0.2)	(0.8)	(0.9)
KP	891.4	906.4	921.7	936.8	951.8	966.7	1045	1135	1239
%	(1.6)	(1.7)	(1.7)	(1.7)	(1.6)	(1.6)	(1.6)	(1.7)	(1.8)
CUR	74.8	75.3	75.5	75.3	75.2	75.2	78.5	85.1	92.1
%	(4.9)	(0.7)	(0.3)	(−0.2)	(−0.2)	(−0.0)	(1.4)	(1.7)	(1.6)
DGAP	94.1	90.0	86.7	84.5	82.3	79.7	55.2	37.9	20.6
%	(−14.8)	(−5.3)	(−4.0)	(−2.6)	(−2.5)	(−3.0)	(−9.7)	(−8.7)	(−15.0)
LPI	114.4	114.9	115.4	115.9	116.3	116.7	118.5	123.6	128.8
%	(−0.1)	(0.5)	(0.4)	(0.4)	(0.4)	(0.4)	(0.3)	(0.8)	(0.8)
TFPI	104.1	104.0	103.8	103.6	103.4	103.2	102.0	103.5	105.0
%	(−0.6)	(−0.2)	(−0.2)	(−0.2)	(−0.2)	(−0.2)	(−0.1)	(0.3)	(0.3)
CP	307.0	303.3	301.8	300.8	300.0	299.4	301.8	310.8	319.9
%	(1.0)	(−1.2)	(−0.5)	(−0.3)	(−0.3)	(−0.2)	(0.4)	(0.6)	(0.5)
CH	300.2	296.5	295.1	294.1	293.3	292.7	294.9	303.3	311.7
%	(1.1)	(−1.2)	(−0.5)	(−0.3)	(−0.3)	(−0.2)	(0.4)	(0.6)	(0.5)
IH	12.7	13.2	13.7	13.7	13.7	13.6	14.8	17.2	18.1
%	(1.3)	(3.9)	(4.0)	(0.0)	(−0.6)	(−0.7)	(3.4)	(2.3)	(0.4)
IP	74.4	76.9	78.2	79.0	79.7	80.4	87.1	96.9	107.8
%	(5.3)	(3.4)	(1.7)	(1.0)	(0.8)	(0.9)	(2.0)	(2.2)	(2.1)
CG	101.4	102.2	103.1	104.1	105.4	106.7	114.5	122.8	131.8
%	(0.8)	(0.7)	(0.9)	(1.0)	(1.2)	(1.3)	(1.4)	(1.4)	(1.5)
IG	18.8	19.7	20.1	20.3	20.4	20.5	21.0	21.1	21.0
%	(−10.4)	(4.8)	(1.7)	(1.1)	(0.6)	(0.5)	(0.3)	(0.0)	(−0.1)
EGS	81.3	88.3	93.9	98.5	102.4	106.0	122.1	138.6	157.2
%	(11.8)	(8.7)	(6.3)	(4.9)	(4.0)	(3.5)	(2.7)	(2.5)	(2.6)
MGS	57.0	59.7	62.1	64.0	65.7	67.1	72.3	74.8	75.0
%	(8.3)	(4.8)	(4.0)	(3.2)	(2.6)	(2.2)	(1.1)	(0.4)	(−0.2)
GDEN	475.1	472.9	473.2	473.1	472.7	472.4	484.9	520.0	564.4
%	(0.2)	(−0.4)	(0.1)	(−0.0)	(−0.0)	(−0.0)	(1.0)	(1.6)	(1.7)

(Continued)

Table 9.1: (*Continued*)

FY	Estimated-Forecasts								
	2010	2011	2012	2013	2014	2015	2020	2025	2030
CPN	275.3	268.2	265.1	263.0	261.4	260.0	259.9	270.6	284.1
%	(−1.9)	(−2.6)	(−1.2)	(−0.8)	(−0.6)	(−0.5)	(0.4)	(1.0)	(0.9)
CHN	269.2	262.4	259.3	257.3	255.7	254.3	254.1	264.3	276.9
%	(−1.8)	(−2.6)	(−1.2)	(−0.8)	(−0.6)	(−0.5)	(0.4)	(0.9)	(0.9)
CGN	95.8	96.7	97.6	98.5	99.5	100.4	106.6	116.0	128.1
%	(0.9)	(0.9)	(1.0)	(1.0)	(1.0)	(1.1)	(1.4)	(1.9)	(2.0)
IPN	67.0	69.2	70.4	71.0	71.5	71.9	77.0	85.7	95.5
%	(5.2)	(3.3)	(1.7)	(0.9)	(0.6)	(0.6)	(1.9)	(2.2)	(2.2)
IHN	13.1	13.6	14.1	14.1	14.0	13.9	15.0	17.6	19.0
%	(1.2)	(4.0)	(4.0)	(−0.1)	(−0.8)	(−0.9)	(3.3)	(2.7)	(1.0)
IGN	18.6	19.4	19.7	19.9	20.0	20.0	20.3	20.7	21.1
%	(−12.5)	(4.2)	(1.6)	(1.0)	(0.4)	(0.3)	(0.4)	(0.4)	(0.3)
JPN	0.28	0.76	0.81	0.69	0.59	0.54	0.85	1.09	1.19
%	(−107.8)	(169.4)	(6.3)	(−15.0)	(−14.3)	(−6.9)	(10.2)	(2.8)	(2.1)
EGSN	69.9	77.3	83.2	87.6	91.1	94.0	105.7	115.4	125.5
%	(8.8)	(10.7)	(7.6)	(5.3)	(4.0)	(3.2)	(2.1)	(1.6)	(1.7)
MGSN	64.9	72.3	77.7	81.9	85.4	88.6	100.6	107.1	110.2
%	(7.9)	(11.4)	(7.5)	(5.3)	(4.3)	(3.7)	(1.9)	(0.9)	(0.5)
PGDE	87.8	86.5	85.9	85.3	84.7	84.1	81.9	81.8	82.5
%	(−2.4)	(−1.5)	(−0.8)	(−0.7)	(−0.7)	(−0.7)	(−0.3)	(0.1)	(0.2)
PCP	89.7	88.4	87.8	87.4	87.1	86.8	86.1	87.1	88.8
%	(−2.9)	(−1.4)	(−0.7)	(−0.4)	(−0.4)	(−0.3)	(−0.0)	(0.3)	(0.4)
PCH	89.7	88.5	87.9	87.5	87.2	86.9	86.2	87.1	88.8
%	(−2.9)	(−1.3)	(−0.7)	(−0.4)	(−0.4)	(−0.3)	(−0.0)	(0.3)	(0.4)
PCG	94.4	94.6	94.7	94.6	94.4	94.1	93.0	94.5	97.2
%	(0.1)	(0.2)	(0.1)	(−0.1)	(−0.2)	(−0.3)	(−0.0)	(0.5)	(0.6)
PIP	90.1	90.3	90.5	90.4	90.2	89.8	88.3	88.2	88.7
%	(−0.1)	(0.3)	(0.1)	(−0.0)	(−0.3)	(−0.4)	(−0.1)	(−0.0)	(0.1)
PIH	102.8	102.8	102.8	102.8	102.6	102.3	101.1	102.2	105.1
%	(−0.1)	(0.1)	(0.0)	(−0.0)	(−0.2)	(−0.3)	(−0.1)	(0.4)	(0.6)
PIG	98.8	98.2	98.1	98.0	97.9	97.6	96.9	98.4	100.8
%	(−2.3)	(−0.6)	(−0.1)	(−0.1)	(−0.2)	(−0.3)	(0.1)	(0.4)	(0.5)
PEGS	86.0	87.6	88.6	89.0	88.9	88.7	86.6	83.2	79.8
%	(−2.7)	(1.8)	(1.3)	(0.4)	(−0.0)	(−0.3)	(−0.6)	(−0.9)	(−0.8)

(*Continued*)

Table 9.1: (*Continued*)

FY	| Estimated-Forecasts								
	2010	2011	2012	2013	2014	2015	2020	2025	2030
PMGS	114.0	121.2	125.2	127.9	130.0	132.0	139.3	143.2	147.0
%	(−0.4)	(6.3)	(3.3)	(2.1)	(1.7)	(1.5)	(0.8)	(0.5)	(0.6)
PMY	120.6	129.6	134.8	138.1	140.8	143.3	152.5	157.4	162.3
%	(−1.7)	(7.5)	(4.0)	(2.5)	(2.0)	(1.7)	(0.9)	(0.5)	(0.7)
PX	103.1	104.1	104.8	105.1	105.3	105.3	105.5	106.0	106.7
%	(0.5)	(1.0)	(0.6)	(0.3)	(0.1)	(0.0)	(0.1)	(0.1)	(0.1)
CPI	96.4	95.7	95.2	94.8	94.4	94.0	92.7	93.8	96.3
%	(−1.3)	(−0.7)	(−0.5)	(−0.4)	(−0.4)	(−0.4)	(−0.1)	(0.4)	(0.6)
PEXY	96.0	97.6	98.7	99.1	99.0	98.8	96.7	93.2	89.8
%	(−2.9)	(1.7)	(1.1)	(0.3)	(−0.0)	(−0.2)	(−0.5)	(−0.8)	(−0.7)
EXR	83.5	85.5	87.5	87.9	87.7	87.2	81.7	73.4	65.6
%	(−10.0)	(2.6)	(2.2)	(0.4)	(−0.2)	(−0.6)	(−1.7)	(−2.3)	(−2.1)
PLAND	70.1	67.8	67.7	67.9	68.2	68.4	70.8	73.3	74.3
%	(−0.5)	(−3.4)	(−0.1)	(0.3)	(0.4)	(0.4)	(0.9)	(0.5)	(0.2)
M2CD	781.9	792.0	801.9	811.4	820.5	829.4	876.3	936.7	1010
%	(1.5)	(1.3)	(1.3)	(1.2)	(1.2)	(1.1)	(1.2)	(1.4)	(1.6)
INTPR	1.65	1.56	1.69	1.64	1.58	1.53	1.39	1.41	1.44
%	(−12.1)	(−5.8)	(8.8)	(−3.3)	(−3.4)	(−3.3)	(−0.6)	(0.5)	(0.3)
INTGB	1.48	1.39	1.49	1.44	1.40	1.36	1.29	1.35	1.43
%	(−7.5)	(−6.1)	(6.9)	(−3.1)	(−3.0)	(−2.8)	(0.2)	(1.3)	(0.9)
WN	94.9	94.5	94.0	93.4	92.8	92.2	91.1	93.4	96.8
%	(−0.2)	(−0.4)	(−0.5)	(−0.6)	(−0.6)	(−0.6)	(0.1)	(0.7)	(0.6)
YE	245.0	241.6	239.1	236.2	233.4	230.9	227.3	235.8	247.1
%	(−2.5)	(−1.4)	(−1.0)	(−1.2)	(−1.2)	(−1.1)	(0.2)	(1.0)	(0.9)
YDH	292.3	288.3	286.3	283.4	280.7	278.3	275.6	285.5	298.3
%	(0.8)	(−1.4)	(−0.7)	(−1.0)	(−1.0)	(−0.9)	(0.3)	(0.9)	(0.8)
YU	34.3	33.2	32.8	33.0	33.2	33.4	35.0	37.3	40.4
%	(−5.7)	(−3.1)	(−1.3)	(0.5)	(0.7)	(0.7)	(1.1)	(1.4)	(1.8)
YDIV	5.1	5.8	6.2	6.4	6.5	6.6	7.2	7.4	7.4
%	(41.9)	(13.4)	(6.6)	(3.6)	(2.4)	(1.9)	(1.2)	(0.3)	(0.0)
YC	40.1	45.5	48.5	50.3	51.5	52.5	56.3	58.2	58.3
%	(41.9)	(13.4)	(6.6)	(3.6)	(2.4)	(1.9)	(1.2)	(0.3)	(0.0)
RYH	88.1	86.6	85.7	85.2	84.8	84.4	83.5	83.7	84.5
%	(−3.7)	(−1.7)	(−1.0)	(−0.6)	(−0.5)	(−0.4)	(−0.1)	(0.1)	(0.2)

(*Continued*)

Table 9.1: (Continued)

FY	2010	2011	2012	2013	2014	2015	2020	2025	2030
				Estimated-Forecasts					
TOPIX	937.9	962.4	1035	1080	1104	1120	1367	1643	1741
%	(3.7)	(2.6)	(7.5)	(4.3)	(2.2)	(1.4)	(5.6)	(2.5)	(0.4)
HFA	1375	1365	1359	1358	1360	1362	1401	1482	1566
%	(−1.3)	(−0.6)	(−0.3)	(0.0)	(0.1)	(0.2)	(0.8)	(1.1)	(1.1)
HNFA	950.0	932.9	914.6	889.4	874.6	863.7	899.2	1044	1182
%	(2.5)	(−1.8)	(−2.0)	(−2.8)	(−1.7)	(−1.2)	(2.3)	(3.1)	(2.1)
HTD	373.6	374.6	375.6	376.6	377.7	379.0	386.3	392.0	394.6
%	(0.2)	(0.3)	(0.3)	(0.3)	(0.3)	(0.4)	(0.5)	(0.3)	(0.1)
SH	13.1	16.0	17.0	16.1	15.0	13.9	11.5	11.3	11.4
%	(−16.7)	(21.7)	(6.7)	(−5.3)	(−6.8)	(−7.2)	(−1.7)	(0.2)	(0.3)
NP	12740	12730	12720	12710	12690	12670	12430	12150	11840
%	(−0.1)	(−0.1)	(−0.1)	(−0.1)	(−0.2)	(−0.2)	(−0.4)	(−0.6)	(−0.7)
NL	6591	6576	6561	6548	6535	6524	6483	6473	6495
%	(−0.3)	(−0.2)	(−0.2)	(−0.2)	(−0.2)	(−0.2)	(−0.0)	(−0.0)	(0.1)
NLE	6247	6219	6193	6172	6155	6142	6142	6172	6196
%	(−0.3)	(−0.5)	(−0.4)	(−0.3)	(−0.3)	(−0.2)	(0.1)	(0.1)	(0.1)
UR(%)	5.22	5.43	5.61	5.74	5.81	5.84	5.26	4.64	4.60
%	(1.0)	(4.0)	(3.3)	(2.2)	(1.3)	(0.3)	(−3.0)	(−1.7)	(0.7)
TXG	47.7	48.2	48.6	48.7	48.6	48.6	51.0	55.1	57.9
%	(6.8)	(1.2)	(0.8)	(0.2)	(−0.1)	(−0.1)	(1.6)	(1.4)	(0.8)
TXI	13.5	13.3	13.2	13.1	13.0	12.9	13.6	15.4	17.1
%	(0.9)	(−2.2)	(−0.1)	(−0.8)	(−1.0)	(−1.0)	(2.4)	(2.5)	(1.8)
TXC	11.2	12.2	12.8	13.1	13.3	13.4	15.2	17.1	17.9
%	(39.0)	(9.3)	(5.3)	(2.2)	(1.2)	(1.1)	(3.3)	(1.7)	(0.5)
GEXGE	85.2	92.7	93.7	94.5	95.2	95.8	99.4	103.9	109.3
%	(0.9)	(8.8)	(1.0)	(0.9)	(0.7)	(0.7)	(0.8)	(1.0)	(1.1)
KLGBT	911.6	941.9	972.8	1004	1036	1069	1238	1406	1582
%	(3.3)	(3.3)	(3.3)	(3.2)	(3.2)	(3.2)	(2.8)	(2.5)	(2.3)
RKLG	191.9	199.2	205.6	212.3	219.3	226.4	255.2	270.4	280.2
%	(3.1)	(3.8)	(3.2)	(3.3)	(3.3)	(3.2)	(1.8)	(0.9)	(0.7)
TB	7.25	6.94	7.17	7.28	7.17	6.93	6.61	9.73	16.44
%	(9.7)	(−4.2)	(3.2)	(1.5)	(−1.5)	(−3.4)	(3.7)	(10.5)	(10.8)
CBP	18.20	16.23	17.06	18.68	18.66	18.36	17.53	20.33	27.08
%	(16.5)	(−10.8)	(5.1)	(9.5)	(−0.1)	(−1.6)	(0.9)	(4.4)	(6.5)

Source: Forecasted and compiled by the author.

be 592.3 trillion yen in FY2020, 536.0 trillion yen in FY2025 and 684.0 trillion yen in FY2030.

As for the real GDE components, real domestic expenditures, including real private consumption, real housing investment and real government investment, will be stagnant in line with the lower growth rates of real GDE in the 2010s and the 2020s. Particularly, the annual average rate of changes in private final consumption expenditure will probably be stagnant at minus 0.17 per cent in the 2010s and remain lower at 0.58 per cent even in the 2020s. In addition, growth rates of real private non-housing investment are also expected to be sluggish in the 2010s and 2020s, and, as a result, in the first half of 2020s the level of non-housing investment will be barely recovered to the level of FY2008 just before the world financial crisis.

On the other hand, real exports of goods and services are expected to continue its fairly steady growth in the 2010s and the 2020s along with a strong growth performance of the world economy. In addition, real government consumption expenditure will probably increase in line with increases of welfare expenditures, which depend on increases in the amount of aged population during the next two decades. As a result, the economic growth of Japan is expected to be led by the steady growth of government consumption and external demands through exports with accumulating government deficits and trade surplus, which may be the similar pattern in the 1990s and the 2000s (see Figure 9.1).

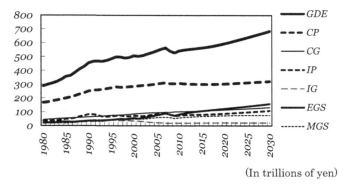

(In trillions of yen)

Figure 9.1:   Real GDE and its major components in the baseline forecast up to FY2030 (Forecasts: FY2010–2030).

Source: Forecasted and developed by the author.

Accordingly, private final consumption expenditure will probably remain stagnant as it was during the lost two decades in the 1990s and the 2000s, in which wage income will continue to be stagnant in the coming two decades up to FY2030 in the baseline forecast. Moreover, behind this situation, household disposable income will be stagnant. As a result, household income share in total of household income and corporate income is expected to decline up until the mid-2020s, from 88.1 in FY2010 to 86.6 in FY2011, to 84.4 in FY2015, to 83.5 in FY2020 and slightly increasing in the latter half of the 2020s to 83.7 in FY2025 and to 84.4 in FY2030. In other words, the corporate sector will probably continue its present behaviors to keep fairly steady profits and to accumulate savings.

With respect to the supply-side of the economy, however, real GDP capacity is expected to grow sluggishly in the 2010s since the world financial crisis damaged the economy and investment behaviors in FY2008–2009, which will result in the lower growth of real GDP capacity in the 2010s. Even in the 2020s, the annual average growth rate of real GDP capacity is expected to be stagnant, depending on the lower growth of the demand-side economy. As a result, total factor productivity (TFPI) will probably be stagnant at negative growth due to the sharp declines in investment in the 2010s and turn to positive growth at 0.2–0.3 per cent in the 2020s, but highly stagnant.

Therefore, these situations will result in macro-imbalances, including high rate of unemployment, large trade surplus and fiscal deficits. It is expected that the rate of unemployment will remain high at around 5.4–5.6 per cent in the 2010s and 4.6–5.0 per cent in the 2020s in spite of declines in the number of active population. As a result, the number of employed will probably be 62.19 million in FY2011, 61.42 million in FY2015, 61.42 million in FY2020 and 61.96 million in FY2030 and, therefore, the stagnant economy will not be able to absorb the bulk of unemployed labor in the baseline forecast.

As for trade balance, the trade surplus is expected to be increasing in the 2010s and in the 2020s and will probably be 6.93 trillion yen in FY2015, 6.61 trillion yen in FY2020, 9.73 trillion yen in FY2025 and 16.44 trillion yen in FY2030. In addition, current balance surplus will be expanding with increases in net income transfers from the rest of the world at 16.23 trillion yen in FY2011, 18.36 trillion yen in FY2015, 17.53 trillion yen in FY2025 and 27.08 trillion yen FY2030, which will be resulted from increases in foreign investment in the rest of the world, particularly from increases in FDI.

On the other hand, it is expected that the government debt outstanding will also increase in the future. The total accumulated national government debts will probably be 941.9 trillion yen in FY2011, following which it will probably be 1,069.3 trillion yen in FY2015, 1,237.7 trillion yen in FY2020, 1,406.2 trillion yen in FY2025 and 1,581.5 trillion yen in FY2030. As a result, the ratio of accumulated government debt to nominal GDE is also expected to increase, in which the ratio will probably worsen to 1.99 in FY2011, to 2.26 in FY2015, to 2.55 in FY2020, 2.70 in FY2025 and to 2.51 in FY2030, as shown in Table 9.1.

As discussed earlier, the deflationary gap is expected to decrease in the future, in which the level of the gap will probably be 79.7 trillion yen in FY2015, 55.2 trillion yen in FY2020 and 20.6 trillion yen in FY2030. Although the deflationary gap will decrease, this may be a result from less dynamism within the Japanese economy. This scenario is because the growth rates of GDP capacity will be stagnant along with the lower growth rates of the demand-side in the 2010s and the 2020s, which may be different from the dynamic economic situation in the 1980s, in which the demand-side was strongly following the strong supply-side growth, as shown in Figure 9.2. In other words, it is expected that Japan will probably lose its economic vitality in both the demand-side and the supply-side of the economy just as the UK and the US experienced in the past, if current Japanese economic trends cannot be rectified with robust policies.

With respect to prices and deflators, it is expected that the current declines will continue by the mid-2020s in the future in the baseline forecast, as demonstrated in Figure 9.3. As the downward spiral continues with the appreciating yen and export declines, the pass-through effect is felt increasingly in the Japanese economy. Yen appreciation to the US dollar will probably continue in the future during the forecasted period, which will be one of the causes of decline in domestic prices and deflators.

According to the baseline forecast, the general deflator in terms of PGDE will continue to decline up until the mid-2020s and slightly increase in the latter half of the 2020s. As a result, PGDE will be declining from 86.5 in FY2011 to 84.1 in FY2015, to 81.9 in FY2020 and will slightly be increasing to 82.5 in FY2030. On the other hand, output prices will

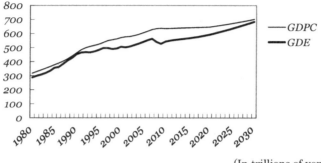

(In trillions of yen)

Figure 9.2: Real GDE (GDP) and real GDP capacity (GDPC) in the baseline forecast, FY2010–2030.

Source: Forecasted and developed by the author.

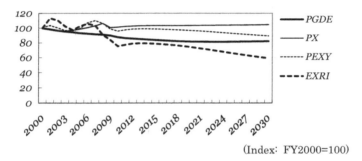

(Index: FY2000=100)

Figure 9.3: PGDE, output price (PX), export price (PEXY) and exchange rate index in the baseline forecast.

Source: Forecasted and developed by the author.

probably be fairly stable depending on the changes in wage rates, import prices and labor productivity. As a result, export prices will be declining depending on changes in output price, exchange rates and wage rates, which will accelerate yen appreciation.

9.2. Household Income Increase Scenario Forecasts

As noted, the household disposable income, as a whole, has been stagnant since the mid-1970s, except for the bubble period, which might have resulted in the long-term stagnation of the demand-side, particularly after the bursting of the bubble economy. Accordingly, this section conducts two alternative policy scenario simulations relating to household income expansion policy scenarios and examines the impacts of policy changes on the economy utilizing the demand-supply integrated econometric model.

In performing the alternative policy simulations from FY2011 to FY2030, we consider two assumptions, in which (1) corporate sector increases dividend yields (the ratio of dividend income to corporate income) for household dividend income by 2 per cent points, and (2) central government reduces corporate income tax by 2.5 trillion yen and the corporate sector increases compensation of employees by the same amounts of corporate income tax cut by 2.5 trillion yen, from FY2011 onward. In the first assumption, as noted earlier, the Japanese corporate sector has increased its accumulated savings in place of increasing wage income, which distorted the income allocation and resulted in the stagnation of household expenditures. Therefore, in this assumption, the corporate sector transfers its profits to the household sector through dividend yield increases by 2.0 per cent, which is equivalent to 1.15 trillion yen in FY2011 in the baseline. Accordingly, we examine the effects of increases of household income and decreases of corporate income with the same amounts between both sectors.

On the other hand, in the second assumption, the central government transfers government money by 2.5 trillion yen, issuing the same amounts of government bonds, to the household sector, during the whole projected period, by way of the corporate sector, Therefore, we examine the impact of household income increases by 2.5 trillion yen on the economy. The amounts of 2.5 trillion yen are equivalent to around 1 per cent of compensation of employees (YE) in the household and hence equivalent to around 45,000 yen per employee (W) in FY2010.

9.2.1. *Household dividend income increase scenario: Scenario A*

In the first place, we examine the impacts of dividend income increase in the household sector on the Japanese economy. In this scenario forecast, the 2 per cent of corporate income shifts to the household sector through dividends. Hence, we examine the impacts of the 2 per cent decrease in the corporate profits and therefore the increase of the household income by the same amounts on the economy.

Table 9.2 shows the impacts of income reallocation from the corporate sector to the household sector on the economy. As a portion of

Table 9.2: The impacts of dividend yield 2 per cent points increases on the economy, FY2011–2030: Scenario A, deviation and per cent deviation in comparison with the baseline forecast.

(in trillions of yen, %)

FY	2011	2012	2013	2014	2015	2020	2025	2030
GDE	1.17	1.98	2.68	3.23	3.61	3.38	2.17	2.54
% dev.	(0.2)	(0.4)	(0.5)	(0.6)	(0.6)	(0.6)	(0.3)	(0.4)
GDPC	0.07	0.19	0.35	0.52	0.68	1.16	1.06	0.96
% dev.	(0.0)	(0.0)	(0.1)	(0.1)	(0.1)	(0.2)	(0.2)	(0.1)
DGAP	−1.10	−1.79	−2.33	−2.71	−2.93	−2.22	−1.12	−1.58
% dev.	(−1.2)	(−2.1)	(−2.7)	(−3.3)	(−3.7)	(−4.0)	(−2.9)	(−7.6)
LPI	0.01	0.03	0.06	0.09	0.12	0.21	0.19	0.18
% dev.	(0.0)	(0.0)	(0.1)	(0.1)	(0.1)	(0.2)	(0.2)	(0.1)
TFPI	0.00	0.01	0.02	0.03	0.04	0.06	0.06	0.05
% dev.	(0.0)	(0.0)	(0.0)	(0.0)	(0.0)	(0.1)	(0.1)	(0.1)
CP	0.64	1.15	1.65	2.12	2.54	3.59	3.48	3.88
% dev.	(0.2)	(0.4)	(0.5)	(0.7)	(0.8)	(1.2)	(1.1)	(1.2)
CH	0.64	1.14	1.63	2.09	2.51	3.53	3.44	3.83
% dev.	(0.2)	(0.4)	(0.6)	(0.7)	(0.9)	(1.2)	(1.1)	(1.2)
IH	0.30	0.50	0.65	0.77	0.86	0.76	0.47	0.56
% dev.	(2.2)	(3.4)	(4.8)	(5.7)	(6.3)	(5.1)	(2.7)	(3.1)
IP	0.29	0.54	0.73	0.86	0.90	0.56	0.15	0.30
% dev.	(0.4)	(0.7)	(0.9)	(1.1)	(1.1)	(0.6)	(0.2)	(0.3)
CG	−0.00	−0.00	−0.02	−0.05	−0.08	−0.31	−0.40	−0.40
% dev.	(−0.0)	(−0.0)	(−0.0)	(−0.0)	(−0.1)	(−0.3)	(−0.3)	(−0.3)
IG	−0.00	−0.03	−0.03	−0.03	−0.04	−0.13	−0.15	−0.10
% dev.	(−0.0)	(−0.2)	(−0.1)	(−0.1)	(−0.2)	(−0.6)	(−0.7)	(−0.5)
EGS	−0.00	−0.02	−0.04	−0.06	−0.08	−0.14	−0.13	−0.12
% dev.	(−0.0)	(−0.0)	(−0.0)	(−0.1)	(−0.1)	(−0.1)	(−0.1)	(−0.1)

(Continued)

Table 9.2: (Continued)

FY	2011	2012	2013	2014	2015	2020	2025	2030
MGS	0.14	0.25	0.35	0.45	0.55	0.92	1.21	1.60
% dev.	(0.2)	(0.4)	(0.6)	(0.7)	(0.8)	(1.3)	(1.6)	(2.1)
GDEN	1.13	2.01	2.90	3.75	4.56	6.76	6.35	6.34
% dev.	(0.2)	(0.4)	(0.6)	(0.8)	(1.0)	(1.4)	(1.2)	(1.1)
CPN	0.58	1.09	1.64	2.21	2.78	4.73	5.00	5.30
% dev.	(0.2)	(0.4)	(0.6)	(0.8)	(1.1)	(1.8)	(1.8)	(1.9)
CHN	0.58	1.08	1.62	2.18	2.74	4.64	4.90	5.18
% dev.	(0.2)	(0.4)	(0.6)	(0.9)	(1.1)	(1.8)	(1.8)	(1.9)
CGN	0.00	0.02	0.07	0.14	0.22	0.66	0.84	0.81
% dev.	(0.0)	(0.0)	(0.1)	(0.1)	(0.2)	(0.6)	(0.7)	(0.6)
IPN	0.27	0.51	0.70	0.86	1.05	1.06	0.90	1.04
% dev.	(0.4)	(0.7)	(1.0)	(1.2)	(1.3)	(1.4)	(1.1)	(1.1)
IHN	0.31	0.51	0.68	0.81	0.91	0.90	0.67	0.79
% dev.	(2.2)	(3.6)	(4.8)	(5.8)	(6.6)	(6.0)	(3.8)	(4.1)
IGN	−0.00	−0.02	−0.00	0.00	0.02	0.03	0.03	0.06
% dev.	(−0.0)	(−0.0)	(−0.0)	(−0.0)	(0.1)	(0.1)	(0.1)	(0.3)
EGSN	−0.07	−0.15	−0.23	−0.30	−0.35	−0.38	−0.27	−0.34
% dev.	(−0.1)	(−0.2)	(−0.3)	(−0.3)	(−0.4)	(−0.4)	(−0.2)	(−0.3)
MGSN	0.04	0.04	0.04	0.03	0.03	0.22	0.71	1.26
% dev.	(0.1)	(0.1)	(0.1)	(0.0)	(0.0)	(0.2)	(0.8)	(1.1)
PGDE	0.02	0.06	0.11	0.18	0.27	0.67	0.73	0.63
% dev.	(0.0)	(0.1)	(0.1)	(0.2)	(0.3)	(0.8)	(0.9)	(0.8)
PCP	0.00	0.03	0.07	0.12	0.19	0.54	0.63	0.57
% dev.	(0.0)	(0.0)	(0.1)	(0.1)	(0.2)	(0.6)	(0.7)	(0.6)
PCH	0.00	0.03	0.06	0.12	0.19	0.53	0.62	0.56
% dev.	(0.0)	(0.0)	(0.1)	(0.1)	(0.2)	(0.6)	(0.7)	(0.6)
PCG	0.00	0.04	0.09	0.17	0.28	0.83	1.00	0.92
% dev.	(0.0)	(0.0)	(0.1)	(0.2)	(0.3)	(0.9)	(1.1)	(0.9)
PIP	0.00	0.02	0.06	0.12	0.20	0.64	0.79	0.71
% dev.	(0.0)	(0.0)	(0.1)	(0.1)	(0.2)	(0.7)	(0.9)	(0.8)
PIH	0.01	0.03	0.08	0.15	0.24	0.83	1.09	1.06
% dev.	(0.0)	(0.0)	(0.1)	(0.1)	(0.2)	(0.8)	(1.1)	(1.0)
PIG	0.00	0.03	0.08	0.16	0.26	0.74	0.85	0.76
% dev.	(0.0)	(0.0)	(0.1)	(0.2)	(0.3)	(0.8)	(0.9)	(0.8)

(Continued)

Table 9.2: (Continued)

FY	2011	2012	2013	2014	2015	2020	2025	2030
PEGS	−0.07	−0.14	−0.20	−0.24	−0.27	−0.22	−0.11	−0.16
% dev.	(−0.1)	(−0.1)	(−0.2)	(−0.3)	(−0.3)	(−0.3)	(−0.1)	(−0.2)
PMGS	−0.21	−0.43	−0.64	−0.84	−1.03	−1.46	−1.34	−1.42
% dev.	(−0.2)	(−0.3)	(−0.5)	(−0.6)	(−0.8)	(−1.0)	(−0.9)	(−1.0)
PX	−0.02	−0.03	−0.03	−0.02	0.01	0.19	0.25	0.22
% dev.	(−0.0)	(−0.0)	(−0.0)	(−0.0)	(0.0)	(0.2)	(0.2)	(0.2)
PMY	−0.27	−0.54	−0.81	−1.07	−1.30	−1.85	−1.69	−1.80
% dev.	(−0.2)	(−0.4)	(−0.6)	(−0.8)	(−0.9)	(−1.2)	(−1.1)	(−1.1)
PLAND	0.33	0.39	0.43	0.46	0.46	0.23	−0.03	−0.03
% dev.	(0.5)	(0.6)	(0.6)	(0.7)	(0.7)	(0.3)	(−0.0)	(−0.0)
EXR	−0.17	−0.34	−0.50	−0.64	−0.76	−0.94	−0.73	−0.68
% dev.	(−0.2)	(−0.4)	(−0.6)	(−0.7)	(−0.9)	(−1.1)	(−1.0)	(−1.0)
M2CD	0.27	0.69	1.21	1.80	2.41	4.56	4.64	4.48
%	(0.0)	(0.1)	(0.1)	(0.2)	(0.3)	(0.5)	(0.5)	(0.4)
INTPR	0.01	0.02	0.02	0.03	0.03	0.04	0.04	0.03
% dev.	(0.6)	(0.9)	(1.3)	(1.7)	(2.0)	(3.0)	(2.5)	(2.3)
INTGB	0.01	0.01	0.02	0.03	0.03	0.04	0.03	0.03
% dev.	(0.6)	(1.0)	(1.4)	(1.8)	(2.2)	(3.1)	(2.4)	(2.1)
WN	0.04	0.11	0.23	0.37	0.53	1.12	1.16	1.06
% dev.	(0.0)	(0.1)	(0.2)	(0.4)	(0.6)	(1.2)	(1.2)	(1.1)
YE	0.33	0.63	1.10	1.64	2.20	3.83	3.61	3.30
% dev.	(0.1)	(0.3)	(0.5)	(0.7)	(1.0)	(1.7)	(1.5)	(1.3)
YDIV	1.02	1.09	1.13	1.15	1.16	1.16	1.19	1.22
% dev.	(17.6)	(17.8)	(17.8)	(17.6)	(17.4)	(16.2)	(16.1)	(16.5)
YDH	1.50	1.83	2.36	2.92	3.47	4.98	4.65	4.33
% dev.	(0.4)	(0.6)	(0.9)	(1.1)	(1.3)	(1.9)	(1.7)	(1.5)
YC	−0.66	−0.64	−0.66	−0.73	−0.84	−1.47	−1.59	−1.38
% dev.	(−1.5)	(−1.3)	(−1.3)	(−1.4)	(−1.6)	(−2.6)	(−2.7)	(−2.4)
HFA	1.42	3.18	5.10	7.02	8.82	12.88	9.51	7.60
% dev.	(0.1)	(0.2)	(0.4)	(0.5)	(0.6)	(0.9)	(0.6)	(0.5)
HNFA	0.59	1.09	1.55	1.96	2.31	2.65	1.45	0.64
% dev.	(0.0)	(0.1)	(0.2)	(0.2)	(0.3)	(0.3)	(0.2)	(0.1)
HTD	0.04	0.03	−0.00	−0.04	−0.10	−1.05	−3.05	−5.97
% dev.	(0.0)	(0.0)	(−0.0)	(−0.0)	(−0.0)	(−0.2)	(−0.7)	(−1.3)

(Continued)

Table 9.2:   (Continued)

FY	2011	2012	2013	2014	2015	2020	2025	2030
RYH	0.24	0.26	0.30	0.35	0.42	0.70	0.73	0.68
% dev.	(0.3)	(0.3)	(0.3)	(0.4)	(0.5)	(0.8)	(0.9)	(0.8)
SH	0.92	0.75	0.75	0.74	0.73	0.34	−0.25	−0.85
% dev.	(5.7)	(4.4)	(4.6)	(5.0)	(5.3)	(2.9)	(−2.2)	(−7.4)
NLE	2.59	5.79	8.87	11.32	12.93	8.96	2.33	2.54
% dev.	(0.0)	(0.1)	(0.1)	(0.2)	(0.2)	(0.1)	(0.0)	(0.0)
UR(%)	−0.04	−0.09	−0.14	−0.17	−0.20	−0.14	−0.04	−0.04
% dev.	(−0.7)	(−1.6)	(−2.4)	(−3.0)	(−3.4)	(−2.6)	(−0.8)	(−0.9)
TXG	0.05	0.23	0.37	0.49	0.57	0.50	0.22	0.30
% dev.	(0.1)	(0.5)	(0.8)	(1.0)	(1.2)	(1.0)	(0.4)	(0.5)
TXI	0.14	0.23	0.32	0.39	0.45	0.56	0.51	0.57
% dev.	(1.1)	(1.8)	(2.4)	(3.0)	(3.5)	(4.2)	(3.3)	(3.4)
TXC	−0.09	−0.02	0.02	0.04	0.04	−0.22	−0.47	−0.45
% dev.	(−0.7)	(−0.2)	(0.1)	(0.3)	(0.3)	(1.5)	(−2.8)	(−2.5)
GEXGE	0.00	−0.02	0.00	0.03	0.05	0.10	0.01	0.02
% dev.	(0.0)	(−0.0)	(0.0)	(0.0)	(0.1)	(0.1)	(0.1)	(0.1)
KLGBT	−0.00	−0.30	−0.67	−1.13	−1.65	−4.13	−5.12	−5.68
% dev.	(−0.0)	(−0.0)	(−0.1)	(−0.1)	(−0.2)	(−0.3)	(−0.4)	(−0.4)
RKLG	−0.48	−0.93	−1.43	−1.96	−2.51	−4.35	−4.28	−4.13
% dev.	(−0.2)	(−0.5)	(−0.7)	(−0.9)	(−1.1)	(−1.7)	(−1.6)	(−1.5)
TB	−0.07	−0.12	−0.17	−0.20	−0.23	−0.38	−0.74	−1.28
% dev.	(−1.1)	(−1.7)	(−2.3)	(−2.8)	(−3.3)	(−5.7)	(−7.6)	(−7.8)
CBP	−0.12	−0.19	−0.27	−0.34	−0.39	−0.59	−0.98	−1.63
% dev.	(−0.7)	(−1.1)	(−1.4)	(−1.8)	(−2.1)	(−3.4)	(−4.8)	(−6.0)

Note: Deviation: (Scenario−Baseline); % deviation: (Scenario−Baseline)/Baseline*100
Source: Simulated and compiled by the author.

the corporate income shifts to the household, the corporate income is expected to decrease while the household income will probably increase in this scenario simulation, in which the corporate income will continue to decrease during the forecasted period, by 0.66 trillion yen in FY2011, by 0.84 trillion yen in FY2015, 1.47 trillion yen in FY2020 and by 1.38 trillion yen in FY2030, as compared to the baseline forecast. On the other hand, it is expected that the household income increase will exceed the corporate income decrease in absolute terms, through indirect positive effects on the whole economy, and the household disposable income will probably increase by 1.50 trillion yen in FY2011, by 3.47 trillion yen in FY2015, by 4.98 trillion yen in FY2020 and 4.33 trillion yen in FY2030, as compared to the baseline forecast. As a result, the indicator (RYH) explaining the ratio of household income to total income of household income plus corporate income, which is employed to represent the household income share in Table 4.4, will probably increase by 0.24 per cent point in FY2011, by 0.42 per cent point in FY2015, by 0.70 per cent point in FY2020 and by 0.68 per cent point in FY2030 as compared to the baseline forecast.

With direct and indirect effects, real GDE and its components, except for real exports of goods and services, will probably have positive impacts, in which real GDE will increase by 0.2 per cent in FY2011, by 0.4 per cent in FY2012, by 0.6 per cent in FY2015 and by 0.6 per cent in FY2020, and thereafter the positive impacts at 0.3–0.4 per cent will be remained up to FY2030, in per cent deviation, as compared to the baseline forecast. It is expected that real household consumption and real housing investment particularly will have large impacts through income effects and net asset effects, in which the real household consumption will increase by 0.8 per cent in FY2015, by 1.2 per cent in FY2020 and by 1.2 per cent in FY2030, in per cent deviation, as compared to the baseline forecast, and the real housing investment will increase by 6.3 per cent in FY2015, by 5.1 per cent in FY2020 and 3.1 per cent FY2030, in per cent deviation, in comparison with the baseline forecast. Furthermore, even in the case of real private non-housing investment, positive effects will be recognized over the tested period in spite of the corporate income decreases.

As for the supply-side, real GDP capacity is expected to increase slightly along with real non-housing investment increases, so that the deflationary gap will decrease by 1.10 trillion yen in FY 2011, by 2.93 trillion yen in FY2015, by 2.22 trillion yen in FY2020 and by 1.58 trillion yen in FY2030, as compared to the baseline forecast. The increases in the supply-side will result from increases in the demand-side economy, as discussed above. Even in this scenario forecast with the limited income transfers, both the demand-side and the supply-side will be stimulated by the household expenditure led demand-side expansion.

With respect to the impacts on prices and deflators, the general deflator (PGDE) is expected to rise by 0.3 per cent in FY2015, by 0.8 per cent in FY2020 and by 0.8 per cent in FY2030, in per cent deviation, as compared to the baseline forecast. On the other hand, output price (PX) will probably decline slightly in the 2010s and rise in 2020s since the yen rate to the dollar will be slightly appreciated along with rises in interest rate, as compared to the baseline forecast.

In this long-term scenario forecast, with the expansion of effective demands, the macro-imbalances will be improved. As for the fiscal balance, with nominal GDP increases, overall tax revenues (TXG) in the central government will probably increase with natural increase in the revenues, by 0.57 trillion yen in FY2015, by 0.50 trillion yen in FY2020 and by 0.30 trillion yen in FY2030, as compared to the baseline projection. As a result, accumulated fiscal deficit (KLGBT) will be improved by 1.65 trillion yen in FY 2015, by 4.13 trillion yen in FY2020 and 5.68 trillion yen in FY2030, in deviation. Moreover, the ratio of the accumulated fiscal deficit to nominal GDP (RKLG) will also be improved by 2.51 per cent points in FY2015, by 4.35 per cent points in FY2020 and by 4.13 per cent points in FY2030, as compared to the baseline forecast.

In addition, the rate of unemployment is expected to be improved through increases in labor demands, by 0.20 per cent point in FY2015, by 0.14 per cent point in FY2020 and by 0.04 per cent point in FY2030, as compared to the baseline projection. In terms of the rise in unemployment, it will probably increase by 25,900 in FY2011, by 129,300 in FY2015, by 89,600 in FY2020 and by 25,400 in FY2030, as compared to the baseline projection.

Concerning trade imbalances, the trade surplus is expected to decline with the expansion of the domestic demand and yen appreciation, by 0.23 trillion yen in FY2015, by 0.38 trillion yen in FY2020 and by 1.28 trillion yen in FY2030, increasing its impacts, as compared to the baseline forecast. Furthermore, the current balance of payment will probably have larger effects by 0.39 trillion yen in FY2015, by 0.59 trillion yen in FY2020 and by 1.63 trillion yen in FY2030 because income transfers, credits will increase along with the increase in FDI position in the rest of the world.

In summary, income reallocation from the corporate sector to the household sector is expected to have positive effects on the whole economy including both household sector and corporate sector, in spite of the limited income reallocation. In other words, the distribution of income, in particular between profits and wages, is crucial to determine the demand-side and the supply-side, in which the appropriate income distribution could improve both on the whole, and achieve domestic demand-led economic growth as experienced in the latter half of the 1980s, as shown in Figures 9.4 and 9.5.

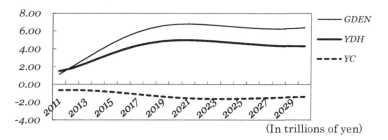

(In trillions of yen)

Figure 9.4: Deviation of nominal GDE, household disposable income (YDH) and corporate income (YC) from the baseline, FY2011–2030.

Source: Simulated and developed by the author.

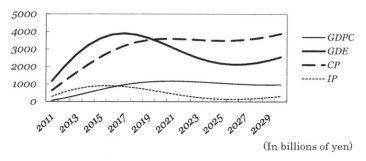

(In billions of yen)

Figure 9.5: Deviation of real GDE, GDP capacity, CP and IP in scenario a from the baseline forecast, FY2011–2030.

Source: Simulated and developed by the author.

9.2.2. *Household wage income and dividend income increase scenario: Scenario B*

Based on the previous scenario forecast Scenario A, we conduct the second scenario forecast. As noted, this scenario simulation examines the impact of income reallocation from the government sector to the household sector by way of the corporate sector, incorporated with Scenario A, as Scenario B.

In accordance with this scenario forecast, as shown in Table 9.3, the household disposable income (YDH) is expected to increase by 5.24 trillion

Table 9.3: The impacts of household disposable income increase on the economy, FY2011–2030: Scenario B, as compared to the baseline forecast.

(in trillions of yen, %)

FY	2011	2012	2013	2014	2015	2020	2025	2030
GDE	4.15	7.61	10.76	13.30	15.17	15.37	11.15	13.14
% dev.	(0.8)	(1.4)	(1.9)	(2.4)	(2.7)	(2.6)	(1.8)	(1.9)
GDPC	0.24	0.71	1.34	2.06	2.79	5.11	5.04	4.85
% dev.	(0.0)	(0.1)	(0.2)	(0.3)	(0.4)	(0.8)	(0.7)	(0.7)
DGAP	−3.91	−6.89	−9.42	−11.24	−12.38	−10.26	−6.12	−8.28
% dev.	(−4.3)	(−8.0)	(−11.1)	(−13.7)	(−15.5)	(−18.6)	(−16.2)	(−40.2)
KP	0.69	2.10	4.03	6.27	8.60	16.91	17.39	17.48
% dev.	(0.1)	(0.2)	(0.4)	(0.7)	(0.9)	(1.6)	(1.5)	(1.4)
CUR	1.26	2.24	3.06	3.66	4.04	3.43	2.13	2.78
% dev.	(1.7)	(3.0)	(4.1)	(4.9)	(5.4)	(4.4)	(2.5)	(3.0)
LPI	0.04	0.13	0.24	0.37	0.51	0.94	0.92	0.89
% dev.	(0.0)	(0.1)	(0.2)	(0.3)	(0.4)	(0.8)	(0.7)	(0.7)
TFPI	0.01	0.04	0.08	0.12	0.16	0.28	0.27	0.25
% dev.	(0.0)	(0.0)	(0.1)	(0.1)	(0.2)	(0.3)	(0.3)	(0.2)
CP	2.27	4.25	6.27	8.23	10.03	14.87	15.26	17.71
% dev.	(0.7)	(1.4)	(2.1)	(2.7)	(3.4)	(4.9)	(4.9)	(5.5)
CH	2.25	4.22	6.21	8.14	9.91	14.65	15.04	17.51
% dev.	(0.8)	(1.4)	(2.1)	(2.8)	(3.4)	(5.0)	(5.0)	(5.6)
IH	1.05	1.83	2.49	3.01	3.39	3.24	2.24	2.76
% dev.	(8.0)	(13.4)	(18.1)	(22.1)	(25.0)	(21.8)	(13.0)	(15.2)
IP	1.05	2.08	2.93	3.52	3.87	2.77	1.11	1.75
% dev.	(1.4)	(2.7)	(3.7)	(4.5)	(4.8)	(3.2)	(1.1)	(1.6)

(Continued)

Table 9.3: *(Continued)*

FY	2011	2012	2013	2014	2015	2020	2025	2030
CG	−0.00	−0.02	−0.07	−0.17	−0.30	−1.18	−1.65	−1.71
% dev.	(−0.0)	(−0.0)	(−0.1)	(−0.2)	(−0.3)	(−1.0)	(−1.3)	(−1.5)
IG	−0.00	0.09	0.29	0.40	0.44	0.22	0.12	0.30
% dev.	(−0.0)	(0.5)	(1.4)	(2.0)	(2.1)	(1.0)	(0.6)	(1.4)
EGS	−0.03	−0.09	−0.15	−0.23	−0.30	−0.56	−0.60	−0.58
% dev.	(−0.0)	(−0.1)	(−0.2)	(−0.2)	(−0.3)	(−0.5)	(−0.4)	(−0.4)
MGS	0.49	0.94	1.40	1.84	2.26	3.86	5.22	7.11
% dev.	(0.8)	(1.5)	(2.2)	(2.8)	(3.4)	(5.3)	(7.0)	(9.5)
GDEN	4.01	7.69	11.53	15.24	18.73	29.19	29.91	31.56
% dev.	(0.8)	(1.6)	(2.4)	(3.2)	(4.0)	(6.0)	(5.8)	(5.6)
CPN	2.07	4.03	6.21	8.54	10.92	19.65	22.06	24.52
% dev.	(0.8)	(1.5)	(2.4)	(3.3)	(4.2)	(7.6)	(8.2)	(8.6)
CHN	2.06	3.99	6.14	8.42	10.75	19.25	21.59	24.04
% dev.	(0.8)	(1.5)	(2.4)	(3.3)	(4.2)	(7.6)	(8.2)	(8.7)
CGN	0.03	0.11	0.27	0.51	0.82	2.67	3.62	3.73
% dev.	(0.0)	(0.1)	(0.3)	(0.5)	(0.8)	(2.5)	(3.1)	(2.9)
IPN	0.96	1.94	2.81	3.53	4.07	4.72	4.26	5.06
% dev.	(1.4)	(2.8)	(4.0)	(4.9)	(5.7)	(6.1)	(5.0)	(5.3)
IHN	1.08	1.90	2.61	3.18	3.62	3.87	3.19	3.90
% dev.	(8.0)	(13.5)	(18.5)	(22.7)	(26.1)	(25.8)	(18.2)	(20.5)
JPN	0.27	0.34	0.35	0.31	0.25	−0.91	−0.82	0.83
% dev.	(38.0)	(45.1)	(53.0)	(54.3)	(45.1)	(−10.2)	(−7.6)	(7.1)
EGN	−0.25	−0.58	−0.92	−1.22	−1.47	−1.75	−1.44	−1.91
% dev.	(−0.3)	(−0.7)	(−1.0)	(−1.3)	(−1.6)	(−1.7)	(−1.2)	(−1.5)
MGN	0.14	0.16	0.15	0.13	0.11	0.72	2.60	4.79
% dev.	(0.2)	(0.2)	(0.2)	(0.1)	(0.1)	(0.7)	(2.4)	(4.3)
PGDE	0.08	0.21	0.42	0.70	1.04	2.73	3.21	3.04
% dev.	(0.1)	(0.2)	(0.5)	(0.8)	(1.2)	(3.3)	(3.9)	(3.7)
PCP	0.02	0.10	0.24	0.45	0.71	2.16	2.69	2.60
% dev.	(0.0)	(0.1)	(0.3)	(0.5)	(0.8)	(2.5)	(3.1)	(2.9)
PCH	0.02	0.10	0.24	0.45	0.71	2.16	2.69	2.60
% dev.	(0.0)	(0.1)	(0.3)	(0.5)	(0.8)	(2.5)	(3.1)	(2.9)
PCG	0.03	0.13	0.33	0.64	1.04	3.32	4.28	4.21
% dev.	(0.0)	(0.1)	(0.3)	(0.7)	(1.1)	(3.6)	(4.5)	(4.4)

(Continued)

Table 9.3: (Continued)

FY	2011	2012	2013	2014	2015	2020	2025	2030
PIP	0.01	0.07	0.21	0.42	0.71	2.53	3.34	3.21
% dev.	(0.0)	(0.1)	(0.2)	(0.5)	(0.8)	(2.9)	(3.8)	(3.6)
PIH	0.02	0.10	0.27	0.54	0.91	3.30	4.66	4.79
% dev.	(0.0)	(0.1)	(0.3)	(0.5)	(0.9)	(3.3)	(4.6)	(4.6)
PIG	0.02	0.11	0.30	0.59	0.96	2.97	3.67	3.53
% dev.	(0.0)	(0.1)	(0.3)	(0.6)	(1.0)	(3.1)	(3.7)	(3.5)
PEGS	−0.25	−0.54	−0.80	−1.00	−1.14	−1.04	−0.69	−0.92
% dev.	(−0.3)	(−0.6)	(−0.9)	(−1.1)	(−1.3)	(−1.4)	(−0.8)	(−1.2)
PMGS	−0.75	−1.60	−2.51	−3.36	−4.13	−6.12	−6.09	−6.91
% dev.	(−0.6)	(−2.3)	(−2.0)	(−2.6)	(−3.1)	(−4.6)	(−4.3)	(−4.7)
PX	−0.06	−0.11	−0.12	−0.09	−0.07	0.69	1.01	0.85
% dev.	(−0.0)	(−0.1)	(−0.1)	(−0.1)	(−0.0)	(0.7)	(1.0)	(0.8)
PMY	−0.96	−2.04	−3.17	−4.24	−5.22	−7.56	−7.69	−8.73
% dev.	(−0.7)	(−1.5)	(−2.3)	(−3.0)	(−3.6)	(−5.1)	(−4.9)	(−5.4)
PLAND	1.18	1.54	1.81	1.92	1.95	1.07	0.08	0.06
% dev.	(1.7)	(2.3)	(2.7)	(2.8)	(2.8)	(1.5)	(0.1)	(0.1)
EXR	−0.60	−1.28	−1.96	−2.57	−2.08	−3.95	−3.37	−3.36
% dev.	(−0.7)	(−1.5)	(−2.2)	(−2.9)	(−3.5)	(−4.8)	(−4.6)	(−5.1)
M2CD	0.95	2.57	4.71	7.17	9.76	19.64	21.31	21.85
% dev.	(0.1)	(0.3)	(0.6)	(0.9)	(1.2)	(2.2)	(2.3)	(2.2)
INTPR	0.03	0.06	0.08	0.11	0.13	0.17	0.16	0.16
% dev.	(2.1)	(3.4)	(5.1)	(6.7)	(8.2)	(12.3)	(11.2)	(10.8)
INTGB	0.03	0.05	0.08	0.10	0.12	0.16	0.15	0.15
% dev.	(2.1)	(3.7)	(5.5)	(7.2)	(8.9)	(12.7)	(11.0)	(10.2)
WN	0.63	1.39	2.28	3.26	4.29	8.63	5.12	5.00
% dev.	(0.7)	(1.5)	(2.4)	(3.5)	(4.7)	(9.5)	(11.4)	(12.0)
YE	3.59	4.76	6.58	8.71	10.95	18.47	18.78	18.42
% dev.	(1.5)	(2.0)	(2.8)	(3.7)	(4.7)	(8.1)	(8.0)	(7.5)
YDIV	1.13	1.54	1.79	1.92	1.97	1.85	1.84	1.96
% dev.	(19.6)	(25.1)	(28.0)	(29.4)	(29.6)	(25.9)	(24.9)	(26.4)
YDH	5.24	6.76	8.95	11.24	13.51	20.41	20.20	19.74
% dev.	(1.9)	(2.4)	(3.3)	(4.2)	(5.0)	(7.7)	(7.3)	(6.8)
YC	0.11	2.34	3.66	4.31	4.51	3.08	2.70	3.47
% dev.	(0.2)	(4.8)	(7.3)	(8.4)	(8.6)	(5.5)	(4.6)	(5.9)

(Continued)

Table 9.3:   (Continued)

FY	2011	2012	2013	2014	2015	2020	2025	2030
HFA	5.01	11.97	19.92	28.04	35.76	55.37	45.99	40.93
% dev.	(0.4)	(0.9)	(1.5)	(2.1)	(2.6)	(4.0)	(3.1)	(2.6)
HNFA	2.12	4.14	6.13	7.92	9.43	11.42	7.21	4.28
% dev.	(0.2)	(0.5)	(0.7)	(0.9)	(1.1)	(1.3)	(0.7)	(0.4)
HTD	−0.45	−0.79	−1.42	−2.21	−3.18	−9.92	−19.22	−29.77
% dev.	(−0.1)	(−0.2)	(−0.4)	(−0.6)	(−0.8)	(−2.6)	(−5.1)	(−7.8)
RYH	0.20	−0.22	−0.39	−0.39	−0.27	0.66	0.90	0.85
% dev.	(0.2)	(−0.3)	(−0.5)	(−0.5)	(−0.3)	(0.8)	(1.1)	(1.0)
SH	3.18	2.77	2.81	2.81	2.76	1.16	−1.38	−4.29
% dev.	(19.9)	(16.3)	(17.4)	(18.7)	(19.8)	(10.1)	(−12.4)	(−38.6)
NLE	9.08	21.26	33.56	43.75	50.77	40.03	15.19	15.56
% dev.	(0.1)	(0.3)	(0.5)	(0.7)	(0.8)	(0.6)	(0.2)	(0.3)
UR(%)	−0.14	−0.32	−0.51	−0.67	−0.79	−0.62	−0.23	−0.24
TXG	0.85	2.18	3.19	3.92	4.43	4.70	4.01	4.60
% dev.	(1.8)	(4.5)	(6.6)	(8.1)	(9.1)	(9.2)	(7.3)	(7.9)
TXI	0.50	0.89	1.25	1.56	1.82	2.37	2.32	2.69
% dev.	(3.8)	(6.7)	(9.5)	(12.0)	(14.2)	(17.5)	(15.0)	(15.7)
TXC	0.35	1.22	1.80	2.14	2.30	1.68	0.92	1.08
% dev.	(2.9)	(9.5)	(13.7)	(16.1)	(17.2)	(11.0)	(5.4)	(6.0)
GEXGE	2.55	2.73	3.07	3.33	3.53	4.00	4.14	4.34
% dev.	(2.8)	(2.9)	(3.3)	(3.5)	(3.7)	(4.0)	(4.0)	(4.0)
KLGBT	1.70	2.26	2.14	1.56	0.66	−4.22	−4.83	−4.82
% dev.	(0.2)	(0.2)	(0.2)	(0.2)	(0.1)	(−0.3)	(−0.3)	(−0.3)
RKLG	−1.32	−2.82	−4.61	−6.53	−8.50	−15.83	−15.58	−15.69
% dev.	(−0.7)	(−1.4)	(−2.2)	(−3.0)	(−3.8)	(−6.0)	(−5.8)	(−5.6)
TB	−0.26	−0.47	−0.66	−0.81	−0.93	−1.52	−2.94	−5.20
% dev.	(−3.8)	(−6.6)	(−9.1)	(−11.4)	(−13.5)	(−23.1)	(−30.2)	(−31.6)
CBP	−0.43	−0.73	−1.07	−1.36	−1.60	−2.47	−4.06	−6.85
% dev.	(−2.6)	(−4.3)	(−5.7)	(−7.3)	(−8.7)	(−14.1)	(−20.0)	(−25.3)

Note: Deviation: (Scenario−Baseline); % deviation: (Scenario−Baseline)/Baseline*100 (%)
Source: Simulated and compiled by the author.

yen in FY2011, by 6.76 trillion yen in FY2012, by 13.51 trillion yen in 2015, by 20.41 trillion yen in 2020 and by 19.74 trillion yen in FY2030, in terms of deviation, as compared to the baseline forecast. These impacts are fairly large, in terms of per cent deviation, at 1.9 per cent in FY2011, at 2.4 per cent in FY2012, at 5.0 per cent in FY2015, at 7.7 per cent in FY2020 and at 6.8 per cent in FY2030, as compared to the baseline forecast, along with the fairly large effects on wage income which may be directly affected by the income transfers from both the corporate sector and the government sector to the household sector. In addition, interestingly, the household income ratio to total income (RYH) is expected to increase by 0.20 per cent point in FY2011 since additional income is reallocated to the household sector, but this ratio will probably decline slightly from FY2012 to FY2016 because corporate income will increase along with an expansion of the economy as a whole. However, this ratio will be increasing in the latter half of the 2010s onward, by 0.66 per cent point in FY2020, by 0.90 per cent point in FY2025 and by 0.85 per cent point in FY2030, in deviation, as compared to the baseline forecast.

As a result, real household consumption expenditure and real housing investment will probably have large impacts, in which particularly real household consumption will have fairly large positive impacts at 0.7 per cent in FY2011, at 1.4 per cent in FY2012, at 3.4 per cent in FY2015, at 4.9 per cent in FY2020 and at 5.5 per cent in FY2030, in per cent deviation, as compared to the baseline forecast. In this scenario simulation, real private non-housing investment is expected to have positive impacts by 1.4 per cent in FY2011, by 2.7 per cent inFY2012, by 4.8 per cent in FY2015, by 3.2 per cent in FY2020 and by 1.6 per cent in FY2030, in per cent deviation, in comparison with the baseline forecast. As a result, real GDE is expected to increase by 0.8 per cent in FY2011, by 1.4 per cent in FY2012, by 2.7 per cent in FY2015, by 2.6 per cent in FY2020 and by 1.9 per cent in FY2030, in per cent deviation, as compared to the baseline forecast and the level of real GDE will likely be 550.7 trillion yen in FY2011, by 577.1 trillion yen in FY2015, by 607.7 trillion yen in FY2020 and by 697.2 trillion yen in FY2030 in this long-term scenario forecast.

These fairly large impacts, in spite of the limited sources of demand stimulus, may result from the net asset effects in the household sector, as discussed earlier. Regarding the impacts on the household assets and liabilities, these stock variables are also expected to have fairly large effects, in which the household financial assets will probably increase by 2.6 per cent in FY2015, by 4.0 per cent in FY2020 and by 2.6 per cent in FY2030 and the household non-financial assets will probably increase by 1.1 per cent in FY2015, by 1.3 per cent in FY2020 and by 0.4 per cent in FY2030, in per cent deviation, as compared to the baseline projection. In addition, the household liabilities will also decrease by 0.8 per cent in FY2015, by 2.6 per cent in FY2020 and by 7.8 per cent in FY2030 in comparison with the baseline forecast.

On the other hand, despite issuing 2.5 trillion yen worth of government bonds as a demand stimulus policy, the central government debt outstanding is expected to decrease from FY2016 onward in comparison with the baseline forecast because the government revenues will increase through the expansion of the economy as a natural tax increase, in which the accumulated central government debt (KLGBT) will be reduced by 0.42 trillion yen FY2016, by 4.22 trillion yen in FY2020, by 4.83 trillion yen in FY2025 and by 4.82 trillion yen in FY2030 as compared to the baseline projection, although in the initial five fiscal years up to FY2015 the government debt outstanding will probably increase. Moreover, the ratio of the central government debt to nominal GDE will probably decrease from initial year by 1.32 per cent points in FY2011, by 8.50 per cent points in FY2015, by 15.83 per cent points in FY2020 and by 15.69 per cent points in FY2030, in deviation, as compared to the baseline forecast.

Regarding trade balance, trade surplus will be reduced by 0.93 trillion yen in FY2015, by 1.52 trillion yen in FY2020 and by 5.20 trillion yen in FY2030, as compared to the baseline projection. In addition, current account will also be reduced by 1.60 trillion yen in FY2015, by 2.47 trillion yen in FY2020 and by 6.85 trillion yen in FY2030 in comparison with the baseline forecast.

With respect to the unemployment problem, the rate of unemployment is expected to be improved by 0.14 per cent point in FY2011, by 0.32 per cent point in FY2012, by 0.51 per cent point in FY2013, by 0.79 per cent point in FY2015, by 0.62 per cent point in FY2020 and by 0.24 per cent point in FY2030 in comparison with the baseline projection. The fairly large positive effects on the unemployment may be dependent on a mix of corporate and government policy as a demand stimulus without increasing the unemployment rate in labor markets along with wage income increases.

As a result of the increases of real GDE, the deflationary gap of Japan is expected to decrease by 3.91 trillion yen in FY2011, by 6.89 trillion yen in FY2012, by 9.42 trillion yen in FY2013, by 12.38 trillion yen in FY2015, by 10.26 trillion yen in FY2020 and by 8.26 trillion yen in FY2030, as compared to the baseline forecast, and the level of the deflationary gap will probably decline to 12.3 trillion yen in FY2030 in this scenario simulation. In addition, nevertheless, GDP capacity will increase through rises in non-housing investment along with the expansion of the economy, which is a very important evidence for improvements in the whole economy because the demand-side economic recovery will result in stimulating the supply side economy even under the current deflationary climate.

In summary, according to this scenario forecast, despite the limited sources of income reallocation from the corporate sector and the government sector to the household sector, fairly large effects will be expected. It seems that many economists, policy makers, politicians and business leaders may underestimate the domestic demand potential. In the long-term scenario simulations, we can elucidate the effects of income reallocation on the economy and recognize the important role of the household sector's expenditures to stimulate the demand-side economy because the size of private final consumption expenditure exceeded 300 trillion yen and its share in real GDE was around 57 per cent, at constant prices, as of FY2010. In other words, we can realize the economic recovery of Japan through stimulating domestic demand, in particular, household consumption expenditure, as simulated in Scenario B.

As demonstrated in Figures 9.6 and 9.7, the impacts of income reallocation from both the corporate sector and the government sector to the household sector could stimulate household expenditures including final consumption expenditure through both income effects and asset effects. This income reallocation has fairly large and long-term effects on the whole economy. Therefore, it could reinforce domestic demand-led economic growth for escaping from the prolonged economic stagnation, as experienced in the 1980s.

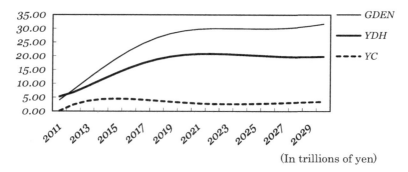

(In trillions of yen)

Figure 9.6: Deviation of nominal GDE, household disposable income (YDH) and corporate income (YC) from the baseline, FY2011–2030.

Source: Simulated and developed by the author.

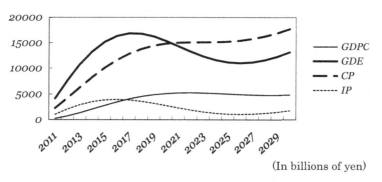

(In billions of yen)

Figure 9.7: Deviation of real GDE, GDP capacity, CP and IP in Scenario B from the baseline forecast, FY2011–2030.

Source: Simulated and developed by the author.

In addition, by taking into account the effects of assets in the household sector, we can see the longer-term impacts of household income increases on the whole economy because accumulated savings affect the household expenditures including consumption and housing investment and lead the demand-side economy as a whole, as discussed in the theoretical model framework section. We can recognize these causations in this scenario forecast.

9.3. Labor Immigration Expansion Scenario Simulation

Japan is now facing the challenge of a negative population growth and an aging society, in which total population has declined since 2008 and the number of workers (labor supply) has also remained stagnant along with declines in economically active population and with the long-term economic slump. Within such a situation, it is planned by the government that the Japanese economy will accept foreign workers through bilateral and multilateral economic cooperation with foreign countries.

Indeed, labor immigration policies have already started experimentally with some countries, which are still permitted only for some specific job markets such as nursing and medical care. However, in the current and future labor markets of Japan, it is indispensable to introduce foreign workers into Japan through economic cooperation.

Accordingly, this section attempts to conduct a long-term labor immigration scenario forecast up to FY2030 and examines its effects on the economy. In this scenario forecast, we assume that the Japanese economy will accept an increase in foreign workers by 50,000, year by year, from FY2011 and henceforth achieve an increase in one million foreign workers in FY2030, as Scenario C. In the scenario simulation, we can anticipate that the expansion of labor immigration will stimulate both the demand-side and the supply-side economies through increasing the number of employed and hence household income.

In implementing this scenario forecast, the number of labor supply which is an endogenous variable in the model, is exogenized because of a Koyck-lag variable in the labor supply function. Therefore, the number of labor supply will increase by 50,000 in FY2011, by 100,000 in FY2012 and by 1 million in FY2030 as compared to the baseline projection. In addition, in this scenario simulation, we assume that immigrant workers will participate in Japanese labor markets, competing with indigenous workers.

With increases in the number of labor force through immigration from the rest of the world, according to the scenario forecast from FY2011 to FY2030 demonstrated in Table 9.4, the number of employed is expected to increase by 45,500 in FY2011, by 220,400 in FY2015, by 447,400 in FY2020 and 904,600 in FY2030, as compared to the baseline projection.

Table 9.4: The impacts of increase in labor immigration by 50,000 year by year on the economy, FY2011–2030: Scenario C, as compared to the baseline forecast.

(in trillions of yen, %)

FY	2011	2012	2013	2014	2015	2020	2025	2030
GDE	0.30	0.77	1.30	1.83	2.83	4.23	5.90	8.13
% dev.	(0.1)	(0.1)	(0.2)	(0.3)	(0.4)	(0.7)	(0.9)	(1.2)
GDPC	0.26	0.55	0.87	1.22	1.59	3.63	5.97	8.60
% dev.	(0.0)	(0.1)	(0.1)	(0.2)	(0.2)	(0.6)	(0.9)	(1.2)
DGAP	−0.04	−0.23	−0.43	−0.61	−0.73	−0.60	0.07	0.47
% dev.	(−0.0)	(−0.3)	(−0.5)	(−0.8)	(−1.0)	(−1.1)	(0.2)	(1.6)
KP	0.04	0.16	0.37	0.66	1.03	3.59	6.92	11.18
% dev.	(0.0)	(0.0)	(0.0)	(0.1)	(0.1)	(0.3)	(0.6)	(0.9)
CUR	0.09	0.23	0.38	0.59	0.64	1.02	1.29	1.68
% dev.	(0.1)	(0.3)	(0.5)	(0.7)	(0.8)	(1.3)	(1.6)	(1.9)
CP	0.18	0.47	0.80	1.16	1.53	3.20	4.70	6.41
% dev.	(0.1)	(0.2)	(0.3)	(0.4)	(0.5)	(1.0)	(1.5)	(2.0)
CH	0.18	0.47	0.80	1.15	1.51	3.16	4.63	6.30
% dev.	(0.1)	(0.2)	(0.3)	(0.4)	(0.5)	(1.0)	(1.5)	(2.0)
IH	0.09	0.21	0.34	0.45	0.55	0.77	0.85	1.00
% dev.	(0.6)	(1.4)	(2.2)	(2.9)	(3.4)	(4.5)	(4.5)	(4.9)
IP	0.07	0.19	0.32	0.46	0.59	1.05	1.45	2.02
% dev.	(0.1)	(0.2)	(0.4)	(0.6)	(0.7)	(1.2)	(1.6)	(2.1)
CG	−0.01	−0.02	−0.03	−0.04	−0.05	−0.07	−0.07	−0.02
% dev.	(−0.0)	(−0.0)	(−0.0)	(−0.0)	(−0.0)	(−0.1)	(−0.1)	(−0.0)
IG	−0.01	0.00	0.02	0.03	0.04	0.07	0.11	0.17
% dev.	(−0.0)	(0.0)	(0.1)	(0.1)	(0.2)	(0.3)	(0.5)	(0.9)
EGS	−0.00	−0.01	−0.03	−0.04	−0.05	−0.10	−0.10	−0.10
% dev.	(−0.0)	(−0.0)	(−0.0)	(−0.0)	(−0.1)	(−0.1)	(−0.1)	(−0.1)
MGS	0.04	0.10	0.18	0.26	0.35	0.75	1.09	1.42
% dev.	(0.1)	(0.2)	(0.3)	(0.4)	(0.5)	(1.0)	(1.4)	(1.7)
GDEN	0.40	1.02	1.70	2.36	2.98	5.33	7.05	8.98
% dev.	(0.1)	(0.2)	(0.4)	(0.5)	(0.6)	(1.0)	(1.3)	(1.5)
CPN	0.21	0.53	0.89	1.27	1.66	3.39	4.86	6.44
% dev.	(0.1)	(0.2)	(0.3)	(0.5)	(0.6)	(1.2)	(1.7)	(2.1)
CHN	0.21	0.52	0.88	1.26	1.63	3.33	4.77	6.33
% dev.	(0.1)	(0.2)	(0.3)	(0.5)	(0.6)	(1.2)	(1.7)	(2.1)

(Continued)

Table 9.4: (Continued)

FY	2011	2012	2013	2014	2015	2020	2025	2030
CGN	0.01	0.04	0.06	0.09	0.11	0.21	0.23	0.16
% dev.	(0.0)	(0.0)	(0.1)	(0.1)	(0.1)	(0.2)	(0.2)	(0.1)
IPN	0.08	0.21	0.37	0.53	0.68	1.25	1.72	2.28
% dev.	(0.1)	(0.3)	(0.5)	(0.7)	(0.9)	(1.6)	(2.0)	(2.3)
IHN	0.09	0.23	0.36	0.49	0.60	0.88	1.01	1.22
% dev.	(0.7)	(1.5)	(2.3)	(3.0)	(3.6)	(4.8)	(4.8)	(5.1)
JPN	0.02	0.04	0.05	0.06	0.06	0.07	0.04	0.06
% dev.	(2.4)	(4.4)	(6.7)	(8.6)	(9.7)	(6.7)	(5.8)	(6.7)
EGN	−0.02	−0.04	−0.08	−0.12	−0.16	−0.27	−0.28	−0.33
% dev.	(−0.0)	(−0.1)	(−0.1)	(−0.1)	(−0.2)	(−0.3)	(−0.2)	(−0.3)
MGN	0.00	−0.00	0.00	0.02	0.03	0.28	0.68	1.07
% dev.	(0.0)	(−0.0)	(0.0)	(0.0)	(0.0)	(0.3)	(0.6)	(1.0)
PGDE	0.02	0.06	0.10	0.14	0.17	0.27	0.28	0.23
% dev.	(0.0)	(0.1)	(0.1)	(0.2)	(0.2)	(0.3)	(0.3)	(0.2)
PCP	0.02	0.04	0.06	0.08	0.10	0.16	0.15	0.08
% dev.	(0.0)	(0.0)	(0.1)	(0.1)	(0.1)	(0.2)	(0.2)	(0.1)
PCH	0.02	0.04	0.06	0.08	0.10	0.16	0.15	0.08
% dev.	(0.0)	(0.0)	(0.1)	(0.1)	(0.1)	(0.2)	(0.2)	(0.1)
PCG	0.02	0.06	0.09	0.12	0.15	0.25	0.25	0.14
% dev.	(0.0)	(0.1)	(0.1)	(0.1)	(0.2)	(0.3)	(0.2)	(0.1)
PIP	0.02	0.06	0.10	0.14	0.17	0.30	0.33	0.26
% dev.	(0.0)	(0.1)	(0.1)	(0.1)	(0.2)	(0.3)	(0.3)	(0.3)
PIH	0.02	0.05	0.08	0.10	0.14	0.26	0.29	0.19
% dev.	(0.0)	(0.0)	(0.1)	(0.1)	(0.1)	(0.2)	(0.3)	(0.2)
PIG	0.03	0.06	0.09	0.12	0.14	0.21	0.20	0.10
% dev.	(0.0)	(0.1)	(0.1)	(0.1)	(0.1)	(0.2)	(0.2)	(0.1)
PEGS	−0.02	−0.03	−0.06	−0.08	−0.11	−0.16	−0.14	−0.16
% dev.	(−0.0)	(−0.0)	(−0.1)	(−0.1)	(−0.1)	(−0.2)	(−0.2)	(−0.2)
PMGS	−0.08	−0.20	−0.34	−0.47	−0.59	−0.92	−0.94	−0.91
% dev.	(−0.1)	(−0.2)	(−0.3)	(−0.4)	(−0.5)	(−0.7)	(−0.7)	(−0.7)
PX	0.01	0.02	0.02	0.03	0.03	0.04	0.04	0.01
% dev.	(0.0)	(0.0)	(0.0)	(0.0)	(0.0)	(0.0)	(0.0)	(0.0)
PMY	−0.10	−0.26	−0.43	−0.60	−0.75	−1.16	−1.19	−1.15
% dev.	(−0.1)	(−0.2)	(−0.3)	(−0.4)	(−0.5)	(−0.8)	(−0.8)	(−0.8)

(Continued)

Table 9.4: (Continued)

FY	2011	2012	2013	2014	2015	2020	2025	2030
PLAND	0.09	0.20	0.29	0.35	0.37	0.28	0.18	0.16
% dev.	(0.1)	(0.3)	(0.4)	(0.5)	(0.5)	(0.4)	(0.2)	(0.2)
EXR	−0.06	−0.16	−0.27	−0.36	−0.44	−0.60	−0.53	−0.45
% dev.	(−0.1)	(−0.2)	(−0.3)	(−0.4)	(−0.5)	(−0.8)	(−0.8)	(−0.8)
M2CD	0.07	0.24	0.51	0.86	1.28	3.91	6.79	10.03
% dev.	(0.0)	(0.0)	(0.1)	(0.1)	(0.2)	(0.4)	(0.7)	(1.0)
INTPR	0.00	0.01	0.01	0.02	0.02	0.03	0.02	0.02
% dev.	(0.2)	(0.5)	(0.7)	(1.0)	(1.2)	(1.6)	(1.4)	(1.1)
INTGB	0.00	0.01	0.01	0.02	0.02	0.03	0.02	0.02
% dev.	(0.2)	(0.5)	(0.8)	(1.1)	(1.3)	(1.7)	(1.4)	(1.0)
WN	0.06	0.12	0.16	0.20	0.23	0.33	0.29	0.15
% dev.	(0.1)	(0.1)	(0.2)	(0.2)	(0.2)	(0.3)	(0.3)	(0.1)
YE	0.54	1.14	1.73	2.30	2.87	5.55	8.05	10.72
% dev.	(0.2)	(0.4)	(0.6)	(0.8)	(1.0)	(1.8)	(2.4)	(2.9)
YDIV	0.01	0.02	0.03	0.03	0.03	0.17	0.11	0.18
% dev.	(0.2)	(0.3)	(0.5)	(0.5)	(0.5)	(0.2)	(0.2)	(0.3)
YDH	0.54	1.09	1.64	2.17	2.70	5.17	7.48	9.95
% dev.	(0.2)	(0.4)	(0.7)	(0.9)	(1.1)	(2.0)	(2.7)	(3.3)
YC	0.08	0.17	0.23	0.26	0.26	0.13	0.09	0.14
% dev.	(0.2)	(0.3)	(0.5)	(0.5)	(0.5)	(0.2)	(0.2)	(0.3)
HFA	0.54	1.62	2.96	4.33	5.60	9.37	11.15	13.70
% dev.	(0.0)	(0.1)	(0.2)	(0.3)	(0.4)	(0.6)	(0.7)	(0.8)
HNFA	0.18	0.48	0.84	1.19	1.50	2.30	2.25	2.09
% dev.	(0.0)	(0.1)	(0.1)	(0.2)	(0.2)	(0.3)	(0.3)	(0.3)
HTD	−0.03	−0.25	−0.35	−0.49	−0.67	−2.05	−3.98	−6.50
% dev.	(−0.0)	(−0.1)	(−0.1)	(−0.1)	(−0.2)	(−0.5)	(−1.1)	(−1.8)
RYH	0.00	0.01	0.02	0.03	0.06	0.19	0.26	0.30
% dev.	(0.0)	(0.0)	(0.0)	(0.0)	(0.1)	(0.2)	(0.3)	(0.3)
SH	0.33	0.57	0.76	0.91	1.06	1.84	2.70	3.62
% dev.	(1.8)	(2.9)	(3.8)	(4.7)	(5.6)	(9.3)	(11.6)	(12.5)
NLE	4.55	8.77	13.04	17.48	22.04	44.74	67.01	90.46
% dev.	(0.1)	(0.1)	(0.2)	(0.3)	(0.4)	(0.7)	(1.1)	(1.4)
UR(%)	0.00	0.01	0.02	0.02	0.03	0.05	0.08	0.10
% dev.	(0.1)	(0.2)	(0.4)	(0.5)	(0.6)	(1.2)	(2.2)	(2.9)

(Continued)

Table 9.4:   (*Continued*)

FY	2011	2012	2013	2014	2015	2020	2025	2030
NL	5.00	10.00	15.00	20.00	25.00	50.00	75.00	100.00
% dev.	(0.1)	(0.2)	(0.2)	(0.3)	(0.4)	(0.8)	(1.2)	(1.5)
TXG	0.10	0.25	0.39	0.50	0.58	0.75	0.86	1.08
% dev.	(0.2)	(0.5)	(0.8)	(1.0)	(1.1)	(1.4)	(1.5)	(1.8)
TXI	0.05	0.12	0.18	0.24	0.29	0.44	0.56	0.73
% dev.	(0.4)	(0.8)	(1.3)	(1.7)	(2.0)	(2.8)	(3.1)	(3.6)
TXC	0.05	0.12	0.19	0.23	0.25	0.20	0.14	0.14
% dev.	(0.4)	(0.9)	(1.3)	(1.6)	(1.7)	(1.3)	(0.8)	(0.8)
GEXGE	0.00	0.03	0.06	0.09	0.12	0.21	0.30	0.39
% dev.	(0.0)	(0.0)	(0.1)	(0.1)	(0.1)	(0.2)	(0.3)	(0.4)
KLGBT	−0.10	−0.32	−0.64	−1.05	−1.51	−4.13	−6.87	−10.03
% dev.	(−0.0)	(−0.0)	(−0.1)	(−0.1)	(−0.1)	(−0.3)	(−0.5)	(−0.7)
RKLG	−0.00	−0.01	−0.01	−0.01	−0.02	−0.03	−0.04	−0.05
% dev.	(−0.1)	(−0.2)	(−0.4)	(−0.6)	(−0.7)	(−1.4)	(−1.7)	(−2.1)
TB	−0.00	−0.02	−0.04	−0.07	−0.11	−0.38	−0.81	−1.10
% dev.	(−0.1)	(−0.3)	(−0.5)	(−0.9)	(−1.5)	(−5.0)	(−7.2)	(−7.3)
CBP	−0.02	−0.04	−0.08	−0.13	−0.18	−0.55	−0.98	−1.44
% dev.	(−0.1)	(−0.2)	(−0.4)	(−0.7)	(−1.0)	(−3.0)	(−4.8)	(−5.8)

Note: Deviation: (Scenario−Baseline); % deviation: (Scenario−Baseline)/Baseline × 100 (%)
Source: Simulated and compiled by the author.

In comparison with the increase in the number of labor supply, the increase in the number of employed (labor demand) will be limited since all of the increased labor supply could not be necessarily absorbed in Japanese labor markets. Therefore, unemployment rate will rise slightly by 0.027 point in FY2015, by 0.049 point in FY2020 and by 0.095 point in FY2030 as compared to the baseline.

As for the demand-side, real domestic expenditure (GDE) is expected to increase by 0.4 per cent in FY2015, by 0.7 per cent in FY2020, by 0.9 per cent in FY2025 and by 1.2 per cent in FY2030, in terms of per cent deviation, as compared to the baseline forecast. It seems that the effects on the demand-side economy may be limited. But, the increase in labor supply is very limited, therefore, the impacts of the labor increase on the economy would be fairly large when we take account of the elasticity of GDE changes to labor supply changes (changes in GDE/changes in labor supply) at 0.97 in FY2015, at 0.89 in FY2020 and 0.81 in FY2030.

The largest effects will probably be recognized in real private final consumption expenditure at 1.5 trillion yen in FY2015, at 3.20 trillion yen in FY2020 and 6.41 trillion yen in FY2030, in terms of deviation, in comparison with the baseline projection, which will be caused by the increase in household income and stimulated by the increase in employment. Therefore, the effects on housing investment will also probably be large at 0.55 trillion yen in FY2015, at 0.77 trillion yen in FY2020 and at 1.00 trillion yen in FY2030, in terms of deviation, as compared to the baseline forecast. Furthermore, private non-housing investment is also expected to have fairly large impacts at 0.59 trillion yen in FY2015, at 1.05 trillion yen in FY2020 and at 2.02 trillion yen in FY2030 in comparison with the baseline forecast.

With respect to the effects on the supply-side economy, with the increase in the number of employed and capital accumulation, GDP capacity will probably be stimulated by 0.2 per cent in FY2015, by 0.6 per cent in FY2020, by 0.9 per cent in FY2025 and by 1.2 per cent in FY2030, in per cent deviation, as compared to the baseline projection. In the 2010s the effects on the supply-side will be weaker, but they will be getting larger than that on the demand-side in the mid-2020s. As a result, deflationary gap is expected to increase in the latter half of the 2020s.

As discussed, these impacts will be brought by way of increases in household income even in this scenario simulation. Particularly, compensation of employee (YE) will probably increase along with the increase in labor, although nominal wage rate will be stagnant with labor supply pressure. As a result, the effects on household disposable income will probably be remarkable at 1.1 per cent in FY2015, by 2.0 per cent in FY2020, by 2.7 per cent in FY2025 and by 3.3 per cent in FY2030, in per cent deviation, as compared to the baseline forecast. Then, as a result of the increase in household income, the percentage share between household disposable income and corporate income (RYH) will probably rise by 0.06 points in FY2015, by 0.19 points in FY2020, by 0.26 points in FY2025 and by 0.30 points in FY2030 in comparison with the baseline forecast.

In summary, as assumed, the expansion of labor immigration is expected to stimulate both the demand-side and supply-side economies through increases in the number of employed and hence household income. The effects on the economy may not be so large, but we can expect the positive and favorable impacts on the economy by way of expanding the household income and its share as well as the previous two alternative scenario simulations, as demonstrated in Figures 9.8 and 9.9. Furthermore, in

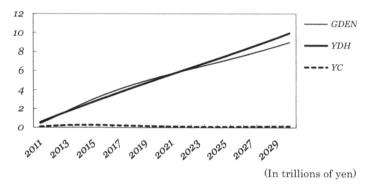

(In trillions of yen)

Figure 9.8:   Deviation of nominal GDE, household disposable income (YDH) and corporate income (YC) from the baseline forecast, FY2011–2030.

Source: Simulated and developed by the author.

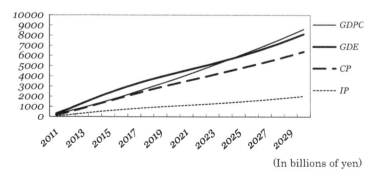

(In billions of yen)

Figure 9.9:   Deviation of real GDE, GDP capacity, CP and IP in Scenario C from the baseline forecast, FY2011–2030.

Source: Simulated and developed by the author.

this scenario forecast, we can recognize that the supply-side will probably have relatively steady effects as well as the demand-side. Therefore, it can be seen that decreases in economically active population and hence labor force will have a large negative effect on the actual economy in Japan.

CHAPTER 10

Concluding Remarks

10.1. Conclusion and Policy Implication

In the present study, the analysis was focused on the macro-economic structure of the Japanese economy, with special attention to the macro demand-side, supply-side and income distribution patterns. An examination was made on how we improve the current long-term deflation, which has been observed since the mid-1970s. Accordingly, we studied the long-term deflationary economy of Japan and its causes with some theories and empirical analyses by employing econometric modeling and forecasting techniques.

Within this volume, we can summarize this study by chapter, as follows.

- **The Japanese Economy after the End of High-Growth Era**

Chapter 2 reviewed the Japanese economic performance in the past decades just after the end of high-growth era, by decade, in order to reveal the current economic stagnation and its causes, considering the world economic environmental changes, including shift to the floating currency system, oil crises and so on. By focusing on economic growth, income distribution patterns and the other major economic indicators, we reviewed the Japanese economy. In reviewing the economy, it can be seen that the growth performance was declining from over 10 per cent annual growth in the 1950s and 1960s to 4–5 per cent in the 1970s and 1980s and to 1–2 per cent in the 1990s and 2000s with declines in the wage income share.

However, even in the oil crises period, the Japanese economy continued its performance with strong investment and R&D expenditures with rises in profit shares and declines in wage income share. This chapter discussed the causes of the structural deflation which has started in the mid-1970s.

● Deflationary Economy of Japan

In Chapter 3, we discussed the structural deflationary economy in the process of economic development by utilizing an intuitive model. According to the model, it seems that the Japanese aggregate supply exceeded the aggregate demand in the early 1970s. Since then, the growth performance has declined depending on the demand-side growth.

In addition, we estimated the Japanese GDP capacity, which is the supply capacity in the economy and hence the deflationary gap with an econometric analysis. According to the results of the estimation of the supply capacity, the deflationary gap has been recognized since the mid-1970s and it increased up to the bursting of the bubble and reached to around 95 trillion yen in FY2008. In addition, we evaluated the estimated supply capacity and its growth by comparing to other estimated measures, including the natural rate of growth of Japan based on Okun's law and the potential growth estimated by the Bank of Japan (BOJ) and by the Economic and Social Research Institute (ESRI) of the Japanese government. In the present study, this GDP capacity has been endogenized in the demand-supply integrated macroeconometric model to analyze the Japanese economy.

● Causes of the Deflationary Economy

In this chapter, we examined the causes of the Japanese structural deflationary economy from the viewpoint of income distribution between profits and wages (wage income) with theories and empirical analyses. Since the end of the high-growth era, profit share has been increasing and hence wage income share declining, which might cause the prolonged stagnation of the demand-side, in particular, household expenditures. Moreover, competing in world market with improving price and non-price competitiveness has resulted in distorting income distribution, which might be attributed to the private corporate sector's behaviors, and deteriorate the deflationary economy of Japan.

In addition, we discussed the distorted income distribution by employing the averaged Tobin's q ratio in the past few decades, based on the latest SNA (System of National Accounts). According to the Tobin's q ratio in the past decades, the ratio of net financial liabilities to total assets in the non-financial corporate sector was very low at 0.4–0.5 on average, which cannot be explained by neoclassical economic theories.

In addition, we examined the causes of the strengthened supply-side, with special focus on the role of technical progress with cost-price incentive induced technical progress, the Solow neutral technical progress and the Hicksian neutral technical progress, on a macro-basis. At the same time, we discussed the effects of the distorted income distribution on the demand-side economy by empirical analyses.

• The Theoretical Model Framework

Chapter 5 discussed the theoretical framework, which is the theoretical mode for developing an econometric model utilized in the present study. The model is a demand–supply integrated type model, in which we emphasized the importance of not only income effects but also asset effects, particular in the deflationary economy. In general, neoclassical growth models, including the Solow–Swan model, are dominant in growth theory. However, it is difficult to apply them to the actual economy, particularly in an open economic system as mentioned by Thirlwall. At the same time, these supply-side growth models cannot explain the Japanese deflationary economy since the demand-side is dominant to determine the growth performance. Therefore, we introduced the demand-supply integrated model approach to examine the structural deflationary economy of Japan.

Furthermore, this chapter examined the relations between income distribution patterns and the Keynes multiplier, theoretically and empirically. The demand-side economic growth model consists of the Keynes multiplier as an accelerator for growth and growth of the independent components as a generator for growth, so that the changes in income distribution patterns affect the growth performance through changes in the multiplier. This chapter also revealed this mechanism and examined the income distribution effects on the growth performance, theoretically and empirically.

• The Demand–Supply Integrated Econometric Model of Japan

Chapter 6 aimed to explain the structure of the demand–supply integrated macro-econometric model of Japan, based on the theoretical model discussed in the previous chapter. The model consists of nine blocks, including

(1) the real expenditure block, (2) the nominal expenditure block, (3) the prices and wage rates block, (4) the production block, (5) the money and finance block, (6) population and labor force block, (7) the income distribution block, (8) the government finance block, (9) the International trade and balance of payment (BOP) block. In addition, the chapter examined the unit root test by employing the ADF (Augmented Dickey–Fuller) Test algorithm.

● **Regression Analysis**

In Chapter 7, we implemented regression analyses, with special attention to the major behavioral equations with reference to the supply-side, the demand-side, the income distribution and prices, based on the theoretical model framework in Chapters 5 and 6. Within the econometric modeling and forecasting techniques, this process is very important to realize the actual economic causations in the multi-equation structural model system as a virtual reality, based on economic theories. We could obtain fairly good results to explain the actual economy within a conventional econometric model framework. In the present study, we had tried to examine the major economic causations between variables by employing rational expectations theories, foreword-looking type models and so on, but the performance of these models was not good in model reliability tests and dynamic simulation tests. Therefore, we did not utilize these models in this study.

However, we introduced not only income effects but also asset/debt effects in the household consumption and housing investment functions, so that the model specification is fairly complex particularly in the real expenditure block (I-S model block). In other words, the study utilized the conventional model that can explain the actual economy more precisely, but did not employ some new methods that cannot explain the actual economy.

● **Dynamic Simulation Tests**

In Chapter 8, we implemented dynamic simulation tests, including a model reliability test, dynamic Keynes multiplier tests, base-money increase scenario simulation test and yen appreciation simulation test in order to examine the effects of policy variable changes on the economy. In the model reliability test, we employed the final test, which is the toughest stress test among the Goldberger tests, in which we were able to get fairly good results and the model could explain actual real GDE within a 2.3 per cent error range in FY1981–2008.

In the dynamic Keynes multiplier tests, we could obtain very interesting results, in which (1) the Keynes multiplier with government investment increase scenario demonstrated fairly high dynamic multiplier at over 2.0 from the third year. These fairly high multipliers depend on not only income effects but also net asset effects, which have not been recognized in the model in utilizing only income effects, (2) the Keynes multiplier with personal income tax cut also presented fairly large impacts on the demand-side because highly stimulated assets and improved liabilities by enhanced household income have positive effects on the demand-side, so that the dynamic Keynes multiplier in the scenario simulations may be higher than that of the theoretical one, reaching to 2.0 in the fourth year even in the case of the personal income tax cut scenario. Within this simulation, the theoretical model discussed in Chapter 5 has been proven.

On the contrary, in the base-money increase scenario, the effects of monetary base increases on the economy were very limited, despite the fairly high Keynes multiplier, because of a liquidity trap in the Japanese economy, which could be explained by the IS-LM model framework. In the yen appreciation scenario, we could recognize the fairly large negative impacts of yen appreciation on the Japanese economy. In this dynamic simulation test, we can easily understand that the over-appreciated yen to the US dollar has accelerated the deflationary economy of Japan.

• Long-Term Scenario Forecasts toward FY2030

In Chapter 9, we conducted long-term economic forecasts and depicted the Japanese economy and its structures up to FY2030 with alternative scenario simulations. We designed and conducted four alternative scenario simulations: (1) the baseline projection that is a most-likely scenario, in which we assumed most of the current policies and trends of the exogenous variables will continue in the future, (2) the scenario forecast that the corporate sector will increase dividend yields by 2.0 per cent for the household sector from FY2011 to FY2030, as Scenario A, (3) the scenario forecast that the government will introduce corporate income tax cut for increasing wage income by 2.5 trillion yen and reallocate its same amounts to the household sector by way of the corporate sector from FY2011 to FY2030, as Scenario B and (4) the labor immigration expansion scenario forecast, as Scenario C, in which the labor immigration will increase by 50,000 year by year from FY2011 and by 1 million in FY2030. In other words, these scenario simulations therefore examined the effects of changes in income distribution patterns through direct and indirect effects.

In the baseline projection, it could be seen that the Japanese economy will probably continue the deflationary economy up to FY2030, in which the annual average growth rate of real GDE will be 0.91 per cent in the 2010s and 1.45 per cent in the 2020s. In line with the low growth rate of the demand-side GDP (GDE), real GDP capacity growth rate is expected to be stagnant and hence the deflationary gap will decline to around 20 trillion yen in FY2030. Therefore, the rate of changes in the general deflator (PGDP) is expected to turn to be positive slightly in the mid-2020s.

In these alternative policy scenarios simulations, on the other hand, we observed relatively large impacts on the economy, despite the limited values added in assumption, through income and asset effects, as discussed in Chapter 5. In other words, we can realize the domestic demand-led growth by improving the distorted income distribution. With income and asset effects through income reallocation, purchasing power in the household sector could be reinforced. As a result, the demand-side and hence overall growth performance could be strengthened in the deflationary economy of Japan.

In addition, we can summarize this study based on theories and evidence on an econometric analysis and recommend some policy implications, as follows.

In the theoretical analysis, we have clarified that the prolonged Japanese deflation is a structural construct which relies on the strong supply-side with a vital capital accumulation and technical progress to cope with severe competition in world markets. On the contrary, the demand-side has been restricted by the stagnant household income with the decrease in household income share since the mid-1970s. At the same time, it was discussed that stock variables, including financial assets, non-financial assets and total liabilities in the household sector, play a significant role in stimulating the household expenditures, such as household consumption and housing investment.

In the econometric analysis, by explicitly employing the estimated GDP capacity, the demand-supply integrated macro-model was constructed in order to analyze the causes of the deflationary economy of Japan. In the regression analysis, the supply-side has been strengthened by the vital investment behavior and technical progress, in which the Solow neutrality with embodied technical progress and the Hicksian neutral technical progress were observed utilizing the Cobb–Douglas production function.

On the other hand, the regression analysis revealed why the demand-side economy was so weak in spite of the strong supply-side, as discussed in the theoretical and empirical analyses. In the regression analysis on real household consumption expenditure and real housing investment, it was clarified that the coefficient of the real debt effect is larger than that of the real asset effect and the increase in household disposable income stimulates the household final consumption expenditure and housing investment through both income effects and asset effects. In addition, in the regression analysis, it was examined that the supply-side GDP capacity base labor productivity contributes to stimulating the demand-side economy through strengthening the price and non-price competitiveness.

In the dynamic simulation tests, we conducted four simulation tests, such as government investment increase scenario, personal income tax cut scenario, monetary base increase scenario as a financial and monetary policy and yen appreciation scenario. In the government investment increase and personal income tax cut scenario simulation tests, it can be seen that the Keynes multiplier was fairly high as compared to the other research projects employing a macro-econometric model. Particularly, in the case of the income tax cut scenario, the multiplier is drastically getting higher from the second year with net asset effects in the household sector. This is because the higher multiplier resulted from not only the income effects but also the asset and the positive debt effects. In other words, the demand stimulus may still be powerful and, therefore, policy makers should reconsider the effects of demand stimulus on the economy within longer term national projects.

On the contrary, it was clarified in the monetary policy simulation test that the effects of the monetary and financial policy were still limited, despite the higher Keynes multiplier, due to the liquidity trap. Accordingly, policy makers should reconsider the policies to stimulate the demand-side of the economy, in particular household sector's expenditure, for example, by reducing the higher interest rates of consumer credit and housing loans thereby stimulating the domestic expenditures.

Concerning the yen appreciation scenario, as discussed in the simulation test, yen appreciation to US dollar has a large negative impact on the economy through decreasing real net exports and accelerates deflation in Japan. Moreover, it is assumed that the yen appreciation results in a vicious circle between deflation and yen appreciation, which causes distorted income distribution by depressing overall corporate income and, as a result, declines in wage income share.

In the long-term forecasts toward FY2030, we performed one baseline and three alternative scenario forecasts, in which the baseline forecast was conducted as a most-likely scenario. According to the baseline forecast in the long-term projection, the Japanese economy will remain stagnant in terms of the demand-side growth, while the supply-side will also be inactive following the weak demand-side economic performance. As a result, the deflationary gap is expected to decline to around 20 trillion yen in FY2030. This will be a problematic situation in which the demand-side and supply-side of the Japanese economy will lose its economic dynamism and eventually hollow out Japan.

At the same time, three alternative policy scenario simulations were conducted. In accordance with the results of these scenario simulations, the Japanese economy is expected to have fairly large positive impacts as compared to the baseline simulation, despite the limited values assumed for stimulating the economy as a demand stimulus.

Accordingly, the long-term scenario forecasts suggest that we need to enhance the household purchasing power for stimulating the demand-side economy because many policy makers, politicians, business leaders and economists underestimate the potential of the Japanese demand-side. It is therefore noteworthy that improvements of the distorted income distribution have an efficient effect to achieve an expanded equilibrium, instead of a declining equilibrium, in the economy. Of course, there is no sufficient policy to solve the Japanese long-term slump completely, so we should combine various policies, as a strong policy package, to stimulate the demand-side and hence the whole economy.

At the same time, it is important to continue strengthening the supply-side economy in Japan. It is worth noting that a strong supply-side with technical progress can stimulate its own demand through reinforcing price and non-price competitiveness, which contributes to enhancing our economic welfare not only in Japan but also in the world economy through international trade and capital transfer.

It is, therefore, indispensable to stimulate the demand-side economy with the strong demand stimulus package while the supply-side is still active, in order to achieve the vital growth performance again, as being discussed, "Demand creates its own Supply." In turn, as for the "over-investment hypothesis" we discussed in Introduction, the Japanese corporate sector has continued vital investment behaviors to cope with severe competition in world markets and to improve price and non-price competitiveness. The strong supply-side is a sort of national asset which allows us to appreciate the active investment behaviors in Japan since we may be able to stimulate the Japanese economy by improving the distorted distribution of income and some demand stimulus policies.

At the same time, we should reconsider the importance of Japanese conventional management system, especially a life-time employment system from the viewpoints of the demand-side and supply-side, because it plays a significant role of maintaining domestic demands as a kind of built-in stabilizer and contributes to strengthening technical progress which is developed and improved by experienced and qualified workers . In particular, major business associations such as the Japan Business Federation, Japan Association of Corporate Executives and the Japan Chamber of Commerce and Industry should reconsider this issue and lead the Japanese economy together with the labor and government.

10.2. Directions for Further Research

In subsequent studies, we will continue this research project and deepen our understanding of the Japanese economy in relation to the roles of the stock variables, including assets and liabilities in the household sector, the corporate sector and the government sector. In addition, we will analyze the role of social infrastructure to stimulate both the demand-side and the supply-side economy. Particularly, it seems that the social infrastructure that is a source of national wealth may affect both the demand-side economy and the supply-side economy in the long run.

In addition, there exist other several problematic issues in the Japanese economy, including external imbalance, regional income inequality, government debt and unemployment problems, which are closely related to the structural deflation; hence there is a need to continue our research on these issues by employing modeling and forecasting techniques. At the same time, we will analyze the hollowing-out problem, as noted, by examining the effects of FDI outflows and of net income transfers from the rest of the world on the Japanese economy in the context of the world economy, in particular Asia and the Pacific.

Bibliography

Adams, F. G., B. Gangnes and S. Shishido (1993). *Economic Activity, Trade and Industry in the US-Japan-World Economy*, USA: Praeger Publisher.

Ando, A., D. Christelis and R. Miyagawa (2003). Inefficiency of Corporate Investment and Distortion of Savings Behavior in Japan, in M. Blomstrom *et al.* (eds.), *Structural Impediments to Growth in Japan*, Chicago: University of Chicago Press, pp. 155–190.

Ando, A. (2002). Missing Household Saving and Valuation of Corporations, *Journal of the Japanese and International Economies*, Vol. 16, No. 2, pp. 147–176.

Domar, E. (1947). Expansion and Employment, *American Economic Review*, Vol. 37, Issue 1, pp. 34–88.

Fisher, I. (1933.) The Debt Deflation Theory of Great Depression, *Econometrica*, Vol. 1, No. 4, pp. 337–357.

Friedman, M. (1968). The Role of Monetary Policy, *American Economic Review*, Vol. 58, Issue 1, pp. 1–17.

Harrod, R. (1939). An Essay in Dynamic Theory, *Economic Journal*, Vol. 49, No. 193, pp. 14–33.

Harrod, R. (1933). *International Economics*, Cambridge: Cambridge University Press.

Hayashi, F. (2006). The Over Investment Hypothesis, in L. R. Klein (ed.), *Long-Run Growth and Short-Run Stabilization: Essays in Memory of Albert Ando*, pp. 275–287, London: Edward Elgar.

Hida, F. *et al.* (2009). The ESIR Short-Run Macro Econometric Model of the Japanese Economy: Basic Structure, Multipliers, and Economic Policy Analyses, Economic Social Research Institute (ESRI), ESRI Home Page.

Hori, M. *et al.* (1998). Structure of Short-term Macro Econometric Model of Japan and Effects of Macro Economic Policy, *Economic Survey*, No. 157, EPA Research Institute.

Horioka, Y. C. (2006). The Causes of Japan's Lost Decade: The Role of Household Consumption, *Japan and the World Economy*, Vol. 18, No. 4, pp. 378–400.

Ito, S. *et al.* (2006). Newly Utilized Method for Estimation of GDP Gap and Potential Growth of Japan, *Bank of Japan Review*, 2006-J-8 (in Japanese).

Kalecki, M. (1944). Professor Pigou on The Classical Stationary State — A Comment, *Economic Journal*, Vol. 54, No. 213, pp. 131–132.

Keynes, J. M. (1936). *The General Theory of Employment, Interest and Money*, Macmillan.

Kido, T., K Nagao and O. Nakamura (2004–2010). Economic Forecasts of Japan and Hokkaido with an Econometric Model Analysis, *Soken Keizai*, Research Institute of Hokkaido Electric Power Co., Ltd., ISSN 0919-6579, Research Paper Series, No. 41–48 (in Japanese).

Kido, T., N. Shimizu, and O. Nakamura (1997–2003). Economic Forecasts of Japan and Hokkaido with an Econometric Model Analysis, *Soken Keizai*, Research Institute of Hokkaido Electric Power Co., Ltd., ISSN 0919-6579, Research Paper Series, No. 33–40 (in Japanese).

Klein, L. R., F. G. Adams, Y. Kumasaka and A. Shinozaki (2007). *Accelerating Japan's Economic Growth: Resolving Japan's Growth Controversy*, Routledge.

Klein, L. R. (1983). *Lecture in Econometrics*, North-Holland.

Klein, L. R. (1978) The Supply-Side, *American Economic Review*, Vol. 68, pp. 1–7.

Kitajima, M. (2011). Lower Decreases in Domestic Demand Deflators in Comparison with the Previous Period, *Weekly Indicators*, No. 981, ESRI (in Japanese).

Krugman, P. (1989). Differences in Income Elasticity and Trends in Real Exchange Rates, *European Economic Review*, Vol. 33, Issue 5, pp. 1031–1046.

Lipsey, R. G. (1960). The Relation between Unemployment and the Rate of Change of Money Wage Rates in the United Kingdom, 1962–1957: A Further Analysis, *Economica*, Vol. 27, No. 105, pp. 1–31.

Lucas, R. (1988). On the Mechanics of Economic Development, *Journal of Monetary Economics*, Vol. 22, pp. 3–42.

Maddala, G. S. (1988). *Introduction to Econometrics*, Macmillan Inc.

Minami, R. (1981). *Japanese Economic Development*, Toyo-Keizai.

Nakamura, O. (2011). Aggregate Demand, Aggregate Supply and Economic Growth of Developing Countries, The Case of Vietnam: Theory and Evidence on an Econometric Analysis, Research Institute of the International University of Japan (IUJ), Working Paper Series, EMS-2011-07.

Nakamura, O. (2010). Economic Structure and Growth Performance of Niigata, Toyama, Ishikawa and Fukui Prefectures: A Comparative Econometric Analysis, *Journal of Econometric Study of Northeast Asia*, Vol. 7, No. 1, pp. 23–45.

Nakamura, O. (2008). Growth Performance of Japan under the Deflationary Economy: An Econometric Analysis, mimeo.

Nakamura, O. (2007). Energy Balances and the Economic Development of China: An Econometric Analysis using the Global Macroeconomic and Energy Model, *Journal of Econometric Study of Northeast Asia*, Vol. 6, No. 1, pp. 57–76.

Nakamura, O. (2002). Reform of Regional Public Finance and Administration: The Case of Hokkaido, An Econometric Analysis, Planning and Administration, *Journal of Japan Association for Planning and Administration*, Vol. 16, No. 3, pp. 58–69 (in Japanese).

Nakamura, O. (1993). Analysis of Hokkaido Economy and its Forecasts to the Year 2000 with a Macro I-O Integrated Model. Paper for the Plenary Session Presentation at the *10th International Conference of Input-Output Association International*, Seville, Spain.

Nakamura, O. (1990). Cohort-Type Demographic Model of Japan, in F. G. Adams and S. Shishido (eds.), *Structure of Trade and Industry in the US-Japan Economy: Integration with Project LINK and Simulation Applications*, Chapter 2, NIRA Study Series, Vol. 3, No. 1, NIRA.

Nakamura, O., M. Sato and T. Shimizu (1996). *International Interactions through International Trade and Capital Transfer within Japan, South Korea and the U.S.: A Pilot Model for the JETRO-WEIS Global Model*, World Economic Information Service (WEIS) (in Japanese).

Okun, A. (1962). Potential GNP: Its Measurement and Significance, *Proceedings of the Business and Finance Statistics Section of the American Statistical Association*.

Phillips, A. W. (1958). The Relation Between Unemployment and the Rate of Change of Money Wage Rates in the United Kingdom, 1961–1957, *Economica*, Vol. 25, No. 100, pp. 283–299.

Pigou, A. C. (1943). The Classical Stationary State, *Economic Journal*, Vol. 53, No. 212, pp. 343–351.

Ramsey, F. (1928). A Mathematical Theory of Saving, *Economic Journal*, Vol. 38, pp. 553–549.

Romer, P.M. (1986). Increasing Return and Long-Run Growth, *Journal of Political Economy*, Vol. 94, pp. 1002–1037.

Rostow, W.W. (1960). *The Stages of Economic Growth: A Non-Communist Manifesto*, Cambridge: Cambridge University Press.

Saito, M. (2008). Substitutability between Household Consumption Expenditures and Corporate Non-housing Investments: Based on the Recent Japanese Capital Accumulation, in S. Ikeda *et al.* (eds.), *Tides to the Contemporary Economics*, oyo-Keizai Sinpo-sha (in Japanese).

Sato, M and O. Nakamura (1996). Simulation System for Global Modeling and Forecasting (*SIMSYS*), mimeo.

Sato, R. and T. Morita (2009). Quantity or Quality: The Impact of Labor Saving Innovation on US and Japanese Growth Rates, 1960–2004, *The Japanese Economic Review*, Vol. 60, No. 4, pp. 407–434.

Shishido, S., A. Kawakami and K. Tamashiro (2010). Policy Alternatives for Japan Toward 2020, in L. R. Klein and S. Ichimura (eds.), *Macro-Econometric Modeling of Japan*, Singapore: World Scientific.

Shishido, S. and O. Nakamura (1992a). Induced Technical Progress Structural Adjustment: A Multi-Sectoral Model Approach to Japan's Growth Alternatives, *Journal of Applied Input-Output Analysis (JAIOA)*, Vol. 1, No. 1, pp. 1–31.

Shishido, S. and O. Nakamura (1992b). Commercial Policy and Restructuring the International Economy, *Journal of Asian Economics*, Vol. 3. No. 1, pp. 97–109.

Shishido, S. and F. G. Adams (1990) Structure of Trade and Industry in the US-Japan Economy: Integration with Project LINK and Simulation Applications, NIRA Study Series, Vol. 3. No. 1, NIRA.

Solow, R. M. (1956). A Contribution to the Theory of Economic Growth, *Quarterly Journal of Economics*, Vol. 79, pp. 65–94.

Solow, R. M. (1960). Investment and Technical Progress, in R. M. Solow (ed), *Mathematical Methods in the Social Sciences*, Stanford: Stanford University Press.

Swan, T. W. (1956). Economic Growth and Capital Accumulation, *Economic Record*, Vol. 32, pp. 334–361.

Thirlwall, A. P. (2002). *The Nature of Economic Growth: An Alternative Framework for Understanding the Performance of Nations*, London: Edward Elgar.

Tinbergen, J. (1942). *Zur Theorie der langfristigen Wiltschaftsentwicklung*, Weltwirtschaftliches Archiv, Bd. 55 (in German).

Tobin, J. (1980). *Asset Accumulation and Economic Activity: Reflections on Contemporary Macroeconomic Theory*, Chicago: The University of Chicago Press.

Tobin, J. (1951). Relative Income, Absolute Income and Saving, in *Money, Trade, and Economic Growth*, New York: Macmillan.

WEIS (2005). *Structure of the JETRO-WEIS Global Model: Development of a Global Energy Sub-Model*, World Economic Information Service (WEIS) (in Japanese).

Working, E. J. (1927). What Do Statistical Demand Curves Show? *Quarterly Journal of Economics*, Vol. 41, No. 2, pp. 212–235.

Appendix A: Macro-Econometric Model of Japan

1. Real Expenditure Block

(1.1) Real gross domestic expenditure

$$GDE = CP + CG + IP + IH + IG + JP + JG + EGS - MGS + SD$$

(1.2) Real household final consumption expenditure

$$\begin{aligned}
CH = {} & 101,692.3 + 0.7412\,(YDH/PCH*100) \\
& \quad (5.66) \qquad (7.22) \\
& - 1,101.92.661\,PCH*(1 + RTXC) \\
& \quad (-3.38) \\
& + 0.04279\,(HFA/PCH*100) \\
& \quad (4.57) \\
& + 0.00845\,(HNFA/PCH*100) \\
& \quad (2.08) \\
& - 0.3887\ (\Delta HTD/PCH*100) - 1,260.94\,INTOR(-1) \\
& \quad (-3.96) \qquad\qquad\qquad\qquad (-2.05)
\end{aligned}$$

OLS(1981−2008)
Adjusted-R^2 = 0.997 SE = 2,466.4 DW = 1.723

(1.3) Real non-profit institution final consumption expenditure

$$\begin{aligned}
CN = {} & -415.952 + 0.003114\,GDE + 0.816975\,CN(-1) \\
& \ (-0.80) \quad\ (2.02) \qquad\qquad (6.90)
\end{aligned}$$

OLS (1981−2009)
Adjusted-R^2 = 0.959 SE = 293.775 DW = 2.368

(1.4) Real government final consumption expenditure

$$CG = CGN/PCG*100$$

209

(1.5) Real housing investment

$$IH = 4{,}495.1 + 0.19633YDH/(PCP^*(1 + RTXC))^*100$$
$$(1.08) \quad (4.25)$$

$$-1{,}273.5\ INTOR(-1)$$
$$\phantom{-1{,}273.5\ }(-3.71)$$

$$+0.00439HTA/PIH^*100 - 0.10367\Delta HTD/PIH^*100$$
$$(2.94) (-2.02)$$

$$-0.16296KH(-1)$$
$$(-4.86)$$

$$+0.31887IH(-1)$$
$$(2.58)$$

OLS(1981−2008)
Adjusted-$R^2 = 0.886$ SE $= 1{,}142.1$ DW $= 1.766$

(1.6) Real private non-housing investment

$$IP = -41838.3 + 0.3761\ \Delta GDE + 0.04104\ (YC + YC(-1)$$
$$(-3.63) \quad (8.91) (2.23)$$

$$-TXC - TXC(-1))/PIP^*100$$

$$+0.03103\ M2CD/PGDP^*100 + 43249.1\ CUR(-1)$$
$$(5.20) (3.55)$$

$$+0.748\ IP(-1)$$
$$(13.16)$$

OLS(1981−2008)
Adjusted-$R^2 = 0.983$ SE $= 1{,}994.8$ DW $= 1.857$

(1.7) Real government investment

$$IG = IGN/PIG^*100$$

(1.8) Real private inventory changes

$$JP = KJP - KJP(-1)$$

(1.9) Real exports of goods and services

$$EGS = (EG + ES)$$

(1.10) Real imports of goods and services

$$MGS = (MG + MS)$$

(1.11) Real private final consumption expenditure

$$CP = CH + CN$$

(1.12) Real inventory stock

$$KJP = -5910.79 + 0.076990\,GDE + 8873.27\,PX/PCP$$
$$\quad\;\;(-0.09)\quad\;(7.01)\qquad\qquad\;(2.44)$$

$$+\,0.471013\,KJP(-1)$$
$$\quad\;(6.62)$$

$$+\,2865.48*(D08)$$
$$\quad\;(2.41)$$

OLS(1981−2009)
Adjusted-R^2 = 0.991   SE = 965.1476   DW = 1.541

(1.13) Real housing stock

$$KH = KH(-1) + IH - DH + SDH$$

(1.14) Real depreciation of housing stock

$$DH = -1525.74 + 0.009399\,KH + 1443.58\,GDE/GDE(-1)$$
$$\quad\;\;(-1.00)\qquad(4.18)\qquad\qquad(1.06)$$

$$+\,0.803277\,DH(-1)$$
$$\quad\;(19.30)$$

OLS(1981−2008)
Adjusted-R^2 = 0.999   SE = 114.4452   DW = 2.412

2. Nominal Expenditure Block

(2.1) Nominal gross domestic expenditure

$$GDEN = CPN + CGN + IPN + IHN + IGN + JPN + JGN$$
$$+\,EGSN - MGSN + SDN$$

(2.2) Nominal private final consumption expenditure

$$CPN = CHN + CNN$$

(2.3) Nominal household final consumption expenditure

$$CHN = CH*PCH/100$$

(2.4) Nominal non-profit institution final consumption expenditure

$$CNN = CN*PCN/100$$

(2.5) Nominal government final consumption expenditure

$$CGN = -6{,}945.66 + 175.7909 \text{ WN} + 0.47934 \text{ GEXSS}(-1)$$
$$(-2.90) \qquad (4.58) \qquad\qquad (2.50)$$
$$+ \ 0.786904 \text{ CGN}(-1)$$
$$(13.55)$$

OLS(1981−2009)
Adjusted-R^2 = 0.999   SE = 639.920   DW = 1.567

(2.6) Nominal private non-housing investment

$$IPN = IP*PIP/100$$

(2.7) Nominal government investment

$$IGN = -8870.27 + 0.681241 \text{ GEXPW} + 1.91027 \text{ GEXTD}$$
$$(-3.38) \qquad (2.08) \qquad\qquad (4.54)$$
$$+ \ 0.767411 \text{ (GEXLA + GEXTT)} - 9308.44 \text{ D98}$$
$$(6.61) \qquad\qquad\qquad (-10.48)$$

OLS(1981−2008)
Adjusted-R^2 = 0.966   SE = 1,299.88   DW = 2.040

(2.8) Nominal private inventory changes

$$JPN = JP*PJP/100$$

(2.9) Nominal government inventory changes

$$JGN = JG*PJG/100$$

(2.10) Nominal exports of goods and services

$$EGSN = EGSN*PEGS/100$$

(2.11) Nominal imports of goods and services

$$MGSN = MGS*PMGS/100$$

3. Prices and Wage Rates Block

(3.1) General deflator of GDE

$$PGDE = GDEN/GDE*100$$

(3.2) Deflator of household final consumption expenditure

$$\ln(PCH) = -\underset{(-0.08)}{0.0560} + \underset{(4.16)}{0.189596}\ln(PX) + \underset{(4.85)}{0.285576}\ln(WN)$$
$$+ \underset{(5.91)}{0.512058}\ln(PCH(-1))$$

C-O (1981−2009)
Adjusted-R^2 = 0.989   SE = 0.004024   DW = 1.955

(3.3) Deflator of non-profit institution final consumption expenditure

$$\ln(PCN) = -\underset{(-0.05)}{0.004637} + \underset{(3.95)}{0.188553}\ln(PX) + \underset{(4.59)}{0.287082}\ln(WN)$$
$$+ \underset{(5.51)}{0.505318}\ln(PCP(-1))$$

C-O (1981−2009)
Adjusted-R^2 = 0.988   SE = 0.004659   DW = 1.935

(3.4) Deflator of government final consumption expenditure

$$\ln(PCG) = -\underset{(-2.25)}{0.693404} + \underset{(7.29)}{0.259166}\ln(PX) + \underset{(6.88)}{0.335449}\ln(WN)$$
$$+ \underset{(7.39)}{0.551485}\ln(PCG(-1))$$

OLS(1981−2009)
Adjusted-R^2 = 0.991   SE = 0.006814   DW = 1.819

(3.5) Deflator of private non-housing investment

$$\ln(PIP) = -\underset{(-0.39)}{0.179680} + \underset{(8.74)}{0.424348}\ln(PX) + \underset{(5.57)}{0.288223}\ln(WN)$$
$$- \underset{(-5.07)}{0.241956}\ln(GDPC(-1)/NL(-1))$$
$$+ \underset{(8.89)}{0.553089}\ln(PIP(-1))$$

C-O (1981–2009)

Adjusted-R^2 = 0.997   SE = 0.004830   DW = 1.702

(3.6) Deflator of housing investment

$$\ln (PIH) = -0.652301 + 0.192431 \ln (PX) + 0.244089 \ln (WN)$$
$$\qquad\quad (-1.14) \qquad (2.25) \qquad\qquad\qquad (3.21)$$
$$+ 0.704039 \ln (PIH(-1))$$
$$\quad (7.27)$$

OLS (1981–2009)

Adjusted-R^2 = 0.959   SE = 0.016565   DW = 1.16

(3.7) Deflator of government investment

$$\ln (PIG) = -0.7162 + 0.46144 \ln (PX) + 0.34848 \ln (WN)$$
$$\qquad\quad (-4.73) \quad (5.58) \qquad\qquad (5.60)$$
$$+ 0.34273 \ln (PIG(-1))$$
$$\quad (3.16)$$
$$+ 0.03415 \, D08$$
$$\quad (2.71)$$

OLS (1981–2009)

Adjusted-R^2 = 0.929   SE = 0.01216   DW = 1.603

(3.8) Output price

$$\ln (PX) = 1.76137 + 0.120073 \ln (PMY) + 0.247875 \ln (WN)$$
$$\qquad\quad (2.22) \qquad (5.82) \qquad\qquad\quad (2.88)$$
$$- 0.198535 \ln (GDPC(-1)/NL(-1))$$
$$\quad (-3.56)$$
$$+ 0.441172 \ln (PX(-1))$$
$$\quad (3.74)$$

C-O (1981–2009)

Adjusted-R^2 = 0.955   SE = 0.012157   DW = 2.047

(3.9) Nominal wage rates

$$DOT(WN) = 4.14957 + 0.3154 \, DOT(PCP) - 1.0473 \, UR$$
$$\qquad\qquad (4.36) \quad (3.13) \qquad\qquad\qquad (-4.16)$$
$$+ 0.3154 \, DOT(GDE/LW)$$
$$\quad (4.44)$$

OLS (1981–2009)

Adjusted-R^2 = 0.902   SE = 0.708   DW = 2.041

(3.10) Export price in terms of local currency

$$\ln(\text{PEXY}) = 0.086566 + 0.908030 \ln(\text{PX}) + 0.305964 \ln(\text{EXR})$$
$$\phantom{\ln(\text{PEXY}) =}(0.07) \qquad (4.40) \qquad\qquad (7.26)$$
$$-\ 0.239279 \ln(\text{GDPC}(-1)/\text{NL}(-1))$$
$$(-2.27)$$

C-O (1981−2009)
Adjusted-R^2 = 0.988   SE = 0.019577   DW = 1.437

(3.11) Consumer price index

$$\ln(\text{CPI}) = -\ 0.473729 + 0.187303 \ln(\text{PX}) + 0.265480 \ln(\text{WN})$$
$$\phantom{\ln(\text{CPI}) =}(-1.08) \qquad (3.63) \qquad\qquad (4.37)$$
$$+\ 0.647058 \ln(\text{CPI}(-1))$$
$$(6.65)$$

C-O (1981−2009)
Adjusted-R^2 = 0.995   SE = 0.005156   DW = 1.624

(3.12) Deflator of exports of goods and services

$$\ln(\text{PEGS}) = -\ 0.049203 + 1.00562 \ln(\text{PEXY})$$
$$\phantom{\ln(\text{PEGS}) =}(-0.36) \qquad (34.81)$$

OLS (1981−2009)
Adjusted-R^2 = 0.977   SE = 0.027106   DW = 1.471

(3.13) Deflator of imports of goods and services

$$\ln(\text{PMGS}) = 0.803257 + 0.827934 \ln(\text{PMY})$$
$$\phantom{\ln(\text{PMGS}) =}(11.07) \qquad (55.09)$$

OLS (1981−2009)
Adjusted-R^2 = 0.991   SE = 0.021096   DW = 1.552

(3.14) Exchange rate (Yen/$)

$$\text{EXR} = 24.0986 + 57.6440\ \text{PEXY}/\text{PGDP<US>}$$
$$\phantom{\text{EXR} =}(3.43) \qquad (5.93)$$
$$-\ 62.9343\ \text{INTGB}/\text{INTGB<US>}$$
$$(-4.10)$$
$$+\ 0.423502\ \text{EXR}(-1)$$
$$(4.20)$$

OLS (1981–2009)

Adjusted-$R^2 = 0.950$ SE $= 10.5893$ DW $= 1.212$

(3.15) Exchange rate index

EXRI = EXR/110.45*100

(3.16) Import price of non-oil and oil products

PMOTY = PMOTS*EXRI/100

(3.17) Crude oil price in terms of local currency

POILY = (POIL/28.23*100)*EXRI/100

(3.18) Import price in terms of local currency

PMY = (POILY*MGOIL + PMOTY*MGOT)/

(MGOIL + MGOT)

(3.19) Real estate prices

$$PLAND = -193.63 + 489.40\,GDE/GDE(-1)$$
$$(-4.49) \quad (4.52)$$
$$+ 0.00738\,PSTOCK + 0.90045\,PLAND(-1)$$
$$(3.05) (20.51)$$

OLS (1981–2009)

Adjusted-$R^2 = 0.963$ SE $= 4.893$ DW $= 1.762$

4. Production Block

(4.1) Real GDP capacity

ln (GDP/(1 − UR/100)*NL*LHRAT))

$$= 0.267797$$
$$ (12.03)$$
$$+ 0.301759\,ln\,((KP*CUR/100)/(1 - UR/100)*$$
$$ (5.63))$$

NL*LHRAT))

$$+ 0.238326\,(IP + IP(-1) + IP(-2))/KP$$
$$ (2.48)$$
$$+ 0.00412\,TIME$$
$$ (3.06)$$

C-O (1981−2008)
Adjusted-R^2 = 0.993   SE = 0.00955   DW = 1.708

(4.1') Real GDP capacity

$$\ln (GDPC) = 0.267797 + 0.301759 \ln (KP*100/100)$$
$$\qquad (12.08) \qquad (5.63)$$
$$+ (1 - 0.301759) \ln ((1 - 2.09/100)*NL*1.099)$$
$$\qquad (***)$$
$$+ 0.238326 (IP + IP(-1) + IP(-2))/KP$$
$$\qquad (2.48)$$
$$+ 0.00412 \, TIME$$
$$\qquad (3.06)$$

(4.2) Real private capital stock

$$KP = KP(-1) + IP - DP$$

(4.3) Real depreciation of capital

$$DP/KP(-1) = -0.046938 + 0.051858 \, GDE/GDE(-1)$$
$$\qquad (-1.46) \qquad (1.51)$$
$$+ 0.921100 \, DP(-1)/KP(-2)$$
$$\qquad (11.36)$$

OLS (1982−2008)
Adjusted-R^2 = 0.882   SE = 0.003800   DW = 2.025

(4.4) Capacity utilization rate of capital

$$\ln (CUR*KP) = -16.8999 + 2.29597 \ln (GDE)$$
$$\qquad (-5.18) \qquad (9.26)$$

C-O (1980−2008)
Adjusted-R^2 = 0.993   SE = 0.027613   DW = 1.916

(4.5) Deflationary gap

$$DGAP = GDPC - GDE$$

(4.6) Total factor productivity (TFP)

$$\text{TFP} = \exp\,(0.263 + 0.238((\text{IP} + \text{IP}(-1) + \text{IP}(-2))/\text{KP})$$
$$+ 0.0041(\text{TIME}))$$
$$= \exp\,(\ln(\text{GDPC}) - 0.301\ln(\text{KP})$$
$$- 0.699\ln((1 - 2.0/100))^*\text{NL}^*1.099))$$

5. Population and Labor Force Block

(5.1) Total population

$$\text{NP} = \text{NP0014} + \text{NP1564} + \text{NP6500}$$

(5.2) Population in the age group of 0 to 14 years

$$\text{NP0014} = -4591.75 + .647563\,\text{NP0014}(-1) - 161.063\,\text{TIME}$$
$$\quad\quad\quad\quad (-5.18)\quad\quad (9.95)\quad\quad\quad\quad\quad\quad (-4.79)$$
$$+ 3.95771\,\text{TIME}^*\text{TIME}$$
$$\quad (4.87)$$

C-O (1981−2008)
Adjusted-$R^2 = 0.999$ SE $= 63.2508$ DW $= 1.435$

(5.3) Population aged over 65 years

$$\text{NP6500} = 95.8119 + 1.02411\,\text{NP6500}(-1)) + 3.36755\,\text{TIME}$$
$$\quad\quad\quad\quad (1.23)\quad\quad (284.97)\quad\quad\quad\quad\quad\quad (2.05)$$

OLS (1981−2008)
Adjusted-$R^2 = 0.999$ SE $= 97.7334$ DW $= 1.794$

(5.4) Population in the age group of 15–64 years

$$\text{NP1564} = 4075.82 + 0.947390\,\text{NP1564}(-1) + 97.4375\,\text{TIME}$$
$$\quad\quad\quad\quad (2.67)\quad\quad (51.78)\quad\quad\quad\quad\quad\quad (9.74)$$
$$- 2.47706\,\text{TIME}^*\text{TIME}$$
$$\quad (-9.87)$$

OLS (1981−2008)
Adjusted-$R^2 = 0.993$ SE $= 184.1280$ DW $= 1.701$

(5.5) Number of labor force

$$NL = -\;129.96 + 8.994\;WN + 0.01196\,(NP1564 + NP6500)$$
$$(-0.26)\quad(4.47)\qquad\qquad(5.80)$$
$$+\;3{,}482.35\,RNLF + .43307\,NL(-1)$$
$$(4.60)\qquad\qquad\;(8.30)$$

OLS (1981−2008)
Adjusted-R^2 = 0.999   SE = 11.054   DW = 1.359

(5.6) Rate of unemployment

$$UR = 18.9484 -\;7.529\;\;\ln(GDE) + 10.388\ln(WN(-1)/$$
$$(0.83)\quad(-7.33)\qquad\qquad(4.45)$$
$$PGDE(-1)) + 9.1290\ln(NL) + 0.83510\,UR(-1)$$
$$(4.17)\qquad\qquad(16.37)$$

OLS (1981−2008)
Adjusted-R^2 = 0.978   SE = 0.1582   DW = 1.910

(5.7) Number of employed

NLE = (1 − UR/100)*NL

(5.8) Number of unemployed

NU = NL − NLE

(5.9) Number of wage and salaried employee

$$NLW = -\;1{,}158.52 + 0.001178\,GDE + 0.4603\,NLE$$
$$(-4.70)\qquad(6.82)\qquad\qquad(8.79)$$
$$-\;7.3576\;WN(-1)$$
$$(-4.06)$$
$$+\;0.69617\,NLW(-1)$$
$$(18.41)$$

OLS (1981−2009)
Adjusted-R^2 = 0.999   SE = 15.007   DW = 1.648

(5.10) Ratio of total working hour to legal working hour

$$LHRAT = 0.29129 + 0.17873\,GDE/GDE(-1)$$
$$(3.03)\qquad(7.72)$$

$$- 0.19512 \, NLE/NL + 0.7373 \, LHRAT(-1)$$
$$(-2.32) \qquad\qquad (7.96)$$

C-O (1981−2009)
Adjusted-R^2 = 0.898   SE = 0.002   DW = 1.855

(5.11) Female labor participation rate

$$RNLF = 0.02304 + 0.02683 \, GDE/GDE(-1)$$
$$(0.77) \qquad (2.50)$$
$$+ \; 0.01086 \, (WN(-1)/PGE(-1)$$
$$(2.41)$$
$$+ \; 0.8518 \, RNLF(-1)$$
$$(9.71)$$

OLS (1981−2008)
Adjusted-R^2 = 0.979   SE = 0.001   DW = 1.392

6. Money and Finance Block

(6.1) Call rate

$$INTCR = - 1.27834 + 1.27436 \, INTOR - 0.002351 - E03M2CD$$
$$(1.83) \qquad (22.02) \qquad\qquad (-2.09)$$

C-O (1981−2009)
Adjusted-R^2 = 0.994   SE = 0.220051   DW = 2.058

(6.2) Prime rate

$$INTPR = 5.42771 - 2.66708 \, M2CD/GDEN + 0.947190 \, INTOR$$
$$(8.96) \quad (-5.91) \qquad\qquad\qquad (21.67)$$

˙ OLS (1981−2009)
Adjusted-R^2 = 0.988   SE = 0.279201   DW = 1.488

(6.3) Government bond yields (10-year bond)

$$INTGB = -1.15596 + 0.796781 \, INTPR$$
$$(-6.48) \quad (18.55)$$

$$+ \ 0.31389 \ \text{INTGB} \text{<US>} - 0.006702 \ \text{EXR}$$
$$\quad (4.83) \qquad\qquad\qquad (-2.98)$$

OLS (1981–2009)
Adjusted-$R^2 = 0.992$ SE $= 0.222131$ DW $= 1.034$

(6.4) Money supply, M2+CD

$$\text{M2CD} = -204277.1 + \ 1.453 \ \text{GDE} + 1.521 \ \text{MB}$$
$$\quad (-4.06) \quad (15.02) \qquad\quad (6.05)$$
$$- \ 5871.72 \ \text{INTGB} + 49773.4 \ \text{D08}$$
$$\quad (-2.23) \qquad\qquad\quad (2.93)$$

OLS (1981–2009)
Adjusted-$R^2 = 0.990$ SE $= 16,137.7$ DW $= 1.564$

(6.5) Stock price (TOPIX)

$$\text{PSTOCK} = - \ 17271.9 + 17863.6 \ \text{GDE}/((\text{GDE} + \text{GDE}(-1))/2)$$
$$\quad (-3.99) \quad (4.09)$$
$$- \ 151.107 \ \text{INTOR-DOT(PGDE)}$$
$$\quad (-3.01)$$
$$+ \ 0.655422 \ \text{PSTOCK}(-1)$$
$$\quad (7.10)$$

OLS (1981–2009)
Adjusted-$R^2 = 0.794$ SE $= 218.9260$ DW $= 2.005$

7. Income Distribution Block

(7.1) Corporate income (before dividends)

$$\text{YCB} = 13.400.0 + 0.562106 \ \text{GDEN} - 3,164.34 \ \text{INTPR}$$
$$\quad (0.77) \qquad (13.03) \qquad\qquad (-8.96)$$
$$- \ 1.01206 \ \text{YW} + 2,5331.5 \ \text{PEXY}/\text{PX} - 7,967.25 \ \text{D08}$$
$$\quad (-14.12) \qquad\qquad (2.35) \qquad\qquad (-2.79)$$

OLS (1981–2008)
Adjusted-$R^2 = 0.917$ SE $= 2,556.72$ DW $= 2.252$

(7.2) Corporate income

$$\text{YC} = \text{YCB} - \text{DIVC}$$

(7.3) Corporate dividend paid

$$DIVC = RDIVC^*YCB$$

(7.4) Wages and salaries per employee

$$\ln(W) = \underset{(3.62)}{2.5615} + \underset{(2.58)}{0.51348}\,WN + \underset{(2.20)}{0.2654}\ln(GDE/GDE(-1))$$
$$+ \underset{(2.21)}{0.4198}\ln(W(-1))$$

OLS (1981–2008)
Adjusted-R^2 = 0.988   SE = 0.012   DW = 1.654

(7.5) Compensation of employees

$$YE = YW + ESC$$

(7.6) Wage and salaried income

$$YW = W^*NLW/100$$

(7.7) Household property income

$$YRH = YIH + YDIV + YROTH$$

(7.8) Household interest income

$$YIH = YIR - YIP$$

(7.9) Household interest income, receivable

$$\ln(YIR) = -\underset{(-2.85)}{4.534} + \underset{(4.27)}{0.5582}\ln(HFA) + \underset{(6.49)}{0.6271}\ln(INTGB)$$
$$+ \underset{(9.35)}{0.5912}\ln(YIR(-1))$$

OLS (1981–2008)
Adjusted-R^2 = 0.968   SE = 0.1181   DW = 1.382

(7.10) Household interest income, payable (consumer debt interest)

$$YIP = -\underset{(-2.56)}{2262.05} + \underset{(4.10)}{0.0135}\,HTD + \underset{(3.33)}{216.74}\,INTGB$$
$$+ \underset{(2.94)}{0.5421}\,YIP(-1)$$

OLS (1981−2008)
Adjusted-$R^2 = 0.972$ SE $= 241.28$ DW $= 1.658$

(7.11) Household dividend income

$$YDIV = RYDIV^*YCB$$

(7.12) Income of incorporated enterprises

$$YU = 79114.8 + .101831\,GDEN - 1573.16\,INTORA$$
$$\;\;\;\;\;(3.99)\;\;\;\;\;\;(4.89)\;\;\;\;\;\;\;\;\;\;\;\;\;\;\;(-7.22)$$
$$- 87399.1\,WN/PCP$$
$$\;\;(-3.05)$$

OLS (1981−2008)
Adjusted-$R^2 = 0.959$ SE $= 1{,}168.17$ DW $= 1.652$

(7.13) Employer's social contributions

$$ESC = -2{,}044.97 + .0714\,YW + .54419\,ESC(-1)$$
$$\;\;\;\;\;\;(-1.33)\;\;\;\;(4.18)\;\;\;\;\;\;\;\;\;(6.01)$$

OLS (1981−2008)
Adjusted-$R^2 = 0.983$ SE $= 1{,}022.2$ DW $= 2.095$

(7.14) Other household property income

$$YROTH = -40{,}927.0 + 41{,}431.1\,GDEN/GDEN(-1)$$
$$\;\;\;\;\;\;\;\;\;(-4.66)\;\;\;\;\;(4.65)$$
$$- 216.74\,INTGB + 0.9426\,YROTH(-1)$$
$$\;\;(-1.98)\;\;\;\;\;\;\;\;\;\;\;\;(24.57)$$

OLS (1981−2008)
Adjusted-$R^2 = 0.959$ SE $= 901.84$ DW $= 2.32$

(7.15) Household income

$$YH = YE + YRH + YU$$

(7.16) Household disposable income

$$YDH = YH + ROTH - TP - POTH$$

(7.17) Household savings

$$SH = YDH - CHN$$

(7.18) Household financial assets

$$\text{HFA} = -86,079.6 + \underset{(3.07)}{1.035}\,\text{YDH} + \underset{(4.26)}{50.5204}\,\text{PSTOCK}$$
$$\phantom{\text{HFA} =}\underset{(-1.76)}{} $$
$$+ \underset{(4.59)}{10,373.5}\,\text{INTGB}(-1)/\text{INTOR}(-1)$$
$$+ \underset{(16.55)}{0.7567}\,\text{HFA}(-1))$$

OLS (1981–2008)
Adjusted-$R^2 = 0.995$ SE $= 27,436$ DW $= 1.930$

(7.19) Household non-financial assets

$$\text{HNFA}/\text{PLAND}^*100 = \underset{(1.79)}{256,195} + \underset{(2.17)}{0.1560}\,\text{YDP}/\text{PLAND}^*100$$
$$- \underset{(-3.13)}{25,596.9}\,\text{INTGB} + \underset{(2.62)}{438,265.4}$$
$$\text{PLAND}/\text{PLAND}(-1)$$
$$+ \underset{(2.91)}{0.4122}\,\text{HNFA}(-1)/$$
$$\text{PLAND}(-1)^*100$$

OLS (1981–2008)
Adjusted-$R^2 = 0.912$ SE $= 34,994.5$ DW $= 1.720$

(7.20) Increment of household total liabilities

$$\Delta\text{HTD} = \underset{(4.11)}{50,329.5} - \underset{(-4.02)}{25858}\,\text{YDP} - \underset{(-3.13)}{3,152.12}\,\text{INTOR}(-1)$$
$$+ \underset{(2.80)}{288.07}\,\text{PLAND} + \underset{(2.64)}{0.50922}\,\Delta\text{HTD}(-1)$$

OLS (1982–2008)
Adjusted-$R^2 = 0.836$ SE $= 5050.93$ DW $= 1.422$

(7.21) Household total assets

$$\text{HTA} = \text{HFA} + \text{HNFA}$$

(7.22) Household total liabilities

$$\text{HTD} = \Delta\text{HTD} + \text{HTD}(-1)$$

8. Public Finance Block

(8.1) Central government personal income tax revenue

$$TXI = -49.418 + 0.017866\,YP + 46,879\,GDEN/GDEN(-1)$$
$$(-3.66)\quad\;\;(2.91)\qquad\qquad(4.01)$$
$$+\,0.7471\,TXC(-1)$$
$$(8.01)$$

OLS (1981–2008)
Adjusted-R^2 = 0.850   SE = 1,489.7   DW = 2.135

(8.2) Central government corporate income tax revenue

$$TXC = RTXC^*YCB$$

(8.3) Effective corporate income tax rate for central government

$$RTXC = -0.66305 + 0.6761\,GDEN/GDEN(-1)$$
$$(-3.60)\quad\;(3.68)$$
$$+\,0.8077\,RTXC(-1) + 0.08440\,D08$$
$$(11.46)\qquad\qquad\;\;(2.76)$$

C-O (1981–2008)
Adjusted-R^2 = 0.877   SE = 0.0277   DW = 2.063

(8.4) Overall corporate income tax paid

$$TC = TXC + TXCL$$

(8.5) Overall personal income tax paid

$$TP = TXI + TXIL$$

(8.6) Overall consumption tax paid by consumer

$$TXCON = RTXCON^*CPN$$

(8.7) Central government consumption tax revenue

$$TAXCON = RTAXCON^*TXCON$$

(8.8) Central government tax revenue in general accounts

$$TXG = TXC + TXI + TAXCON + TXOTH$$

(8.9) Source for local allocation tax

GEXLAB = 0.32*TXI + 0.325*TXC + 0.295*TAXCON + TXLA

(8.10) Central government disbursement for local allocation tax

GEXLA = GEXLAB + GEXLAD

(8.11) Central government total expenditures in general accounts

$$GEXGE = GEXSS + GEXLF + GEXED + GEXND + GEXPS$$
$$+ GEXDF + GEXEC + GEXFD + GEXPW$$
$$+ GEXOTH$$

(8.12) Central government expenditure for social welfare in general accounts

$$GEXSS = -437.875 + 0.846317\,NP6500 - 617.238\,D8990$$
$$(-1.20)\quad\ \ (31.70)(-2.16)$$
$$+\,2147.44\,D99$$
$$(4.81)$$

OLS (1981–2008)
Adjusted-R^2 = 0.989   SE = 433.9338   DW = 1.081

(8.13) Central government expenditure for local finance in general accounts

$$GEXLF = 389.340 + 0.987496\,GEXLAB$$
$$(1.21)\quad\ \ (40.86)$$

OLS (1981–2008)
Adjusted-R^2 = 0.985   SE = 346.1535   DW = 2.073

(8.14) Central government expenditure for education in general accounts

$$\ln(GEXED) = 1.09004 + 0.118384\ln(GRVGE)$$
$$(1.75)\quad\ \ (1.20)$$
$$+\,0.721440\ln(GEXED(-1))$$
$$(4.68)$$

OLS (1981–2008)
Adjusted-R^2 = 0.854   SE = 0.050928   DW = 1.929

(8.15) Central government expenditure for public services

$$\ln (\text{GEXPS}) = -0.044061 + 0.113643 \ln (\text{GRVGE})$$
$$(-0.12) \quad (1.70)$$
$$+ 0.936465 \ln (\text{GEXPS}(-1))$$
$$(25.95)$$
$$- 0.02318 \text{ TIME}$$
$$(-3.45)$$

OLS (1981−2008)
Adjusted-R^2 = 0.996   SE = 0.013152   DW = 1.213

(8.16) Central government expenditure for economic cooperation

$$\text{GEXEC} = -278.079 + 0.003872 \text{ GDEN} + 1.27620 \text{ U}$$
$$(-6.54) \quad (19.08) \quad (6.44)$$
$$- 29.9079 \text{ TIME}$$
$$(-9.65)$$

OLS (1981−2008)
Adjusted-R^2 = 0.963   SE = 38.8607   DW = 1.198

(8.17) Central government expenditure for national defense

$$\text{GEXDF} = 271.646 + 0.004382 \text{ GDEN} + 0.490488 \text{ GEXDF}(-1)$$
$$(1.63) \quad (4.35) \quad (5.18)$$

C-O (1981−2008)
Adjusted-R^2 = 0.996   SE = 46.3532   DW = 1.622

(8.18) Central government expenditure for foods in general accounts

$$\text{GEXFD} = 2109.83 + 3241.59 \text{ GRVGE/GDEN} - 125.351 \text{ TIME}$$
$$(7.42) \quad (3.34) \quad (-8.99)$$
$$+ 1.58881 \text{ TIME*TIME} + 71.0926 \text{ D87}$$
$$(6.22) \quad (1.48)$$
$$+ 478.736 \text{ D2001}$$
$$(10.47)$$

OLS (1981−2008)
Adjusted-R^2 = 0.963   SE = 46.1664   DW = 1.26

(8.19) Central government expenditure for public works in general accounts

$$\text{GEXPW} = 1157.25 + 0.869248 \, (\text{GEXPWOR} + \text{GEXPWSU})$$
$$(2.45) \quad\;\; (17.78)$$

OLS (1981−2008)
Adjusted-$R^2 = 0.924$ SE $= 676.0988$ DW $= 2.435$

(8.20) Central government revenue prior to government bond revenue

$$\text{GRVGEB} = \text{TXG} + \text{GRVOTH}$$

(8.21) Central government bond issued

$$\text{GRVGB} = \text{GEXGE} - \text{GRVGEB}$$

(8.22) Central government revenue in general accounts

$$\text{GRVGE} = \text{TXG} + \text{GRVGB} + \text{GRVOTH}$$

(8.23) Local government household income tax revenue

$$\text{TXIL} = \text{RTXIL*YH}(-1)$$

(8.24) Local government corporate income tax revenue

$$\text{TXCL} = \text{RTXCL*YCB}(-1)$$

(8.25) Central government bonds outstanding

$$\text{KLGB} = \text{KLGB}(-1) + \text{GRVGEB} - \text{GEXED}$$

(8.26) Total national government debts outstanding

$$\text{KLGBT} = \text{KLGB} + \text{KLGOT}$$

(8.27) Ratio of accumulated government debt to nominal GDE

$$\text{RKLG} = \text{KLGB/GDEN*}100$$

9. International Trade and BOP Block

(9.1) Real merchandise exports

$$\ln \text{EXG} = -\,0.2941 + 0.3429 \ln \text{TWM}$$
$$(-0.73) \quad (2.55)$$

$$- 0.3853 \text{ PEXIY/EXRI/PTW}$$
$$(-5.06)$$
$$+ 1.3171 \ln (\text{GDPC/NL})$$
$$(3.67)$$

OLS (1980–2008)
Adjusted-R^2 = 0.988   SE = 0.044   DW = 1.523

(9.2) Real merchandise imports of crude oil and oil products

$$\ln (\text{MGOIL}) = - 1.90156 + 0.834229 \ln (\text{GDE})$$
$$(-2.33) \quad (13.39)$$
$$- 0.200364 \ln (\text{POIL*EXRI/PX})$$
$$(-14.57)$$
$$+ 0.106251 \text{ D08}$$
$$(3.79)$$

OLS (1980–2009)
Adjusted-R^2 = 0.912   SE = 0.024780   DW = 1.771

(9.3) Real merchandise imports of non-oil and oil products

$$\text{MGOT} = - 36037.3 + 43473.4 \text{ GDE/GDE}(-1))$$
$$(-1.73) \quad (2.17)$$
$$- 5614.67 \text{ PMOTS*EXRI/PX}$$
$$(-3.01)$$
$$+ 0.96918 \text{ MGOT}(-1)$$
$$(18.68)$$

OLS (1981–2009)
Adjusted-R^2 = 0.960   SE = 2,107.03   DW = 1.903

(9.4) Nominal merchandise exports in BOP in terms of local currency

$$\text{EGNB} = 12996.0 + 9.34138 \text{ EXGN}$$
$$(2.82) \quad (122.15)$$

OLS (1996–2008)
Adjusted-R^2 = 0.999   SE = 3,328.50   DW = 1.026

(9.5) Nominal merchandise imports in BOP in terms of local currency

$$MGNB = -16748.9 + 9.46495 \, MGN$$
$$\quad\quad\quad (-5.30) \quad (155.05)$$

OLS (1996–2008)
Adjusted-$R^2 = 0.999$ SE $= 2{,}965.32$ DW $= 1.203$

(9.6) Nominal service imports in BOP

$$MSNB = -4028.24 + 1.20034 \,(MCN^*10 - MGB)$$
$$\quad\quad\quad (-0.52) \quad (19.12)$$
$$\quad\quad + 13028.1 \, D08$$
$$\quad\quad\quad (4.67)$$

OLS (1997–2008)
Adjusted-$R^2 = 0.978$ SE $= 2{,}520.85$ DW $= 2.155$

(9.7) Nominal service exports in BOP

$$ESNB = -3384.89 + 1.34530 \,(EXCN^*10 - EGB)$$
$$\quad\quad\quad (-0.82) \quad (25.34)$$
$$\quad\quad + 11556.7 \, D08$$
$$\quad\quad\quad (2.96)$$

OLS (1997–2008)
Adjusted-$R^2 = 0.987$ SE $= 3{,}400.37$ DW $= 1.925$

(9.8) Nominal merchandise exports

$$EXGN = EXG^*PEXY/100$$

(9.9) Nominal merchandise imports

$$MG = MGOT + MGOIL$$

(9.10) Nominal merchandise imports of non-oil and oil products

$$MGOTN = MGOT^*PMOTY/100$$

(9.11) Nominal imports of oil and oil products

$$MGOILN = MGOIL^*POILY/100$$

(9.12) Nominal merchandise imports in local currency

$$MGN = MGOILN + MGOTN$$

(9.13) Trade balance in local currency

$$TBG = EGNB - MGNB$$

(9.14) Service balance in local currency

$$TBS = ESNB - MSNB$$

(9.15) Income transfer, credits in local currency

$$EINB = -5988.6 + 0.0612 \text{ FA}(-1) \times EXR(-1)$$
$$ (-1.22) \quad (10.62)$$

$$+30116.9 \text{ (INTGB/INTGB<US>)}$$
$$ (9.82)$$

$$-102.77 \text{ EXR}(-1) - 6319.72 \text{ D08}$$
$$ (-2.89) (-3.10)$$

C-O (1992–2008)
Adjusted-R^2 = 0.897   SE = 1,326.2   DW = 2.169

(9.16) Income transfer, debits in local currency

$$\ln(MINB) = -7.476 + 1.888 \ln(\text{INTGB<US>})$$
$$ (-1.90) \quad (2.56)$$

$$+0.6511 \ln(FL(-1)^*EXR(-1))$$
$$ (2.32)$$

$$+0.53777 \ln(MINB(-1))$$
$$ (3.40)$$

OLS (1992–2008)
Adjusted-R^2 = 0.835   SE = 0.0214   DW = 1.781

(9.17) Income balance in local currency

$$TBI = EINB - MINB$$

(9.18) Current balance of payment in local currency

$$CBP = TBG + TBS + TBI + TBC$$

(9.19) Merchandise exports in US$

$$EGNBS = EGNB/EXR^*1000$$

(9.20) Merchandise imports in US$

$$MGNBS = MGNB/EXR*1000$$

(9.21) Trade balance in US$

$$TBGS = EGNBS - MGNBS$$

Appendix B: Variable List and Data Sources

Variable List (Variable (Endogenous (D)/Exogenous (X)) : Definition)

CG (D): real government consumption expenditures (2000 constant prices, chain-linked)

CGN (D): nominal government consumption expenditures

CH (D): real household final consumption expenditure (2000 constant prices, chain-linked)

CHN (D): nominal household final consumption expenditure

CN (D): real non-profit organization consumption expenditure (2000 constant prices, chain-linked)

CNN (D): nominal non-profit organization consumption expenditure

CP (D): real private final consumption expenditures (2000 constant prices, chain-linked)

CPI (D): consumer price index (CPI.2005=100)

CPN (D): nominal private final consumption expenditures

DGAP (D): deflationary gap (GDPC-GDE)

DH (D): depreciation of real residential stock (2000 constant prices)

DIVC (D): corporate dividend paid

DP (D): depreciation of real private capital stock (2000 constant prices)

EG (D): real merchandise exports (2000 constant prices)

EGN (D): nominal merchandise exports

EGNB (D): nominal exports (f.o.b.)

EGNBS (D): nominal exports in terms of US$ (f.o.b.)

EGS (D): real exports of goods and services (2000 constant prices)

EGSN (D):	nominal exports of goods and services
EINB (D):	income transfers, credits in BOP
ES (D):	real service exports (2000 constant prices)
ESC (D):	employer's social contribution
ESN (D):	nominal service exports
ESBNS (D):	nominal service exports in terms of $US
EXR (D):	exchange rate (yen/$)
EXRI (D):	exchange rate index (EXRI.2000 = 100)
FA (X):	foreign assets in terms of billion US$
FL (X):	foreign liabilities in terms of billion US$
GDE (D):	real gross domestic expenditures (2000 constant prices, chain-linked))
GDEN (D):	nominal gross domestic expenditures
GDPC (D):	real GDP capacity (2000 constant prices)
GEXDF (D):	central government expenditure for defense
GEXEC (D):	central government expenditure for economic corporation
GEXED (D):	central government expenditure for education
GEXFD (D):	central government expenditure for foods
GEXGE (D):	central government total expenditure in general accounts
GEXLF (D):	central government expenditure for local finance
GEXLAB (D):	central government expenditure for local allocation tax before an adjustment
GEXLA (D):	central government expenditure for local allocation tax (LAT)
GEXLAD (X):	supplementary budget for LAT
GEXND (D):	central government expenditure for national debts
GEXOTH (X):	central government other expenditures
GEXPS (D):	central government expenditure for public service
GEXPW (D):	central government expenditure for public works
GEXPWOR (X):	central government expenditure for public works: budgetary base
GEXPWSU (X):	supplementary for central government expenditure for public works

GEXSS (D):	central government expenditure for social security
GEXTD (D):	central government treasury disbursement
GRVGB (D):	government bond revenue in general accounts
GRVGE (D):	general accounts government revenue
GRVGEB (D):	general governments' revenue without bond revenue
GRVOTH (X):	other government revenue in the general accounts
HFA (D):	household financial assets
HNFA (D):	household non-financial assets
HTA (D):	household total assets
HTD (D):	household total financial liabilities
INTCR (D):	call rate
INTGB (D):	government bond yield (10-year bond)
INTOR (X):	basic discount rate and basic loan rate (previously indicated as official discount rates)
INTPR (D):	prime rate
IG (D):	real government investment (2000 constant prices, chain-linked)
IGN (D):	nominal government investment
IH (D):	real housing investment (2000 constant prices, chain-linked)
IHN (D):	nominal housing investment
IP (D):	real private non-residential investment (2000 constant prices, chain-linked)
IPN (D):	nominal private non-residential investment
JG (D):	real government inventory changes (2000 constant prices, chain-linked)
JGN (D):	nominal government inventory changes
JP (D):	real private inventory changes (2000 constant prices, chain-linked)
JPN (D):	nominal private inventory changes
KH (D):	real residential stock (2000 constant price)
KLGB (D):	central government bonds outstanding
KLGOT (X):	other national debts outstanding
KLGBT (D):	total national government debts outstanding
KP (D):	real private capital stock (2000 constant prices)

KJP (D):   real private inventory (2000 constant price)
LHL (D):   legal working hours, per month
LHRAT (D):   ratio of total working hours to legal working hours
LHT (D):   total working hours, per month
LPI (D):   labor productivity index (LPI.2000 = 100)
MG (D):   real merchandise imports (2000 constant prices)
MGN (D):   nominal merchandise imports
MGNB (D):   nominal imports (f.o.b.)
MGNS (D):   nominal imports in US$ (f.o.b.)
MGOIL (D):   real crude oil and oil products imports
MGOILN (D):   nominal crude oil and oil products imports
MGOT (D):   real merchandise imports excluding crude oil and oil products
MGOTN (D):   nominal merchandise imports excluding oil and oil products
MGS (D):   real imports of goods and services (2000 constant prices)
MGSN (D):   nominal imports of goods and services
MINB (D):   income transfers, debits in BOP
MS (D):   real service imports (1994 constant prices)
MSN (D):   nominal service imports
MSNBS (D):   nominal service imports in terms of $US
M2CD (D):   money supply, M2 plus CD
MB (X):   monetary base
NL (D):   number of labor
NLE (D):   number of employed
NLW (D):   number of waged and salaried employees
NP (D):   total population
NP0014 (D):   population in the age group of 0 to 14 years
NP1564 (D):   population in the age group of 15 to 64 years
NP6500 (D):   population aged over 65 years
NTOTH (X):   household other net transfer
NU (D):   number of unemployed
PCG (D):   implicit deflator of CG
PCI (D):   per-capita income in terms of US$

PCH (D):	implicit deflator of CH
PCN (D):	implicit deflator of CN
PCP (D):	implicit deflator of CP
PEGS (D):	implicit deflator of EGS
PEXY (D):	export price in terms of local currency
PGDE (D):	implicit deflator of GDE
PGDP (D):	implicit deflator of GDP
PIG (D):	implicit deflator of IG
PIH (D):	implicit deflator of IH
PIP (D):	implicit deflator of IP
PJG (X):	implicit deflator of JG
PJP (D):	implicit deflator of JP
PLAND (D):	real estate price
PMG (D):	import price in local currency base
PMGS (D):	implicit deflator of MGS
PMOTY (D):	import price of non-oil and oil products in local currency base
PMS (X):	import price in terms of US$
POIL (X):	crude oil price ($/barrel)
POILY (D):	crude oil price in local currency base (POILY.2000 = 100)
POTH (X):	household other payments
PSTOCK (D):	stock prices (TOPIX base)
PTW (X):	world import deflator in dollar terms
PX (D):	output price
RDIVC (X):	ratio of dividend profits to corporate income
RKLG (D):	ratio of accumulated government debt to nominal GDE
RNLF (D):	female labor participation rate
ROTH (D):	household other receipts
RTXC (X):	effective corporate tax rate for central government
RTXCL (X):	effective corporate tax rate for local government
RTXIL (X):	effective personal income tax rate for local government
RTXCON (X):	consumption tax rate

RTAXCON (X):	rate of central government consumption tax revenue to total consumption tax
RYDIV (X):	ratio of dividend income of household to corporate income
SH (D):	savings in households
TAXCON (D):	central government consumption tax revenue
TBC (X):	balance on current transfer in terms of local currency
TBG (D):	trade balance in local currency
TBGS (D):	trade balance in terms of $US
TBI (D):	income balance in terms of local currency
TBS (D):	service balance in local currency
TC (D):	total corporate tax paid for central and local governments
TFP (D):	total factor productivity
TIME (X):	time trend
TP (D):	total personal income tax paid for central and local governments
TWM (X):	real total world imports in US dollar
TXC (D):	central government corporate income tax revenue
TXCL (D):	local government corporate income tax revenue
TXG (D):	central government total tax revenue
TXI (D):	central government personal income tax revenue
TXIL (D):	local government personal income tax revenue
UR (D):	rate of unemployment
W (D):	wages and salaries per employee
WN (D):	nominal wage rates
YC (D):	corporate income
YCB (D):	corporate income (prior to dividend)
YDH (D):	household disposable income
YDIV (D):	household dividend income (including private unincorporated enterprises)
YE (D):	compensation of employees
YHOT (D):	other household income

YH (D):	household income (including private unincorporated enterprises)
YIR (D):	household interest income, receivable
YIP (D):	household interest income, payable (consumer debt interest)
YRH (D):	household property income
YROTH (D):	household other property income
YU (D):	income of private unincorporated enterprises
YW (D):	wage and salaried income

Data Sources

Economic and social Research Institute (ESRI), Cabinet Office, Central Government of Japan

Ministry of Finance

Ministry of General Affairs

Ministry of Economy, Trade and Industry

Ministry of Welfare, Health and Labor

Bank of Japan (BOJ)

International Financial Statistics (IFS), IMF

Appendix C: Keynes Multiplier with Asset Effect in a Theoretical Model

Demand-side

$$Y_d = C + I + G^* + E^* - M \qquad (1A)$$

$$C = C_d(Y_w, A) + C^*(p, r, N, \dots) = \gamma Y_w + \varepsilon A + C^* \qquad (2A)$$

$$A = A(-1) + \Delta A \qquad (3A)$$

$$= A(-1) + \eta Y_w + \Delta A^* \quad (\Delta A = \eta Y_w + \Delta A^*)$$

$$I = Id(Y_c) + I^*(r, p, K(1), \dots) = \mu Y_c + I^* \qquad (4A)$$

$$M = Md(Y_d) + M^*(p, e, \dots) = \lambda Y_d + M^* \qquad (5A)$$

$$Y_w = \theta Y_d \quad (Y_i = Y_w + Y_c = Y_d) \qquad (6A)$$

$$Y_c = (1 - \theta)Y_d \qquad (7A)$$

Therefore,

$$C = (\gamma + \varepsilon\eta)Y_w + \varepsilon A(-1) + \varepsilon\Delta A^* + C^*$$

$$= (\gamma + \varepsilon\eta)\theta Y_d + \varepsilon A(-1) + \varepsilon\Delta A^* + C^* \qquad (8A)$$

$$I = \mu Y_c + I^* = \mu(1 - \theta)Y_d + I^* \qquad (9A)$$

$$M = \lambda Y_d + M^* \qquad (10A)$$

Consequently,

$$Y_d = (1/(1 - (\gamma + \varepsilon\eta)\theta - \mu(1 - \theta) + \lambda))W \qquad (11A)$$

$$(W = (C^* + G^* + I^* + E^* - M^* + \varepsilon A(-1) + \varepsilon\Delta A^*))$$

Accordingly, the Keynes multiplier in the demand-side model with assets effects, as follows.

$$m = 1/(1 - (\gamma + \varepsilon\eta)\theta - \mu(1 - \theta) + \lambda).$$

where Y_d, Y_i, C, C_d, I, I_d, G, E, M, M_d, Y_w, Y_c, p, r, A, N, e, θ and ε refer to demand-side GDP (gross domestic expenditure, GDE), income-distribution-side national income, overall consumption, consumption dependent on Y_d, overall investment, investment dependent on Yd, government expenditure, exports, overall imports, imports dependent on Y_d, wage income, corporate income, prices, rate of interest, net financial assets, total population, foreign exchange rate, wage income share and marginal propensity to consume out of net asset, respectively. And * means variables independent of Y_d in IS model [Equation (1A)].

Appendix D: Unit Root Test with the Augmented Dickey–Fuller Test for the Other Major Variables: with Trend and Intercept

Variable	Level	First difference	Second difference
EXR	−1.40	−3.64**	−6.10***
PMY	−1.33	−4.07***	−6.80***
POIL	−1.34	−4.19***	−5.41***
PX	−1.50	−3.17	−4.49***
PEXY	−1.42	−3.95**	−5.43***
PCP	−0.80	−2.91	−4.39***
PCG	−0.15	−2.96	−5.16***
PIP	−1.44	−2.34	−3.20
PIH	−1.04	−3.37*	−6.49***
PIG	−1.45	−2.82	−3.98**
PEGS	−1.60	−3.66**	−5.24***
PMGS	−1.41	−4.06**	−6.93***
GDEN	0.38	−2.75	−5.30***
CPN	0.84	−2.49	−5.67***
CGN	0.78	−2.80	−6.86***
IPN	−1.07	−2.47	−4.55***
IHN	−0.73	−5.29***	−8.84***
IGN	−0.36	−2.52	−6.73***
EGSN	−1.96	−2.50	−5.66***
MGSN	−2.15	−1.62	−3.75**
WN	0.25	−2.55	−4.80***
YW	−0.12	−2.28	−4.49***
YCB	−2.41	−4.51***	−6.11***
YDH	−0.41	−2.72	−6.46***
YU	−0.95	−5.65***	−8.09***
YRH	1.73	−5.09***	−7.96***
HFA	0.55	−3.36*	−6.48***
HNFA	−1.30	−2.34	−4.73***
HTD	0.59	−2.31	−3.52*

(*Continued*)

(*Continued*)

Variable	Level	First difference	Second difference
M2CD	−0.44	−2.46	−4.62***
MB	−1.62	−3.63**	−6.47***
PSTOCK	−1.79	−3.72**	−7.00***
PLAND	−1.22	−2.20	−4.01**
INTOR	−2.52	−3.62**	−4.86***
INTCR	−2.73	−4.57***	−5.87***
INTPR	−2.23	−4.11**	−7.11***
INTGB	−2.04	−4.13 **	−7.01***
GEXGE	−0.27	−4.64***	−7.36***
GRVGE	−0.48	−5.12***	−7.63***
TXC	−1.52	−2.39	−3.58*
TXI	−1.72	−4.05**	−6.24***
EXG	−1.88	−4.24**	−6.43***
MGOIL	1.39	−5.03***	−7.36***
MGOTH	−2.38	−4.03**	−6.06***

Note: *, ** and *** indicate the significance at 10%, 5% and 1%, respectively.

Level, First Difference and Second Difference with Trend and Intercept
Level: $\Delta Y = \alpha + \beta\ Trend + \delta Y(-1) + u$
First difference: $\Delta(\Delta Y) = \alpha + \beta\ Trend + \delta \Delta Y(-1) + u$
Second difference: $\Delta(\Delta(\Delta Y)) = \alpha + \beta\ Trend + \delta \Delta(\Delta Y(-1)) + u$

ADF Critical Values Within Level, First Difference and Second Difference

	Level	First Difference	Second Difference
1%	4.324	4.339	4.356
5%	3.581	3.588	3.595
10%	3.225	3.229	3.233

Note: Sample: FY1980–2008.
Source: Estimated and compiled by the author.

Appendix E: Major Exogenous Variables for the Baseline Forecast, FY2010–2030

FY	2010	2011	2012	2013	2014	2015	2020	2030
POIL($/b)	85.0	95.0	95.0	95.0	95.0	95.0	95.0	95.0
(%)	(22.9)	(11.8)	(0.0)	(0.0)	(0.0)	(0.0)	(0.0)	(0.0)
INTOR(%)	0.300	0.300	0.300	0.300	0.300	0.300	0.300	0.300
(%)	(−60.0)	(−16.7)	(200.0)	(0.0)	(0.0)	(0.0)	(0.0)	(0.0)
GEXPW(tril.)	7.329	7.329	7.329	7.329	7.329	7.329	7.329	7.329
(%)	(−19.2)	(0.0)	(0.0)	(0.0)	(0.0)	(0.0)	(0.0)	(0.0)
JG(trillion)	0.205	0.205	0.205	0.205	0.205	0.205	0.205	0.205
(%)	(0.0)	(0.0)	(0.0)	(0.0)	(0.0)	(0.0)	(0.0)	(0.0)
TWM($)	8411	8705	9010	9325	9652	9990	11865	16736
(%)	(4.5)	(3.5)	(3.5)	(3.5)	(3.5)	(3.5)	(3.5)	(3.5)
PTW($)	143.8	148.1	152.6	157.1	161.9	166.7	193.3	259.7
(%)	(4.0)	(3.0)	(3.0)	(3.0)	(3.0)	(3.0)	(3.0)	(3.0)
INTGB<US>	4.40	4.20	4.20	4.20	4.20	4.20	4.20	4.20
(%)	(0.0)	(−4.5)	(0.0)	(0.0)	(0.0)	(0.0)	(0.0)	(0.0)
PGDP<US>	127.0	129.5	132.1	134.8	137.5	140.2	154.8	188.7
(%)	(2.5)	(2.0)	(2.0)	(2.0)	(2.0)	(2.0)	(2.0)	(2.0)
RTXCON, %	5.00	5.00	5.00	5.00	5.00	5.00	5.00	5.00
(%)	(0.0)	(0.0)	(0.0)	(0.0)	(0.0)	(0.0)	(0.0)	(0.0)
FA (b. $)	5,518	5,573	5,628	5,685	5,742	5,799	6,095	6,732
(%)	(2.0)	(2.0)	(2.0)	(2.0)	(2.0)	(2.0)	(2.0)	(2.0)
FL (b. $)	3,354	3,421	3,489	3,559	3,630	3,702	4,088	4,983
(%)	(1.0)	(1.0)	(1.0)	(1.0)	(1.0)	(1.0)	(1.0)	(1.0)

Note: POIL: crude oil price ($/b), INTOR: basic discount rate and basic loan rate, GEXPW: central government public works expenditure, JG: real government inventory changes, TWM; real world trade, PTW: deflator of TWM, INTGB<US>: US government bond yield (30-year bond), PGDP<US>: US general deflator of GDP, RTXCON: consumption tax rate.

Source: Assumed by the author.

Index